REPRESENTATIVE DEMOCRACY

REPRESENTATIVE DEMOCRACY

Public Policy and
Midwestern Legislatures
in the Late Nineteenth Century

BALLARD C. CAMPBELL

Harvard University Press
Cambridge, Massachusetts
and London, England
1980

Library of Congress Cataloging in Publication Data
Campbell, Ballard C 1940-
    Representative democracy.

    Includes bibliographical references and index.
    1.   Legislative bodies—Middle West—Voting—History.
2.   Middle West—Politics and government. I. Title.
JK2484.C35   328.77077'09   80-12775
ISBN 0-674-76275-4

PREFACE

The finishing touches were applied to this book as the earliest caucuses and primaries of the 1980 presidential race were beginning, and as the crisis in American foreign policy erupted over developments in Iran and Afghanistan. The national preoccupation with these events dramatizes how much the pace of political life in the United States has come to revolve around the federal government, the presidency, and world affairs, and thus provides an instructive counterpoint to the character of public activities a century ago. The way Americans governed themselves in the late nineteenth century resembled less the political patterns of our own times than those of the earlier part of last century. This older polity was highly decentralized and primarily concerned with domestic political matters. It was a political system in which, among the several levels of government, the states had the greatest control over the direction of public policy and in which state legislatures were the centers of lawmaking.

This book examines several of these older state legislatures in the late nineteenth century. Such a study is needed to correct several imbalances in the writing of American governmental history. American historiography has dealt unkindly with the American state legislatures. They have been the objects of some of the most derisive comments made about any political institution in the United States. More typically, scholars have avoided the study of state legislatures altogether; to say that these forums are almost forgotten institutions in our past politics is scarcely an exaggeration. One objective of this book is to restore state legislatures to their appropriate place in the study of nineteenth-century governance.

American federalism necessarily enters this story. The role of the older state legislatures can be understood only within the jurisdictional relationship that prevailed between the states and the central government during the nineteenth century. Although popular norms prescribed limits on the scale of all governmental activity during those years, constitutional interpretation and political practice granted the largest share of policy-making prerogative over domestic subjects to the states and their legislatures. Prior to the New Deal, the national government had a comparatively small part in directing the internal affairs of state. By examining the activities of subnational government, a historical study of state legislatures focuses attention on the most influential but least-studied side of the federal equation before its balance tilted toward Washington.

The second objective of this book is to emphasize the centrality of policy to the governmental process. Government's primary function is to make authoritative decisions; its chief challenge is to resolve conflicts between competing interests that seek divergent goals. Systematic analysis of policy content and policymaking, therefore, is an essential but frequently neglected chapter of political history. A policy orientation provides one of the thematic scaffolds for this book. The study identifies the contested legislative issues in the late-nineteenth-century Midwest, discusses their broader policy context, and shows the relation between the substance of policy proposals and legislative decisions. Each subject under consideration, therefore, was a reference that helped guide lawmakers to a policy position. Yet the roots of legislative behavior were extremely complex, as is clear from a multivariate analysis of roll call votes taken from fifteen legislative sessions.

The term "public policy" warrants a word of explanation. I use it to mean the authoritative rules that government sets for society. This definition is admittedly broader than others, and perhaps it is too loosely construed for some observers of public policymaking who prefer a narrower and more restrictive concept. It can be argued, however, that present-day definitions of policy as rationally integrated programs of action have few analogues in nineteenth-century America, although governments in the past did make decisions that affected society and that reflected explicit and implicit assumptions about the obligations of public authority. The purpose of this study is not to resolve definitional differences, but to explain the basis of legislative disputes over what government should do.

I take great pleasure in acknowledging the individuals who helped me during the many years of work on this book. Allan G. Bogue of the University of Wisconsin suggested the need for a study of state legislatures, directed my dissertation about them, and remained a loyal supporter of the project through its subsequent evolution. Aage R. Clausen of Ohio State University offered counsel at several stages of my work, beginning with my initial methodological formulations. John Post and Clay McShane of Northeastern University provided constructive comments on earlier versions of several chapters. Advice I received from Aida Donald of Harvard University Press led to some substantial improvements in the book. Dorothy Whitney worked very hard to make my writing more literate and comprehensible.

Wendy Campbell bore many of the burdens of this book, beginning with our collaborative coding of the 1,105 roll calls on which the roll call analysis rests. Many of my ideas about the meaning of these data emerged during our discussions of the project. She then kept the children at bay while I attempted to transform early notions into coherent and verified statements.

The American Philosophical Society provided a timely research grant during the middle phase of my work. The Charles Warren Center for Studies in American History at Harvard University made it possible for me to take a year away from teaching for research and writing during the last stage of the project. I am grateful to the director of the Center and its professors for their support. I have special appreciation for the many librarians who gave me uniformly courteous and professional assistance. In order not to omit particular people inadvertently, I draw attention only to the libraries that I used the most: the university, state, law, and historical society libraries of Illinois, Iowa, and Wisconsin, and especially the State Historical Society of Wisconsin; the Chicago Historical Society; the state library of Massachusetts; the libraries of Harvard University and Harvard Law School; and Northeastern University Library. The staffs and facilities of the computation centers of the University of Wisconsin in Madison and Northeastern University in Boston were equally instrumental in furthering my research.

B.C.

For Wendy, Cynthia, and Erica

CONTENTS

TABLES

1

INTRODUCTION

If Americans have shared any political belief, it has been the faith in representative government. From this attachment to republicanism evolved the chief agency of public policymaking in the American past, the state legislature. The primacy of legislative authority, an idea nurtured in colonial and Revolutionary experience, blossomed into a dominant political reality in the early national period of the United States. State legislatures enjoyed broad and relatively unrestricted grants of authority during those years. Reactions against their expansive powers led later to a curtailment of some prerogatives, but throughout the nineteenth century the state legislatures retained a wide scope of jurisdiction. For most of American history they were the focal points of policymaking on domestic affairs.

Given their historical role, state legislatures have not received the study they deserve. When the nation turned increasingly to national political leadership in the twentieth century, attention swung away from the states toward Washington. Political commentators observed deridingly at midcentury that state legislatures had languished with the inversion of the federal order. As political relationships changed, so did scholarly perspectives. Historians and political scientists began to center their gaze on national political institutions, and the state legislatures of the nineteenth century were nearly forgotten.[1]

In the last century the preponderance of power lay with the state governments. State and local officials, not policymakers in Washington, performed the tasks of government that intruded most often on daily lives. James Bryce, whose *American Commonwealth* remained a standard portrayal of American government for decades after its publication in 1889, recognized the order of this relationship. While an American seldom may "be reminded of the Federal Government," Bryce wrote, the citizen comes into frequent contact with his state and its legal creations, local government.

> His direct taxes are paid to officials acting under State laws. The State, or a local authority constituted by State statutes, registers his birth, appoints his guardian, pays for his schooling, gives him a share in the estate of his father deceased, licenses him when he enters a trade . . . marries him, divorces him, entertains civil actions against him, declares him a bankrupt, hangs him for murder. The police that guard his house, the local boards which look after the poor, control highways, impose water rates, manage schools—all these derive their legal powers from his State alone.

Fiscal relationships corroborated Bryce's observation. State and local expenditures exceeded those of the national government throughout the nineteenth and early twentieth centuries, until World War II. And even if school employees were excluded, state and local workers outnumbered civilian personnel in the federal establishment by a ratio of two to one early in the twentieth century. But neither of these indices fully captures the locus and scope of policy initiative and administration over domestic affairs. These responsibilities resided primarily at the subnational level of government throughout the 1800s.[2]

Unflattering assessments of government and especially of state government have helped to divert historical attention away from the implications of these facts. Writings about political life from the Civil War through the Progressive Era and the 1920s are laden with the themes of corruption, ineptitude, and irrelevancy. Some of the sharpest condemnations were reserved for the legislatures of the states. Following James Bryce's comment that "State legislatures are not high-toned bodies," commentator after commentator voiced similar, though less understated, criticisms. A composite of these complaints portrayed the state legislatures as staffed with unqualified and dishonest lawmakers, controlled by bosses and their political machines, and submissive to the will of corporations, which bought legislative favor when they could not coax or demand it. At best, state legislatures were inept; at worst they were sinkholes of "bottomless corruption." A corollary of this thinking was the indictment of political parties. Aside from their handling of the few matters that advanced their competitive position, parties displayed no leadership, had few principles, and acted indifferently to popular demands. Thus the public progressively lost faith in the institutions in which they had formerly placed their trust.[3]

The understanding of American governance in the nineteenth and early twentieth centuries has undergone considerable refinement in recent years, but old stereotypes persist. Does the conventional wisdom accurately describe the character of state legislature policymaking? Were these forms such blots on the record of American democracy? This book reopens these questions by looking at the legislatures of Illinois, Iowa, and Wisconsin during the 1880s and 1890s.

The study focuses on conflict over public policy. This concentration is consistent with the fundamentals of representative government, whose primary function is orderly resolution of the competition between group interests and conflicting goals. As decision-making agencies faced with varied demands but constrained by limited resources, governments are obliged to choose some policy options and reject others. At stake in many such disputes are psychic as well as material consequences because outcomes seldom satisfy all supplicants. Focus on conflict, therefore, directs attention to the most sensitive nerve of the body politic. Because government has the dual obligation of rendering authoritative decisions and simultaneously preserving the integrity of the regime and the legitimacy of its current managers, disagreement tests severely the resiliency of policymakers and ultimately of the whole polity. Yet the successful resolution of these challenges depends upon consensus over certain issues and procedures. Areas of agreement, therefore, are an essential component of legislative policymaking.

A series of specific inquiries guided the analysis. What issues divided lawmakers? What was the structure of their responses to these controversies and how are they explained? Because of the importance of political parties in the American past, partisan influences are one logical source of legislative conflict to be examined. But constituent expectations and legislators' personal attitudes also are factors that bear on legislative decision-making. Then too, the patterns of electoral politics that placed lawmakers in office, and the way legislators organized their deliberative bodies and conducted their proceedings, can affect lawmaking. So can the interest groups that sought specific policy outcomes. As these speculations imply, the study is based on the assumption that legislative policymaking is a complex process in which a variety of potential influences swirled and interacted. The task of legislative research is to identify these determinants of behavior and evaluate their relative impact on legislative outcomes.

The validity of generalizations about the wider field of knowledge on the basis of a case study is governed, in part, by the setting in which the actors and institutions under examination performed. Most of the following comments about the midwestern legislatures are based on observations about houses of representatives. The lower houses contained more members than did senates, and representatives served shorter terms and smaller constituencies than did senators. Although these distinctions can affect legislative behavior, the structural differences between the two chambers are not sufficiently large to inhibit generalizations about the legislative process, which derived mainly from the actions of lower houses. All enacted legislation and many identical issues appeared before both bodies. And each branch of the legislature functioned within the same political and socioeconomic environment and the same local historical tradition.

Examination of three states insures that the peculiarities of any one do not bias the discussion. Illinois, Iowa, and Wisconsin are contiguous states, permitting this study to be phrased in regional terms. The three jurisdictions do not make up the entire Middle West, but their geographic similarity distinguishes them from the other major regions of the United States. Observations about the Illinois and Wisconsin legislatures rest mainly on analyses of the biennial meetings of 1887 through 1895 while the study of the Iowa house draws on data from the five regularly scheduled sessions of 1886 through 1894. For some questions, a broader chronological and spatial perspective is used.

Partisan competitiveness was a major consideration in the selection of the time and place studied. Republicans dominated state government in the Midwest between the Civil War and the Great Depression; Democrats mounted the greatest challenge to this hegemony in the late 1880s and early 1890s. Voters in Iowa in 1889 and in Illinois in 1892 elected their first Democratic governor since Civil War days, while in Wisconsin the election of 1890 elevated only the second Democrat since 1854 to the state's highest office. The Democracy's upsurgence was translated into legislative places as well. Democrats won the majority of house seats in Illinois and Wisconsin in 1890 and 1892. The Iowa branch of the party came as close to capturing a house majority in 1889 as at any time between 1852 and 1932. Political tides turned quickly, however, as Republicans reinstated their rule in 1893 and 1894. This succession of party turnovers and the relatively close partisan margins in the lower houses represent the apex of two-party competition at the state level in the upper Midwest in the late nineteenth and early twentieth centuries. Since partisan conflict is likely to be greater in legislatures where each party has a sizable delegation than in chambers where one faction monopolizes the seats, the sessions of 1886 through 1895 offer an appropriate political setting in which to examine the impact of party on policy.[4]

These were not quiet years in the Midwest. The period opened with the Haymarket riot of 1886 in Chicago, an eruption that sent emotional shock waves around the country, and with a similar but less publicized clash between labor and civil authority near Milwaukee. The Pullman strike of 1894 and the depression of the mid-1890s closed the ten years spanned by the study. The nativist crusade of the American Protective Association, an anti-immigrant and anti-Catholic organization formed in Clinton, Iowa, in 1887, symbolizes the social strains that accompanied class and economic tensions throughout the era. In the background less dramatized but more pervasive changes were occurring in the social order. Urbanization, industrialization, technological innovation, and increased national integration steadily reshaped the old America, while rising immigration eroded its traditional cultural landscape. The growth of labor and commercial organizations, the emergence of an urban middle class, and the proliferation of ethnic institutions were by-products of these changes as well as stimulators of new ones. The last decades of the nineteenth century, some say, marked the transition from a world of isolated agrarian and rural communities to a more integrated and technologically dependent society.

The upper Middle West was a microcosm of this transformation. Change had diversified its social and economic structure so that by the 1880s and 1890s Illinois, Iowa, and Wisconsin each displayed a heterogeneous composite of economic, social, and population patterns. Yet no state was a mirror reflection of its neighbors. Both forms of variation, between states and within each state, contains the kinds of environmental differences that facilitate examination of the connection between constituency and legislative behavior.

A balance between agricultural and nonagricultural activities had emerged in the region by 1890. Illinois had the most developed industrial base of the three states. Approximately two of every five gainfully employed males in the state worked in trade, transportation, manufacturing, and mechanical occupations, which was slightly greater than the proportion engaged in agriculture, mining, and fishing. Iowa, by contrast, was still primarily a farming state. Fifty-eight percent of its adult males labored in agriculture or extractive industries, twice the number at work in commerce and industry. Occupational patterns in Wisconsin fell between those of its two southern neighbors. Farmers and kindred workers outnumbered commercial and industrial employees 48 percent to 34 percent in the Badger State.[5]

Despite rising competition from trade and manufacturing, commercial agriculture was still of major importance in the region. As with the economy as a whole, factors of change had diversified midwestern agriculture by the latter decades of the 1800s. The Corn Belt dominated farming in much of the upper two-thirds of Illinois, parts of southern Wisconsin, and the lower two-thirds of Iowa. Wheat was an important market commodity in northwestern Iowa, southern Illinois, and the western counties of Wisconsin. By the late nineteenth century dairy farming had replaced wheat as the dominant form of agriculture in Wisconsin. Dairying also figured prominently in northeast Iowa, as well as in northern Illinois where truck farming had begun to attract commercial attention.[6]

Within this pattern of horticulture and husbandry, which defies rigid geographical classification, many farmsteads fell short of the yeoman ideal. Tenants worked a third of the farms in Illinois and more than a quarter of those in Iowa in 1890. Owners, by contrast, ran all but a small proportion of Wisconsin's farms. Extractive industries also supported the economies of rural areas. Coal mining was a major industry in several counties of central and northern Illinois and south-central Iowa. The forests sustained the economy of northern Wisconsin. Lumber and timber ranked first in value among Wisconsin's manufactured products and accounted for nearly a fourth of all wages around 1890.[7]

The growth of industry contributed to the region's urban growth. With a population of over a million in 1890, Chicago ranked as the nation's second largest city, overshadowing all midwestern urban rivals. Milwaukee, a fifth the size of the Windy City, stood sixteenth in the country, and was Wisconsin's biggest metropolitan center. Iowa had no urban equivalent: Des Moines, the state's capital and largest city, counted only 50,000 inhabitants in 1890. But situated on Iowa's river boundaries were many lesser cities, such as Dubuque, Clinton, Davenport, and Burlington along the Mississippi, and Sioux City and Council Bluffs along the Missouri. Smaller cities also dotted the urban landscape in Illinois and Wisconsin. Peoria, Quincy, Springfield, Rockford, Joliet, and Bloomington in Illinois each exceeded 20,000 people, and Racine, La Crosse, Oshkosh, Eau Claire, and Sheboygan in Wisconsin each had 15,000 residents by 1890. Using the conventional threshold of 2,500 people to designate an "urban" place, 45 percent of Illinois' population resided in cities, large and small, as did a third of Wisconsin's and a fifth of Iowa's inhabitants.

The cities lured a substantial portion of the millions of immigrants who settled in the upper Mississippi Valley. Six of every seven residents of Milwaukee in 1890 claimed foreign birth or foreign-born parents. Chicago's foreign stock constituted more than three-quarters of its population. Immigrants and their children made up almost as large a fraction of the residents of La Crosse and Davenport and more than one-half of Peoria's inhabitants. Roughly one-third of the population of Des Moines, more Yankee than most middle-sized cities in the region, were first- and second-generation immigrants. With so many of their residents of recent European background, the larger cities possessed a distinctively foreign quality. But immigrant groups located in rural settings too, as the perusal of census figures and contemporary plat maps attests. For example, Scandinavians and, to a lesser degree, Germans resided more often in the country than in the city. Immigrants and their American-born children composed 74, 49, and 43 percent respectively of the total populations of Wisconsin, Illinois, and Iowa in 1890.

The cultural diversification of the Midwest dated from the arrival of American southerners, who had settled in southwestern Illinois and southeastern Iowa during the early nineteenth century. Their cultural legacy persisted for several generations in these areas, but by midcentury New Englanders, Yorkers, Buckeyes, Hoosiers, and natives of the Keystone State outnumbered southerners. A rising flow of natives from the British Isles and northwestern Europe joined these transplanted northerners. Germans were the most numerous of the foreign settlers. Together with their American-born children, they constituted one-half of Wisconsin's foreign stock and roughly two-fifths of that of Illinois and of Iowa. Swedes, Norwegians, and Danes ranked second among the number of first- and second-generation immigrants in Iowa and Wisconsin, and fourth in Illinois behind the Germans, Irish, and the British (including Scots). Nearly as many Irishmen as Scandinavians lived in Iowa, but not in Wisconsin where descendants of Norsemen considerably exceeded the sons and daughters of the Emerald Isle. Many Englishmen, Scots, and Welshmen also made their homes in each state. Less numerous but distinctive by virtue of their customs, color, or local concentration were Poles, Dutch, Swiss, Bohemians, Austrians, Belgians, and American blacks.

Whatever their origin, the newcomers brought their folkways and customs, of which religion held prime importance. The Catholic church, which thrived with the arrival of Irishmen, Poles, Austrians, and many of the Germans, Dutch, and Swiss, intruded on the older Protestant tradition of the region. Federal census enumerators in 1890 recorded the Roman Catholic church as the largest religious body in each of the three states. Most Scandinavians and many Germans belonged to the Lutheran church, which was well represented in each state but especially in Wisconsin. Methodists, Congregationalists, Baptists, Episcopalians, and Presbyterians, by contrast, counted mostly "old Americans" among their adherents. Methodists, the largest of these old-line Protestant denominations in the Midwest, were particularly numerous in Iowa. Richard Jensen's estimate of pietistic and liturgical orientations among church members gives a suggestive overview of the distribution of religious belief in the region. In Illinois the number of liturgicals, to which Jensen assigns most Catholics, German Lutherans, and Episcopalians, equaled the number of pietists, which included most Methodists, Congregationalists, and Baptists but also other Protestants. Liturgical groups substantially outnumbered pietists in Wisconsin while pietists were more than twice as numerous as members of liturgical faiths in Iowa.[8]

These varied ancestries and religions created a rich ethnic heterogeneity in the Midwest. Census information only hints at the texture of life styles and social customs indigenous to these peoples. Time would lessen traditional attachments as assimilation eroded old social distinctions and weakened the sociopsychological identities that linked individuals to particular cultural referents. But in the late nineteenth century the bonds of ethnicity had fundamental relevance to social relations.[9]

Terms such as "Yankees" and "German Lutherans" can imply, however, greater social and behavioral uniformity than actually existed. The fact that the members of each particular ethnic subculture had a common ancestral and religious background did not mean that they all shared similar attitudes. The network of individuals in an ethnic collectivity contained a range of practices and personalities, and the cohesion of ethnic cultures changed over time. The recognition of these intragroup variations cautions against overdetermining the impact of ethnic influences on political behavior. Yet intergroup ethnic contrasts, both real and presumed in the life of the day, should not be underestimated. They played a substantial role in the political controversies of the late nineteenth century.

2
ELECTING
REPRESENTATIVES

Every two years during the late nineteenth century voters chose representatives for all 153 house seats in Illinois and for the 100 seats in the houses of Iowa and Wisconsin. But not all midwesterners could participate in the selection. Women, all those under twenty-one, certain wards of the state, and unnaturalized aliens in Illinois and Iowa had no legal franchise. Wisconsin extended suffrage to immigrants who declared their intention to become citizens, a provision that significantly affected the demography of the state's electorate. By 1895 immigrants outnumbered native-born voters in more than one-half of Wisconsin's seventy counties.[1]

The county was the most common unit of representation to the lower house, but important exceptions existed. In Iowa single counties, each entitled to one house member, made up most districts. The more populous counties elected two representatives at large while thinly populated counties combined to form a small number of multicounty districts. In Wisconsin the integrity of single counties was not always preserved, despite the constitutional specification that Assembly districts be "in as compact form as practicable." Districts in the Badger State ranged from single wards in Milwaukee, to combinations of parts of two counties, to collections of six whole counties in the relatively unpopulated north. Most Wisconsin Assembly districts, however, consisted of a portion of a county, while a lesser number embraced an entire county.[2]

House districts in Illinois differed considerably from those in Iowa and Wisconsin. The Illinois constitution of 1870 provided for three representatives for each of fifty-one legislative districts. Under a system of cumulative voting, voters had three ballots to cast any way they chose: three votes for one candidate, one vote for three candidates, or other variants possible under this system of balloting. Because they were few in number, house constituencies in Illinois contained larger populations than those in Iowa and Wisconsin. Most Illinois districts embraced two or more counties, but a few districts consisted of very populous single counties. Only Cook county, which contained Chicago's burgeoning population, violated this arrangement. The act of 1882 apportioned Chicago into nine legislative districts and thus allotted the city 18 percent of the seats in the house. By 1890, however, federal census enumerators found 28 percent of Illinois' residents in Chicago, where the largest house district had become four times as populous as the smallest downstate district. Without a state census to keep track of intradecennial population change, Illinois waited until the publication of the national census before reapportioning its legislative districts. In 1893 Chicago gained five additional districts (fifteen seats), which gave the city 27 percent of the house seats.

Large population disparities also existed between the smallest and largest districts in Iowa and Wisconsin. The largest house unit in each state was four times the size of the smallest district. Changing concentrations of population and constitutional restrictions produced inevitable inequalities in constituent populations. The population of Chicago, for example, doubled in the 1880s, and Milwaukee came close to doing so. Relatively free of constitutional constraints on the shape of its representational units, Wisconsin adjusted its Assembly districts to accommodate population shifts more easily than did Iowa and Illinois. Milwaukee's proportion of Assembly seats, for example, approximated the ratio of its inhabitants to the whole state population. Yet apportionments in all three states provided greater equity than the extremes in district sizes suggest. The majority of districts did not deviate greatly from the median constituency size.[3] Malapportionment of urban districts was not a serious problem in these states. But politicians did redraw district boundaries to suit their partisan interests when the opportunity arose.

Parties served as the primary recruiting agency for staffing government, including the state legislatures, during the late nineteenth century. Nearly all midwestern state representatives during these years won their legislative seats as Republicans or Democrats. County party conventions nominated candidates for the state legislature in the early fall of the election year. Individual campaigns for the house generally lasted only one or two months, and sometimes not that long. But these nominees ran as part of the larger party ticket, which included the candidates for governor and other state constitutional offices. In Illinois and Wisconsin, where state and national election years coincided, party slates also listed the candidates for Congress and, quadrennially, for President. Iowa held state elections in odd-numbered years.

The state party convention, usually held in the summer prior to November elections, preceded the nominations for state legislature. Besides selecting candidates for statewide offices, conventions issued state party platforms. These documents addressed both state and national affairs, and the two types of planks were often interspersed within the statement. The mixture reflected the impact of federalism on elections and party organization. From the standpoint of electioneering and balloting, all elections in nineteenth-century America were local activities. Voters balloted for all candidates in local election units, which formed the basis of political party organization. Party activists campaigned within these several jurisdictions to lure voters to their candidates, those for state representative as well as for President.

State platforms did not offer integrated proposals of governmental action, but neither were they issueless. Platforms addressed national issues such as the tariff, currency policy, and voting rights in the South more consistently than they articulated positions on state affairs, although the balance varied with time and place. The emphasis was partially attributable to the different types of elections. Discussion of national issues predominated during Presidential election years, whereas state concerns received proportionally greater attention during off-year elections. Form followed function: state platforms serviced the needs of the entire party slate, not just the candidates for state government. Party strategists emphasized issues that they thought would benefit the party collectively in each particular balloting contest.

In 1886, a non-Presidential election year, the Illinois and Wisconsin platforms gave particular attention to labor issues in the wake of the Haymarket and Bay View riots. Two years later, when Presidential candidates headed party slates, few state issues appeared in these election statements. But between 1889 and 1891 platform emphasis focused on topics under state jurisdiction and especially on the conflict over liquor in Iowa and compulsory education in Illinois and Wisconsin. Eighteen ninety-two was another Presidential election year; yet the continuing fight over school policy was reflected in Illinois platforms, which mixed state and national planks. The construction and unusual length of these 1892 documents indicates that Republican and Democratic leaders had decided to wage a vigorous campaign along two jurisdictional fronts. With the onset of economic depression in 1893, platform format shifted once more. Reference to social policy virtually disappeared in 1893 and 1894, as discussion centered on economic issues of national jurisdiction and on mutual accusations of party responsibility for the "hard times."[4]

Despite these topical fluctuations, several motifs continually recurred in party platforms. The G.O.P. usually reminded the electorate that Republicans had preserved the Union during the Civil War. To dramatize this boast, the party regularly praised the "gallant" military records of Republican candidates. The image of "the immortal Lincoln" was invoked for similar purposes and to accentuate the pledge of generous funding of pensions for Union veterans. Democrats too promised equity for veterans and revered past party heroes, a strategy designed in part to counter charges that the Democracy harbored the legacy of slavery. Democrats placed greater emphasis, however, on the protection of individual personal liberty and on opposition to "paternalism" and "centralization," themes commonly offered in response to Republican proposals for a protective tariff.

Pledges of "economy" in government and denunciation of Republican fiscal "extravagance" similarly found favor with Democratic platform writers. While Republicans also promised governmental frugality, they placed more emphasis on the promotion of industrial and economic "progress." Except for references to the tariff and currency policy, details regarding implementation were either vague or nonexistent. Both parties, however, denounced "monopoly" and "trusts," and habitually heralded the laboring man, whose interests they vowed to support. Each party, moreover, invariably denigrated the objectives of its rival as self-interested and characterized its own motives as responsive to the public welfare. The tactic was cleverly crafted: platform writers sought to turn public suspicion of partisanship to their own partisan advantage.

Party strategists chose these themes deliberately. Their platforms were intended primarily as election-year rhetoric and only secondarily as a list of specific policy recommendations. Editorialists and lawmakers did, on occasion, remind legislators of substantive platform provisions. Yet the dominant feature of these documents was an evocative appeal to partisan sympathies. The emphasis flowed from the relationship between the broadly based pattern of voter loyalty to party, straight-ticket voting, and high voter turnout, which characterized popular politics in the late-nineteenth-century Midwest. Close competition between the parties and an electorate composed of diverse occupational, economic, ethnic, and sectional groups further shaped the context in which party tacticians planned campaigns. Efforts to rejuvenate customary party voting habits can be seen as their attempt to minimize the divisive influences that could destroy heterogeneous voter coalitions. The generalized partisan images that stand out so prominently in the state platforms of the era were crafted with this purpose in mind. They served as common campaign motifs for each party's assortment of candidates.[5]

Patterns of voter participation in Wisconsin suggest the close integration of legislative races with the general party campaign. Nearly as many Wisconsinites voted for Assembly candidates as for President in the elections of 1884, 1888, and 1892. In Assembly races, roll off (the difference between the vote for all Assemblymen and for President) averaged 1.6 percent for the three contests (see table 2.1).[6] In the 1960s a somewhat

Table 2.1.   Average roll off and drop off in Wisconsin (percent), 1884-1894 and 1960-1970.

Period	Roll off			Drop off		
	Assembly	Governor	Congress	Assembly	Governor	Congress
1884-1894	1.6	0	0.5	8.8	7.4	10.3
1960-1970	6.4	0	3.1	30.0	26.1	24.8

Source: Election returns printed in *Wisconsin Bluebook* for appropriate years.

wider margin (6.4 percent) occurred between the votes for the two offices. Roll off in the Illinois house races of 1888 and 1892 paralleled the Wisconsin pattern. These data imply, although they offer no certain proof, that during the late nineteenth century most voters cast their votes for a party slate, making little distinction between major state and federal offices.[7] Regardless of the exact magnitude of straight-ticket voting, voter participation rates indicate that Wisconsinites sustained a higher interest in state legislative races in the late nineteenth century than in the mid-twentieth century. Drop off (the change, usually a decline, in the total vote for a particular office between a Presidential and non-Presidential pair of elections) in Wisconsin Assembly races between 1884 and 1894 averaged not quite 9 percent. By the 1960s, this figure had increased to 30 percent. The vote for governor and, to a lesser degree, for Congress underwent a similar change between the two time periods (see table 2.1). These patterns suggest two fundamental characteristics of state legislative campaigns in the 1880s and early 1890s: voters balloted for legislative candidates about as often as they did for higher offices, and they usually supported the whole party ticket. The two tendencies, of course, were closely related.

The major parties used elaborate organizations to nurture these voter habits. A state central committee and its chairman oversaw party interests on a statewide basis. Representation on the central committee was by congressional district in each of the three midwestern states. The hierarchical structure of these organizations in Iowa was neatly outlined in the Democratic party's "Rules of Organization" in 1893. Besides the state central committee, party procedure called for organizations in congressional districts, in joint judicial, senatorial, and representative districts in each county, and in local voting precincts. In Cook county, Illinois, each party maintained a microcosm of its statewide body: besides their congressional and state senatorial district committees, Republicans and Democrats each sponsored a county central committee, based on ward representation. Rural committees had an analogous geographical apportionment. The

Democratic committee of Fulton county, Illinois, for example, allotted a seat to each of the county's twenty-six townships.

These organizations performed several important electoral functions. The hierarchical committee structures served as communications networks through which instructions and inquiries filtered down from the state central committee to local organizations, while tactical suggestions and requests for assistance passed up to the top campaign echelons. Local party workers polled potential voters, providing state leaders with surveys of current voter sentiment. And party committees sponsored rallies to generate voter interest in the campaign.

The Democratic rally in Litchfield, Illinois, in early October 1892 illustrates the nature of one such gathering. Ten thousand visitors reportedly flocked into Litchfield for the event, a crowd that temporarily doubled the size of the small central Illinois town. In the afternoon three thousand people marched in a parade, which concluded with addresses by the local congressman, the candidate for the state senate, and William L. Mounts, a candidate for state representative. Mounts stood for election in Morgan and Macoupin counties, but Litchfield lay in adjacent Montgomery county. Mounts' visit to Litchfield suggests that party rather than the individual candidate was the unifying theme of this rally.

Nightfall brought more festivities, highlighted by a parade of two thousand torchbearers and a fireworks display. Speeches by gubernatorial candidate John Peter Altgeld, U.S. Senator John M. Palmer, and the chairman of Montgomery county's Democratic central committee climaxed the evening's activities. The "enthusiasm was intense," according to the *Daily Illinois State Register*, a Democratic paper, which reported that the audience of five thousand "remained to the end." Partisan sympathies may have inflated the *Register*'s attendance estimate, but the general tempo of events in Litchfield was replicated in other midwestern localities during the campaign season.[8]

The extent to which candidates for the state legislature separated their own campaign from the general partisan effort remains an open question. Some legislative nominees at least devoted considerable time to their own race. Riley Briggs made fifty speeches, sometimes two a day, in his district in western Iowa during the six weeks prior to his election in 1889. Although Democrat John Dayton stumped "the county from beginning to end" during the 1893 race, he failed to protect his house seat from the Republican landslide in Iowa that year. Wisconsin State Senator Willet S. Main visited many communities in Dane county during his 1888 campaign. Illinois Representative Archibald Hopkins recorded in his journal that his 1892 campaign cost him "much time and $503.50—all used in a legitimate way."[9]

The evidence is unclear about how closely legislative candidates integrated their personal campaigns with the larger party effort, but there were numerous advantages in such a merger. The party provided workers to help turn out the vote, writers to generate partisan propaganda, money to distribute it and finance other costs, seasoned tacticians to advise political novices, and most important, a general symbolic mantle that reminded voters of party tradition. Given these resources and the entrenched status of the two-party tradition in the United States by the 1880s, most successful candidates for the state legislatures understandably joined forces with the Republicans or the Democrats. Nearly all occupants of the 1765 seats in the Illinois, Iowa, and Wisconsin houses that met between 1886 and 1895 maintained at least nominal affiliation with one of these two parties (see table 2.2).

The size of a party's legislative delegation depended on the cumulative results of elections in each of the state's legislative districts, no two of which were exactly alike. Analysis of the social and economic features of these constituencies provides clues to the ecological basis of party electoral success, and it also helps to identify the groups that were represented in each legislative district.

In the late-nineteenth-century Midwest, population concentration bore only a slight relation to party success in state legislative elections. In Illinois the two major parties won roughly equal shares of the seats in urban districts while in the Badger State they traded control of such districts (see table 2.2).[10] In Iowa, Democrats outnumbered Republicans in each session among the few urban constituencies. Democrats showed greater electoral success in the cities than did the Republicans; yet only the labor parties of 1887, the one sizable third-party delegation in the midwestern legislatures between 1886 and 1895, had clear urban roots. Both of the major parties drew the large majority of their delegations from the countryside and small towns, which were the largest category of constituencies in each state.

Since population concentration did not hold the key to party electoral success, what did? To answer this question, a variety of ethnic, economic, and other constituency features were correlated with the party affiliation of state representatives.[11] These tests were supplemented with analysis of the 1892 election returns for state representative in Illinois and Wisconsin and the gubernatorial elections in Iowa from 1883 to 1893. Among all the factors considered, ethnicity stood out as the best indicator of the difference between Democratic and Republican districts. Economic characteristics, by contrast, showed few close connections to electoral patterns.

Ethnicity had a pervasive impact on state elections in Iowa. The proportion of Catholics among constituents, for example, produced the high-

Table 2.2. Party strength in Illinois, Iowa, and Wisconsin legislatures, 1886 to 1895.

| State and year | House seats (N) Urban[a] | | | Rural | | | Democrats Seats (%) | | Governor Vote | Winner |
	Demo-cratic	Repub-lican	Third party	Demo-cratic	Repub-lican	Third party	House	Senate	Demo-cratic %	Party
Illinois										
1887	13	15	8	50	65	2	41%	35%	—	R
1889	18	18	0	54	62	1	47	29	47%	R
1891	21	15	0	56	58	3	50	47	—	R
1893	21	15	0	57	60	0	51	57	49	D
1895	20	27	1	41	64	0	40	33	—	D
Iowa										
1886	9	2	0	29	60	0	38	38	49	R
1888	7	1	1	26	63	2	33	31	45	R
1890	7	2	0	38	48	5	45	40	50	D
1892	10	2	0	35	52	1	45	50	49	D
1894	9	7	0	12	72	0	21	32	42	R
Wisconsin										
1887	5	6	8	24	52	5	29	18	40	R
1889	11	12	0	18	59	0	29	18	44	R
1891	17	5	1	49	28	0	66	58	52	D
1893	22	9	0	34	35	0	56	79	48	D
1895	7	24	0	12	57	0	19	39	38	R

a. Districts with 50% or more of population residing in incorporated places of at least 2,500.

est correlation with legislative party affiliation in six sessions, 1884 through 1892 and 1896. The greater the ratio of Catholics to the total population of a legislative district, the more likely voters were to send a Democrat to the statehouse in Des Moines. Constituencies with the largest numbers of Germans and Irish also were especially hospitable to Democratic candidates. Most Yankees, Scandinavians, and Methodists, on the other hand, voted Republican. By contrast, no equivalent pattern emerged in correlations between party affiliation and agricultural characteristics, such as farm tenancy, farm wealth and valuation, or type of agricultural production.[12] Gubernatorial elections in Iowa followed a pattern similar to that of legislative elections. The combined product of five ethnic variables (Catholics, Scandinavian immigrants, German immigrants, Yankees, and southerners) accounted for between 61 and 74 percent of the statistical variation in the Democratic vote for governor among Iowa's ninety-nine counties during the six elections held between 1883 and 1893. The introduction of population concentration and agricultural characteristics into the multiple correlation models, however, added little additional explanatory power to the regression calculations.[13]

Assembly races in Wisconsin displayed an analogous connection with the ethnocultural composition of constituencies. Catholicism produced the highest statistical association with the party affiliation of Assemblymen among all variables tested. The distribution of Germans (the variables German and German Lutheran) yielded coefficients nearly as high. Concentrations of manufacturing workers, in contrast, did not significantly differentiate Republican from Democratic Assembly districts.[14] Democrats tended to have a higher rate of electoral success in urban than in rural constituencies, and Republicans scored their most consistent victories in country districts, but this relationship was partially the artifact of the high proportion of Catholics and Germans among the populations of Wisconsin's cities. Neither ethnic group was predominantly urban. Catholics and Germans resided throughout eastern Wisconsin and constituted the population majority in numerous rural counties. Measured cumulatively, four ethnic variables (Catholic, German, Scandinavian, German Lutheran) accounted for 61 percent of the variation in the vote for Democratic Assembly candidates in the election of 1892.[15]

The connection between constituents' cultural background and party success in Iowa and Wisconsin can be summarized by classifying legislative constituencies by their ethnic tendencies and noting the rate at which various units elected Democrats (see table 2.3).[16] Despite the unavoidable imprecision in the ethnic typology, the index suggests the extent to which culture affected electoral outcomes. In both Iowa and Wisconsin, Mixed Catholic, German Catholic, and German Lutheran districts usually sent Democrats to the statehouse. Conversely, Yankees and Scandinavians

Table 2.3. Democratic party affiliation of representatives by Ethnic District in Iowa and Wisconsin houses, 1886 to 1895.

Ethnic District	Number of seats per session		Percentage of Democratic representatives[a]			
	Iowa	Wisconsin	Iowa		Wisconsin	
	1886–1892[b]	1893–1895	1886–1892	1894	1893	1895
Mixed Catholic	6	14	89%	80%	86%	28%
German Catholic	4	10	94	75	80	30
German Lutheran	3	4	75	75	100	50
Mixed German	7	—	93	71	—	—
Mixed Lutheran and Catholic	6	14	32	0	86	50
German Protestant	—	5	—	—	40	0
Scandinavian	3	7	0	0	0	0
Mixed	—	22	—	—	50	9
Low Yankee	11	15	39	8	47	7
Middle Yankee	29	9	31	11	0	0
High Yankee	29	—	22	7	—	—

a. Average (mean) percentage of seats per session won by Democrats among the total number of seats in each district classification.

b. Data are averages because reapportionments in Iowa changed the distribution of districts between certain sessions; figures do not total 100 because of rounding. Dashes indicate that category is not applicable.

generally sent Republicans. The record of the Scandinavian districts was unblemished in this respect: they did not choose a single Democratic representative during the seven sessions recorded in table 2.3. In vivid contrast, Democratic nomination to the state legislature in a German Catholic constituency in Iowa was virtually tantamount to election.

The elections of 1893 in Iowa (for the session of 1894) and of 1894 in Wisconsin (for the session of 1895) dealt Democrats a severe blow, and drastically reduced their house membership. The G.O.P. onslaught seated Republicans in districts that traditionally had sent Democrats to the state capitol. Republicans swept nearly all Yankee constituencies and captured a larger number of German districts than they had in earlier elections. Despite the G.O.P. incursion into enemy territory, however, the ties between ethnicity and party persisted. The massive Democratic losses in the mid-nineties confined the party's few house victories to its most hospitable localities, the districts with large German and Catholic populations (see table 2.3).

Culture left its imprint on elections in Illinois too. In the legislative sessions of 1883 through 1893 Illinois Democrats fared best in the Southern and Catholic districts while Republicans scored consistent victories in the Low Yankee and Middle Yankee districts (see table 2.4). And like their colleagues in Iowa and Wisconsin, Illinois Republicans regularly captured the majority of seats in Scandinavian districts. A party standoff occurred in the Mixed German districts and the Mixed Lutheran and Catholic districts; the presence of large numbers of Protestant Germans and Scandinavian Lutherans in these constituencies presumably explains much of the Republican strength there. The Illinois High Yankee districts, however, present a curious contrast to electoral patterns in Iowa and Wisconsin. There the G.O.P. consummated a stable political marriage with Protestants of old American roots, but in Illinois the parties battled to a draw in similar constituencies.

Sectionalism explains this apparent paradox. All but one of the nine High Yankee districts were located in southern Illinois (see table 2.4).[17] Since early in the nineteenth century, Democrats had maintained an electoral stronghold in that section of Illinois while Republicans dominated politics in the north. This pattern resulted largely from differing migratory and settlement patterns. Natives of border and southern states had settled southern and west central Illinois before the Civil War. Disproportionately Democratic, their traditional partisan sympathies lingered in this region throughout the nineteenth century. Native American migrants from the northeastern United States, on the other hand, took up residence in northern and east-central Illinois, and tended to be Republicans. So too were the majority of Scandinavians, German Protestants (with the apparent exception of many German Lutherans), and British immigrants, most of whom settled in northern Illinois.[18]

The interconnection among ethnicity, sectionalism, and party loyalty is evident in the partisan makeup of the Illinois house between 1883 and 1893. The Yankee districts are most instructive on this point. Low Yankee constituencies in northern Illinois usually elected Republicans while in the south the same category of districts customarily elected Democrats. Generally speaking, the greater the proportion of Yankees among a constituent population, the greater the rate of Republican victories to the statehouse. Conversely, as the ratio of southerners to Yankees increased, Democratic fortunes improved. Democrats challenged Republicans most in southern Illinois, therefore, in areas where substantial residues of southern sociopolitical tradition remained.[19] The three Mixed Catholic districts, the only constituencies outside Cook county containing numerous Catholics or Germans, displayed an analogous pattern. Democrats split the Mixed Catholic districts with Republicans in the north, but always won control of the one Mixed Catholic constituency in southern Illinois.

Agricultural contrasts between northern and southern Illinois accen-

Table 2.4. Party affiliation of representatives by Ethnic District and region in Illinois houses, 1883 to 1893.

| Ethnic District | Number of seats per session | | | Percentage of districts with party house majority[a] | | | | Republicans |
| | Cook county | North | South | Democrats | | | | |
				Cook county	North	South	Total	Total
Mixed Catholic	12	6	3	46%	50%	100%	62%	36%
German Catholic	6	0	3	42	—	67	50	44
Mixed German	3	0	3	0	—	83	42	50
Mixed Lutheran and Catholic	9	0	0	44	—	—	44	50
Scandinavian	0	6	0	—	0	—	0	92
Low Yankee	0	24	9	—	23	94	42	58
Southern	0	0	18	—	—	67	67	33
Middle Yankee	0	15	9	—	0	83	31	69
High Yankee	0	3	24	—	0	54	48	46
Summary	30	54	69	40	18	70	46	51

a. The party that won two or three of the three seats in each district is denoted the majority party in the district. Calculations were based on the number of districts won by each party, totaled for six sessions and expressed as a percentage of all seats, for each district classification.

tuated the regional differences within the state. Farms in southern Illinois were smaller, had lower valuations, and produced commodities of lower market worth than farms in the north. Wheat cultivation was concentrated in the southern quarter and the south-central portion of the state, which were also the areas of greatest southern settlement. Chicago, located in the northeastern corner of Illinois and the center of its industrial activity, increased the disproportions in the state's economic geography. But smaller concentrations of manufacturing and mining dotted the state, notably in Rock Island, Henry, LaSalle, and Peoria counties in the north, Adams and Sagamon counties in central Illinois, and St. Clair county in the south. Broadly put, Cook county, the north, and the south constituted three distinct socioeconomic regions in the Prairie state.

Ethnicity, economic contrasts, and historic regionalism were all connected to electoral patterns in Illinois. The vote for Democratic and Republican legislative candidates in 1892, studied in detail, varied moderately in relationship to ethnicity, but regionalism also explained considerable variation in party electoral strength. Controls for ethnicity in regression analysis demonstrated regionalism's independent association with the balloting. Removal of Chicago from the calculations did not alter the impact of regionalism but did reduce the ethnic correlations, which fell to the level of the coefficients produced by economic variables. Social and economic characteristics, in other words, account for some of the variation in Republican and Democratic strength in the 1892 legislative races, particularly when Chicago is included in the analysis, but traditional partisan loyalties common to the several regions of Illinois appear to have had an equally close relationship to electoral outcomes.[20] The form of this analysis, however, may accentuate the comparative significance of regionalism in Illinois' political landscape. The large size of the state's legislative districts possibly masks some social influences on voting behavior that operated within localized social structures.

However ethnic and economic conditions interacted with sectionalism in Illinois, the two parties drew the majority of their house delegations from different regions of the state. More than one-half of the Democrats who sat in the house between 1887 and 1895 represented southern districts, in comparison with 29 percent who won their elections in northern constituencies outside Cook county. The south, Chicago, and the three districts bordering the Illinois River between Tazawell and LaSalle counties in central Illinois constituted the most fertile electoral turf for the Democrats. Illinois Republicans recruited 61 percent of their representatives from northern districts, including Cook county. Had the east-west line of sectional demarcation been dropped southward one tier of counties in *eastern* Illinois, a site of entrenched Republicanism, the regional bias in party strength would have been further accentuated.

Prior to 1870, when Illinois had single-member legislative districts, persistent sectionalism in the state's politics had resulted in Democratic monopolization of southern constituencies and Republican domination of most northern districts. To moderate the rigidity of this partisan geography, writers of the state's new constitution in 1870 instituted a system of "minority representation" whereby each legislative district had three house members. By allowing voters to cast three votes in any combination they chose, including half-votes, the constitutional planners correctly assumed that some voters in each district would pool their ballots and elect a representative of the minority party. This scheme did not end the political regionalism in Illinois, but it did seat Democratic and Republican legislators in previously one-party districts.[21]

The political parties adjusted to the new arrangement by nominating either one or two (and occasionally three) candidates for the lower house in accordance with their assessment of party strength in each district. In the election of 1892, for example, the slates of house candidates in twelve districts listed two Republicans and one Democrat, while in seventeen other districts the party tickets contained two Democrats and one Republican. Republicans outpolled Democrats by an average of 15 percent in the former set of districts while in the latter group Democrats edged the G.O.P. by an equivalent margin. Despite a clear partisan tendency in both collections of districts, the minority party won a seat in each constituency.

The real battleground for control of the house in 1892 took place in the remaining twenty-two districts. Here, each major party ran two candidates, and the margin between the Democratic and Republican vote was close. The construction of these slates reflected past competitiveness, as twelve of the twenty-two districts had recorded at least one turnover in majority party status during the five preceding elections. Republicans had captured eight of the remaining ten districts, but the margin of party strength had been sufficiently close in all to attract a Democratic two-candidate challenge. Only three of the twenty-nine uncompetitive districts, by contrast, had experienced a partisan turnover in the five previous elections. Careful construction of tickets coupled with stable party loyalties among voters and the system of minority representation insured a sizable minority party delegation in each session. But in exchange for *party* competition at the statehouse, the new scheme of representation sacrificed competition between *individuals,* save that offered by third parties, in close to one-half of the lower house districts.[22]

The pattern of partisan representation to the Illinois house during the 1880s and early 1890s was remarkably stable. In the six elections between 1882 and 1892, when the legislature operated under the same apportionment act, a switch in majority party status occurred in only 32 out of 255 possible turnovers. Since many of the turnovers represented an aberrant

Republican or Democratic triumph in an otherwise politically stable district, the index artificially inflates political instability, since in such an election sequence two turnovers are recorded: one at the victory of the minority party and another when the district returned to its former party allegiance. If a party "swing" district is defined as one in which more than one sequence of party alterations occurred, then only four of Illinois' fifty-one house districts can be called highly competitive. Two such swing districts were in Chicago and two were in central Illinois, located among the "border" counties that marked the sectional fault line of party strength in the state. No turnovers occurred in thirty-six house districts between 1882 and 1892. Six of the fifteen districts that had at least one party turnover were in Chicago, where on average a quarter of the house seats per election recorded changes in majority party status. Fewer party alterations occurred elsewhere, particularly in northern Illinois, where only 7 percent of the house districts changed party representation.

The addition of the ethnic characteristics of constituencies to this analysis draws the pattern of party stability and competition into clearer focus. House districts were divided into those with no party turnovers ("stable" districts) in the sessions of 1883 through 1893 and those with at least one interparty switch ("competitive" districts), and the two types of constituencies were distributed according to their partisan, ethnic, and sectional attributes (see table 2.5). Two distinct electoral battlegrounds emerged from the analysis. Seven of the nine competitive districts in northern Illinois contained sizable Catholic and German populations; six

Table 2.5. Stable and competitive districts and majority party by Ethnic District and region in Illinois houses, 1883 to 1893.[a]

Ethnic District	North			South		
	Stable		Com-	Stable		Com-
	Republican	Democratic	petitive	Republican	Democratic	petitive
Catholic and German	1	4	7	0	1	2
Scandinavian	2	0	0	—	—	—
Southern	—	—	—	2	4	0
Yankee	11	1	2	2	8	4
Total	14	5	9	4	13	6

a. The majority party was the party that won two or three of the three seats in each multi-member house district.

of these were in Chicago. Competitiveness also characterized the Catholic and German districts in southern Illinois, but in this region Yankee districts witnessed the greatest number of party turnovers. Three of the four competitive Yankee districts were in central-southeastern Illinois, the approximate meeting ground of Yankee and southern traditions. The other district qualified as a low Yankee constituency and contained a fair number of Germans and Catholics.[23]

Partisan stability figured prominently in the political geography of all three midwestern states, not just Illinois. In elections in Iowa between 1883 and 1897 an average of only one-fifth of the house districts recorded a party turnover. And this rate was considerably inflated by the Democrats' loss of twenty-four seats in 1893, the largest single partisan shift in the Iowa house in the late nineteenth century. Elections to the Wisconsin state senate between 1867 and 1894 evidenced a similar partisan stability. Four-fifths of the senatorial races, on average, returned the incumbent party (though not necessarily the same senator) to the statehouse in Madison. Partisan instability increased over time in Wisconsin, however, and the rate of party turnovers for the period 1882-1894 was twice that of the period 1867-1881.[24]

Partisan continuity and ethnic voting were the two main political currents of midwestern legislative elections in the late nineteenth century. Economic class played a less significant part in determining the party makeup of the state houses. These observations correspond to the conclusions of several scholars who have analyzed popular voting behavior in the Midwest for the same years. Although recent studies have not focused on legislative races, they have documented persistent patterns of party preference among particular ethnic groups and have argued that economic class and occupational function had relatively less impact on voter behavior.[25]

Still, the fact that ethnicity accounted for only a portion of the variance in voters' partisan choices suggests that personal economic status may have had greater impact on elections than is currently acknowledged. Ethnic background and economic position can be interactive phenomena, which jointly affect socioeconomic status. Separating the contribution of economic class from more general socioeconomic influences on voter decisions, however, is one of the most difficult methodological problems of historical political analysis.[26]

Whatever the precise effect of ethnic background on voter behavior, political activists thought it was influential. Many party leaders and candidates for elective office viewed the electorate as a composite of distinct ethnocultural groups and recognized the importance of cultural issues to their political behavior. Such evidence reveals only indirectly, of course, the motivational wellsprings of mass political behavior, but it certainly tells something about the perceptions of politicians. "A time-worn axiom of American politics," wrote V. O. Key, an eminent student of the subject, "proclaims the proposition that politicians keep their ears to the ground. Different politicians keep their ears to different sorts of soil . . . "[27] Successful politicos knew who their clients were and how they wanted to be led.

Scant material has survived to show how candidates for the state legislature perceived the context of their campaigns. But available documents indicate that the ethnic factor entered into electoral calculations. Wisconsin State Senator Willet S. Main recorded in his diary that Democrats had selected his opponent in 1888" to get Rep. norwegian votes." A major objective of his campaign tour of Dane county, Main noted, was to retain the support of this bloc. In Iowa, campaign broadsides could interject both religious and cultural issues into house elections. Shortly before election day in 1887, Catholic clergy in Iowa county charged that Democratic candidate Abraham Owens was "a renegade Catholic," "an enemy of the Cross," and religiously "offensive," and that therefore he was "not a fit and proper person to represent a Christian community in the General Assembly." A Republican circular distributed in Johnson county, Iowa, several years later, which had originally been printed in the "Bohemian" language, contended that the Democratic house candidate "made the Bohemians a great deal of trouble" and was "an enemy of the saloon"—a potentially devastating charge in a state where the liquor issue had troubled politics for a generation. By contrast the circular portrayed the Republican candidate as "a man who always drinks his glass of beer," reprinting his pledge to support the manufacture of liquor in Iowa regardless of party caucus policy on the question.[28]

Men active in other political roles similarly paid close attention to the ethnic voter. A Republican activist in northwest Iowa suggested to Congressman George Perkins that the party should prepare broadsides promising enforcement of prohibition and including church resolutions in support of the policy.[29] Following the Democratic upsurgence in Illinois in the early 1890s, U.S. Senator Shelby Cullom's local correspondents lamented Republicans' inattentiveness to "the Catholic vote" and to German Lutherans.[30] Close attention to key ethnic voters fills the correspondence of Ellis B. Usher and Edward C. Wall, chairmen of the Wisconsin Democratic state committee in the late 1880s and early 1890s, as well as the letters of other party luminaries in the state.[31] Carter Harrison, Jr., remembered that catering to the cultural interests of ethnic groups had eased the way for subsequent discussion of economic issues during his first mayoralty campaign in Chicago at the end of the nineteenth century.[32] Congressman William Lorimer from Chicago overcame the liability of his Republicanism among voters of recent European ancestry by adopting the role of broker rather than antagonist. Lorimer's electoral success, according to his biographer, lay in mediating conflicts among diverse ethnic groups and avoiding divisive cultural issues.[33] Clues to the likely behavior of ethnic groups on election day that reached party strategists through personal experience or written communications were verified by canvassing voters. Both parties conducted polls in the 1890s and recorded voters' nationality and language skills in these surveys. Foreign language tracts were available for voters unable to read English.[34]

Admittedly selective, these illustrations make the point. Many party leaders in the 1880s and 1890s understood that electoral success required the construction of a pan-ethnic coalition. They saw the electorate as composed of blocs of distinct ethnic groups and realized that a false step on certain cultural issues could dislodge customary party loyalties. It is unrealistic, however, to assume that all politicos fully appreciated the nature of the ethnic dimension of their political universe: levels of individual awareness of the environment vary. Those who manifest ethnic behavior, furthermore, are not necessarily aware that they are doing so. Cognizance of ethnicity has two sociopsychological components: self-perception and the perception of identities assigned by others. Republicans, closely connected to Yankee subcommunities and thereby to the country's traditionally dominant cultural norm, appeared to display less sensitivity to ethnic diversity and its political ramifications than did Democrats, whose constituents embraced a wider spectrum of ethnic backgrounds. But whatever the variations in politicians' perceptions of the Midwest's ethnic collage, it affected their political fortunes.

The stability of the political order in the late-nineteenth-century Midwest was tested by a series of short-term intrusions, themselves derivatives of the political culture. From the mid-eighties to the mid-nineties a combination of these divisive elements jarred the political system: heightened complaints from labor and agriculture, incipient third-party activity, zealous prohibitionists, new levels of cultural conflict, and the most devastating depression of the century. The resiliency of the political order was strained by these pressures and, in the end, party patterns were altered.

Labor made considerable organizational progress in the late 1870s and early 1880s in the industrial centers of the Midwest. In 1886 coalitions of workingmen's groups in Chicago and Milwaukee pressed for an eight-hour day. Due to a complexity of events, this campaign triggered brief but deadly confrontations between the authorities and labor demonstrators in each city. The Haymarket and Bay View riots shocked people, including workingmen, throughout the country. The harsh reaction of the economic and political establishment galvanized diverse labor organizations into cooperative political action. A coalition of socialists, trade unionists, and members of the Knights of Labor formed the People's party in Milwaukee and the United Labor party in Chicago and other parts of Illinois prior to the election of 1886. Both organizations enjoyed short-run success. The Illinois workers' party captured eight of Chicago's twenty-seven house seats and one additional seat in the district containing East St. Louis, while some Chicago Democrats won with labor's endorsement. The Milwaukee organization won six of that city's ten Assembly seats. But labor's bid for independent representaton went no further. Opponents' denunciation of labor "anarchy" and socialism, factional problems among the labor coalitions, and fusion tickets fielded by the major parties in Chicago and Milwaukee effectively undermined the workers' political movement. Subsequently other labor groups ran independent candidates but elected only two to the midwestern houses.[35]

Fluctuating commodity prices and agricultural change unsettled many farmers in the Midwest, yet they made little headway toward independent political action. Farmer organizations did nominate some candidates on their own, but the large majority of farmers clung to their traditional party allegiance. Few candidates of independent farmer parties won a house seat. The last remnants of the Greenback movement survived in Iowa during the election of 1885 and to a lesser extent in Illinois in 1886, when the Greenback party fused with one of the major parties, usually the Democrats, in some local races and ran separately in others. No Greenbacker, however, won independently. The most significant agricultural third-party success occurred in 1890 when the Farmer's Mutual Benefit Association (FMBA) elected three representatives in southeast Illinois.

The FMBA typified a variety of farmer organizations that sprouted in response to agricultural grievances in the 1880s and later joined forces to form the Populist party. But Populism too failed to disrupt two-party dominance in the upper Midwest. Rural Populists outside the South were centered in the wheat-producing states of the Great Plains. The comparative economic stability of corn, hog, and dairy farming in the upper Midwest stunted the growth of third-party protest. Populism, in fact, was as much an urban as a rural phenomenon in Illinois and Wisconsin. But farmers and industrial workers, divided over goals and by mutual suspicions (some fueled by ethnic differences), failed to sustain a viable third-party coalition in the early 1890s. Throughout their time of troubles agricultural organizations continued instead to urge farmers to support those candidates of the major parties who promised or endeavored to work in their interest.[36]

The economic complaints of farmers and workers affected political behavior in the Midwest, but cultural issues had a greater impact in producing fluctuations of party strength at the statehouse in the late 1880s and early 1890s. Few controversies were as politically explosive as the debate over liquor in Iowa. The prohibition of alcoholic beverages emerged as a prominent issue in the state in the mid-1870s, and by the 1880s it had become the most consistently divisive question in Hawkeye politics. Yielding to pressure from prohibitionists, Republicans endorsed an antiliquor position in the late 1870s and became more outspoken on the issue in the 1880s. This new stance cost the party dearly. Republicans lost supporters during the decade, especially among German Protestants, while Democrats, who took a more permissive stand on liquor, benefited from their defection. Owing largely to the party's defense of "personal liberty" and its opposition to "sumptuary" legislation such as prohibition, Democrats elected Horace Boise as governor in 1889 and held Republicans to an even 50 percent of the house seats. Republicans regained a few house districts in the next canvass but failed to unseat Boise. These two campaigns marked the Iowa Democracy's best showing since the Civil War.[37]

The major parties in Illinois and Wisconsin approached the liquor question gingerly during the 1880s and early 1890s, and refrained from making the issue a centerpiece of their campaigns. But Prohibitionists were active there as in Iowa. In 1886, for example, the Prohibition party ran candidates in seventy-one of the one hundred Wisconsin Assembly districts and in forty of the fifty-one house districts in Illinois. Prohibitionists intensified their efforts during the decade in the Prairie state: after running only seventeen house candidates in 1884, they put up a nominee in all but two constituencies in the early nineties. While not lacking candidates, they did lack voters. The antiliquor party elected only one member to the lower house in Illinois, Iowa, and Wisconsin between 1885 and 1894. But their potential threat was greater than their annual balloting performance in years of close electoral margins between the major parties. Since voters sympathetic to the "dry" crusade came primarily from Republican ranks, G.O.P. leaders cast a wary eye on Prohibition party activists.[38]

The Illinois Edwards law and the Wisconsin Bennett law, compulsory education statutes passed in 1889, had a greater effect than the liquor issue on altering party fortunes in these two states. Both laws required the instruction of basic subjects in English and mandated stringent regulation of school attendance. Passed without much legislative controversy, the school laws provoked wide denunciation from many foreign-speaking groups and from Catholics. Democrats manipulated the imbroglio to advantage in their successful election campaign of 1890 and kept the issue alive in 1892, when they won again. As in Iowa, the defection of German Protestants, especially Lutherans, from the G.O.P. upset the delicate coalitions that apportioned voter support between the two parties.[39]

The school laws were not the sole determinant of voter decisions in these contests. Evidence from voter studies indicates that in any election most voters remain loyal to their customary party preferences. But a relatively small shift of balloting support from one party to the other, coupled with the abstention of some voters, can significantly affect electoral outcomes. The McKinley Tariff of 1890, enacted under a Republican administration, probably stimulated some temporary voting aberrations of this kind.[40] It is reasonable to suppose that voter behavior in 1890 and in other elections in the late-nineteenth-century Midwest can be explained largely in terms of the way in which party manipulation of short-run factors interacted with the traditional partisan voting habits of the electorate. Democratic leaders, for example, appear to have pooled state-level cultural issues and some national economic questions into a generalized motif that charged Republicans with an agressive "paternalism" that infringed individual autonomy. Whatever the combination of elements explaining voter behavior, many Republicans sensed the main sources of their political woes in the early years of the 1890s. "In this state," Willet Main noted of the Republican loss in Wisconsin in 1890, "the Bennett Law slaughtered us and the McKinley bill buried us."[41]

The defeats forced Republicans to rethink their strategy. The aim of the revision of G.O.P. tactics was the return of the Germans, thousands of whom had deserted the party on account of its cultural policy. The chairman of the Illinois Republican state committee characterized the exodus of Germans, especially Lutherans, from the Republican fold in unequivocal terms to Senator Cullom: "You never saw anything like it in all your political experience." Henry C. Payne, master G.O.P. strategist in Wisconsin, told Jeremiah Rusk, a former governor, "The worst feature of the situation is the almost hopeless task of getting back our German Republicans without whose help it is impossible to carry Wisconsin." Worried Republicans in Iowa urged party leaders to avoid prohibition. Although the dry faction of the party ignored the advice, Iowa Republicans moderated their stand on liquor in the 1893 gubernatorial campaign after an epic convention struggle over the issue. But at the various Democratic headquarters in the Midwest it was business as usual. The party had previously capitalized on the "intolerance" issue and now alleged that the growth of the American Protective Association represented the latest episode in Republican anti-Catholicism and cultural aggression.[42]

Omitted from these calculations was the depression, which cast the country into economic gloom in the summer of 1893 and changed the context of the elections of 1893 and 1894. It transformed the Democrats from the party of personal liberty, in power in both the Midwest and Washington, into the party of "hard times." The reaction against Democrats cut across both ethnic and economic lines, and swept Republicans to victory in Wisconsin and Illinois in 1894.[43] In Iowa, where in the previous year Republicans had overwhelmed Democrats, the extent of the impact of the depression is an open question. The new Democratic bimetallist monetary proposal, offered as an economic corrective, may have alienated many Germans, who reportedly were fiscal conservatives and apprehensive of monetary reforms. At the same time, the Iowa Republicans' new platform position on liquor, which proclaimed that "prohibition is no test of Republicanism," seems to have been crucial in regaining German votes in the state. Whatever the reasons, the depression year elections decimated the Democratic delegations. The party lost twenty-five house seats in Iowa and thirty-seven in Wisconsin. In the Illinois house, where the system of minority representation cushioned legislative parties from the full effects of voter shifts, the Democratic delegation shrank by seventeen seats. Never again would that generation of midwestern Democrats control their state legislatures.[44]

3

THE LAWMAKERS
AND LAWMAKING

In Forrest Crissey's fictionalized account of Illinois politics in the late nineteenth century, old pol William Bradley wrote to his political protégé in unflattering terms about state legislators:

> And so you resent my statement that I'd rather have a son of mine caught stealing scab sheep than see him elected to a legislature? Well, perhaps that was putting it strong. In fact, I'll admit that I did bear down hard on a whole lot of good men when I bunched the entire legislative field in that sort of an omnibus knock.

Unfortunately, Crissey refrained from providing many specifics, both about the individuals he had in mind and about the criteria on which he so offhandedly distinguished "good men" from rascals.[1] But whatever Crissey's opinion, historians must proceed on the assumption that any large gathering of human beings contains all kinds of personalities, and they must free the evidence of past politics from its biases. Fortunately, enough evidence exists concerning the 1,375 individuals who sat in the fifteen sessions being studied to permit some generalizations about them.

The typical midwestern representative of the late nineteenth century was a middle-aged white male serving his first term at the statehouse. Most legislators were in their late thirties, their forties, or their early fifties. At an average age of forty-five, they were only a few years younger than their later counterparts of the mid-twentieth century, but the first group compared unfavorably with the second in terms of legislative experience. During the late nineteenth century, freshmen predominated in each house. On average only a quarter of the members of any one session returned to the next meeting. Rarely did a member accumulate many years of legislative service. Less than 4 percent of the midwestern delegates served for three consecutive terms. Partisan representation of individual constituencies was relatively stable from one session to the next, but individual representation was not. Those incumbents who were returned to office tended to come from the stable political districts.[2]

Abbreviated legislative tenure was the norm at the statehouse throughout the nation during most of the 1800s. The trend in state legislative experience over the course of the nineteenth and twentieth centuries forms a gently sloped U-shaped curve. Reelection of incumbents was more common in the early decades of the 1800s, when state legislatures met annually, than during the latter half of the century, when biennial sessions prevailed. The pendulum reversed its swing in the twentieth century as proportions of first-termers declined, so that by the middle of the century freshmen lawmakers constituted a minority in most house sessions. During the 1950s 85 percent of the state legislators in Illinois and roughly 66 percent of Iowa's and Wisconsin's representatives had served previously. The long-run pattern of tenure in the United States House of Representatives was similar to the statehouse pattern, but in the twentieth century the percentage of experienced members increased much more sharply in Washington than in the states.[3]

Though relatively homogeneous in terms of age and legislative experience, the midwestern statehouse representatives were culturally diverse. The 1893 Wisconsin Assembly (for which the largest file of ethnic information was gathered) illustrates this point. The social origin of virtually every Assemblyman in that session derived from one of seven ethnic groups: Irish Catholic, German Catholic, German Lutheran, Continental Protestant (non-Lutheran Protestants of northern European descent), British Protestant, Yankee, and Scandinavian. Yankees made up a quarter of the Assembly, Catholics another quarter, German Lutherans and Continental Protestants (most of whom were of German background) a similar proportion; and Britishers and Scandinavians together counted for roughly a fifth of the membership. Clear patterns of party affiliation prevailed among each ethnic group. Four-fifths of the Catholic Irish, all the German Catholics, three-quarters of the German Lutherans, and two-thirds of the Continental Protestants sided with the Democracy in this session and together constituted more than two-thirds of that party's delegation. Two-thirds of the Republicans were Yankees, Britishers, or Scandinavian Lutherans. Three-quarters of the legislators from these groups were affiliated with the G.O.P. Although each partisan delegation was ethnically heterogeneous, Democratic Yankees and Britishers, as well as Republican Catholics and Germans, formed small ethnic minorities in the parties.[4]

The early 1890s marked the peak of political conflict in Wisconsin during the late nineteenth century. If ethnicity bears any relationship to legislative party affiliation, the 1893 Assembly should show it. The question is whether the ethnic configuration of this session in Wisconsin was typical of all three midwestern states. Unfortunately, information about the social origins of legislators in that wider arena is scarce. Knowledge about two attributes of lawmakers, their national ancestry (including generational status) and their religion, is needed to construct a full ethnic profile. The case of legislators of German descent illustrates this need for data on religion as well as national origin to test completely the relationship between party and ethnicity. Of the 159 representatives in the fifteen sessions studied who are known to have been of German or Swiss ancestry, 58 percent were Democrats. The addition of religious information accentuates the ethnic contrast in their party ties. All fifteen of the known Catholics in the group were Democrats, as were four of every five of the German Lutherans. A slight majority of the Continental Protestants, on the other hand, sided with the Republicans. Religious background was not located for one-half of the Germans, 56 percent of whom stood with the Republicans.[5]

A close relation existed, nonetheless, between many specific religious traditions and national ancestry. For example, Yankees came from non-Lutheran Protestant backgrounds, virtually all Scandinavians in the Midwest clung to Lutheranism, and Irishmen usually embraced Catholicism. Since religion indexes broad ethnic divisions, a denominational profile of legislators suggests the connection between ethnicity and party affiliation in the Midwest. This composite (see table 3.1), based on all available religious information (on the occupants of 531 of the 1765 legislative seats in the fifteen sessions), displays a pattern analogous to the association between party and religious background in the 1893 Wisconsin Assembly (not shown tabularly). More than 90 percent of the Catholics were Democrats compared with only 15 percent of the Methodists and Congregationalists, while Evangelicals, Christians, and United Brethren (in effect, German Methodists) came close to the Methodists' partisan preferences, as did the Unitarians, Universalists, and Quakers, 77 percent of whom sided with the G.O.P. Republicanism decreased sequentially among Baptists, Dutch Reformed, and Presbyterians. Lutherans and Episcopalians were the only sizable Protestant denominations that were more likely to affiliate with Democrats than with the G.O.P. Comparatively low rates of Republicanism also prevailed among men who claimed no particular Protestant denomination, or whose Protestant denomination was not known. Whatever the actual religious views of the last two groups, the distribution of their partisan affiliation as well as that of the other church groupings is consistent with the general picture contained in recent studies of the midwestern electorate in the late 1800s, which find higher rates of Republicanism among members of evangelical church denominations.[6]

Table 3.1. Religious background of representatives by party affiliation (percentage) in three midwestern states, 1886 to 1895.

Religious background	Republican (N = 299)	Democratic (N = 232)	Total (N = 531)
Catholic	8%	92%	79
Episcopalian	29	71	24
Lutheran	38	62	45
Presbyterian	63	37	63
Dutch Reformed	72	28	7
Baptist	73	27	26
Unitarian, Universalist, Quaker	77	23	22
Evangelical, Christian, United Brethren	80	20	30
Methodist, Congregational	85	15	159
"None"	34	66	61
Unknown Protestant	53	47	15

To build a larger sample of legislators' cultural origin in the three midwestern states, all available data on both religious background and national ancestry were pooled into a composite index. Yankees, Methodists, Congregationalists, Britishers, Scandinavians, and several smaller kindred groups were classified as the "core" culture. Catholics, German Lutherans, central and eastern Europeans (most of whom probably were Catholic), and Irishmen were put into a "peripheral" category, located at the other pole of the index. The residual groups, primarily Continental Protestants, Germans, and Swiss for whom religious background was unknown, and native-born Americans of southern background, were placed in an "intermediate" category.[7] While this nomenclature was adopted mainly for referencing convenience, the order of the index entries does indicate a scale of decreasing social and ethnic status. In northern states during the late nineteenth century Yankees had the greatest social prestige and economic power. In their eyes, at least, they constituted the social elite; numerically as well as historically, they represented the traditional heart of American culture. From their perspective (and that of their close cultural kin, the Britishers and Scandinavians), Catholics of all ancestries and German Lutherans threatened the compatibility of the social milieu, whereas non-Lutheran Protestant Germans, Southerners, Episcopalians, and Baptists, though not at the top of the order, were more acceptable. This scale implies that gradations of acceptability were measured in terms of social proximity to the traditionally dominant ethnic groups in the United States.

Such an interpretation is mainly conjectural because interethnic perceptions and their social meaning during the nineteenth century have not yet
been fully documented, but even if it is only partially valid these gradients
of social distance and ethnic status help to explain the political impact of
ethnocultural diversity in America.

Whatever its status implications, the composite index of cultural
background shows that the typical Republican lawmaker had his roots in
an ethnoreligious world very different from that of the modal Democrat
(see table 3.2). Core culture and Republicanism went hand in hand. The
G.O.P. claimed nearly four of every five legislators (78 percent) placed in
the core classification and recruited more than two-thirds of its house delegations from this group. By comparison, only one of every eighteen Republicans (6 percent) possessed a peripheral background. Men of this origin sided with the Democrats by more than a six-to-one margin (87 percent) and constituted 44 percent of the party's legislative contingent; in
Wisconsin, well over half (58 percent) of the Democrats came from this
group. Party affiliation was more equally apportioned among the men of
intermediate backgrounds, who on average constituted a larger fraction of
the Democratic than of the Republican party in each of the three states.
Despite some variations in these party proportions from one state to another and from one session to another, the relationship between cultural
background and party affiliation was strikingly similar for the three states.
The magnitude of these associations (measured by gamma coefficients)
ranged from 0.71 in Illinois to 0.73 in Iowa and to 0.79 in Wisconsin. To
the extent that Yankees, Methodists, Congregationalists, and kindred
groups represented the traditional core of American ethnic culture, and
Catholics, Lutherans, and other peripheral affiliates lay largely outside
this social preserve, Republicans recruited their legislative delegation essentially from the cultural establishment while Democrats found their followers more frequently among ethnic outsiders.

Table 3.2. Cultural classification and party affiliation of Illinois, Iowa, and Wisconsin representatives, fifteen sessions (N = 847).

Cultural classification	Illinois		Iowa		Wisconsin		All three states[a]	
	R (N)	D (N)	R (N)	D (N)	R (N)	D (N)	R (%)	D (%)
Core	94	33	127	34	97	23	78%	22%
Intermediate	53	51	36	41	33	30	50	50
Peripheral	11	74	2	22	13	73	13	87

a. Percentages are for rows, indicating the party distribution of each cultural
classification.

The ethnic composition of the midwestern houses was the product of three factors: the ethnic structure of each state's population, the connection between ethnicity and party electoral support, and the relative number of seats occupied by party legislative delegations. The last two factors tempered but did not control the basic relationship between ethnicity and statehouse seats: the larger the size of an ethnic population in a state, the greater the number of its members likely to win seats. The preponderance of Yankees in Iowa, for example, was replicated in the ethnic makeup of that state's lower house, and the large number of Catholics and Germans in the Wisconsin Assembly reflected the social composition of that state. This difference between the two states, moreover, extended to the composition of each party in the two legislatures: both Republicans and Democrats in Iowa drew more heavily on core-culture adherents than did their partisan counterparts in Wisconsin. As for Illinois, the social profile of its legislature fell into a middle position, but it resembled the Wisconsin Assembly more than the Iowa house.[8]

The virtually complete ethnic profile that has been constructed of the 1893 Wisconsin Assembly shows convincingly that the cultural origins of legislators tended to complement those of their constituents. Constituencies with large peripheral populations usually elected lawmakers of German or Catholic backgrounds. Of the forty-two Catholic and German districts (see the categories of Ethnic District in table 2.3) for which legislators' ethnicity is known, Germans and Catholics held thirty-five seats in comparison with five held by Yankees and Britishers. Three of the Yankees represented Mixed Lutheran and Catholic constituencies, some of which included substantial numbers of Scandinavians. In the thirty Yankee and Scandinavian legislative units, by contrast, Yankees, Britishers, and Scandinavian Lutherans occupied twenty-seven Assembly places compared with only three occupied by men of Catholic or German background, and two of the three were Continental Protestants. The ethnically mixed constituencies, the main party battleground for control of the Assembly, sent an ethnically diverse batch of representatives to the 1893 meeting. Party electoral trends reinforced these patterns: Democrats obtained their greatest successes in the Catholic and German districts, and Republican candidates did best in Scandinavian and Yankee communities. But party affiliation did not wholly determine the cultural consistency between constituents and Assemblymen. British and Yankee Democrats and Catholic and German Republicans, ethnic minorities in their party delegations, tended to represent constituents of similar backgrounds.

The Irish in the 1893 Wisconsin Assembly displayed a distinctive hold over the Mixed and Mixed Catholic and Lutheran constituencies. Ten of the fifteen Irish Catholics won their seats in these districts. Irish politicians reportedly were particularly adept at cultural accommodation, a form of politics very useful in ethnically diverse localities. Their talents were usually at the disposal of Democrats, who claimed 90 percent of the Catholic Irish legislators in all of the fifteen sessions held in the three states. The Irish connection with the Democracy was so close, to some minds at least, that the biographer of the legislators in the 1883 Illinois house completed his profile of one Irish Catholic with the remark: "To say that he is a Democrat is but to state what the reader must have already inferred." The Irish were highly overrepresented among Democratic lawmakers from Chicago, where they constituted two-thirds of the party's legislative delegation in the 1880s and early 1890s. The pattern suggests further confirmation that Irishmen excelled as political brokers in culturally heterogeneous settings.[9]

In 1894 and 1895, however, the number of Irish Democratic lawmakers declined sharply.[10] It is true that they tended to represent politically unstable districts, the first to fall during partisan swings; but could it be that political instincts convinced some of them not to run in the years that were to prove disastrous for the midwestern Democracy? In any case, the enlarged Republican majorities in the 1894 and 1895 houses altered the cultural profiles of these bodies. Legislators with core origins, who had held 43 percent of the seats in earlier sessions, increased their proportion to 62 percent in the depression years. Representatives of peripheral ties shrank from 25 to 16 percent of the total membership of the three legislatures between the two periods.

Partisan turnovers, however, did not automatically forecast a change in the ethnic background of a district's representative, as is demonstrated by the following analysis of the transfer of thirty-seven Democratic seats to Republicans in Wisconsin between 1893 and 1895. Of the thirteen districts with German Democratic Assemblymen in 1893 that went to Republican lawmakers whose nationality is known, eight retained German representatives while four switched to Yankees and Britishers. German constituencies with German Democratic Assemblymen in 1893 that changed to Republican representation in 1895 displayed an even stronger preference for delegates of Teutonic background. Of the districts in this category for which legislator ancestry is known for both sessions, seven elected Germans and only one chose a Yankee. Similarly, Democratic Yankee and British Assemblymen who watched their seats go Republican in 1895 saw men of similar social backgrounds, not Germans, take their old places. Since national origin does not fully index ethnic background, it is possible that ethnic change was greater than these data imply. Most of the German Democrats in the 1893 Wisconsin Assembly were Catholic or Lutheran, but in all likelihood the majority of the seventeen German Republicans in the 1895 session were non-Lutheran Protestants.

The strong tendency of each stable political district to elect representatives of similar ethnic backgrounds helped to perpetuate the cultural contrast between the partisan delegations in the depression years. None of the nineteen Yankee and British Republicans in the 1895 Assembly, for example, replaced a German colleague who had sat in the 1893 meeting (where precious few German Republicans were found anyway), nor did any of the Democratic districts with German Assemblymen in 1893 switch to Democrats of known Yankee, British, or Scandinavian ties in 1895. The cultural distinction that existed between the parties prior to 1894 proved quite durable in the early depression years.[11] Old political habits die slowly: the association between cultural background and officeholding in the Midwest and in other regions of the United States predated the Civil War, and its legacy was to continue after World War II.[12]

The midwestern lawmakers were occupationally as well as culturally diverse. Roughly 33 percent of the representatives cited farming as their source of livelihood. But many of them also pursued other activities that went unreported in their short official biographies, which were compiled from information that lawmakers supplied. Some delegates apparently had political motives for concealing such occupations as bank president, utility company director, or agricultural landlord. Despite its flaws, the data still suggest the proportion of farmers among the legislative population. They constituted a larger fraction of the Iowa house (47 percent) than of the Illinois and Wisconsin houses (31 and 30 percent respectively), a pattern consistent with the economic differences among the three states.[13]

Law ranked as the second most common occupation. Seventeen percent of the lawmakers in the three midwestern states claimed this profession as their chief pursuit. The proportion was highest in Illinois (24 percent), somewhat lower in Iowa (18 percent), and lowest in Wisconsin (10 percent). Like some self-designated farmers, some attorneys preferred to omit their other sources of livelihood, apparently because the law raised fewer questions about economic loyalties than did many other pursuits. The relative economic neutrality of the law in comparison with other occupations perhaps helps to explain why a higher proportion of attorneys existed in the national House of Representatives, where a majority of members customarily claimed legal careers. Whatever the explanation, law usually constituted less than a quarter of the occupations of state representatives, both in the Midwest and elsewhere in the nineteenth and twentieth centuries.[14]

The lawyers tended to be five years younger than the average midwestern state legislator. Farmers, by contrast, were four years older, on average, than their typical legislative colleague. The youngest midwestern delegates—in their mid-twenties and early thirties—included numerous attorneys but few farmers. In some states during the early twentieth century the age differential between the two groups spanned twenty years.[15] The contrast in ages was due to the nature of their occupations and the necessity that lawmakers take up temporary residence in the capital city during the session. Lawyers' work allowed more flexible schedules than did farming, which was governed by the seasons. The age profile of the midwestern farmer legislators suggests that many waited until their sons or employees could run their farms before seeking legislative office. Legal activities lacked similar constraints; some business could be delayed until after the session and other matters could be transacted from the capital. The public visibility and personal contacts that legislative service offered, moreover, could boost a fledgling legal career but had little bearing on farming.

Roughly 30 percent of the midwestern representatives were engaged in business. Half of this group were merchants while the remainder followed banking and insurance, manufacturing, real estate, lumbering, or coal mining. Physicians and newspaper publishers appeared regularly in the legislatures, as did teachers, clergy, and engineers; 9 percent of the members of the house pursued such "professional" careers. Service, sales, and blue-collar employees occupied 11 percent of the seats in Illinois and 9 percent in Wisconsin, but only 1 percent in Iowa. The small contingent of skilled and semiskilled workers was the only occupational group that showed a partisan tendency. And only in Wisconsin, where sales, service, and blue-collar employees were twice as numerous among Democrats as Republicans, did a clear relationship exist. Unlike ethnic background, occupation was a poor predictor of party affiliation.

The wealth and socioeconomic status of the midwestern legislators were not systematically investigated for this study. But the reading of hundreds of biographies and the occupational profile constructed from them suggest that the legislators were decidedly middle-class. Both Democrats and Republicans recruited their delegations mainly from the more eminent citizens of small town and rural America, not from men of great wealth or nationally recognized professional achievement, or from the lowest rungs of the occupational ladder. Young lawyers, the presidents of small banks, country doctors, local newspaper publishers, urban contractors, insurance agents who doubled as real estate entrepreneurs, merchants and manufacturers of various types, cattlemen, dairymen, and established farmers filled most of the places in the midwestern houses during the late nineteenth century.

Government during that era was a white male preserve. In this respect the state legislatures paralleled other political and economic institutions. Yet, by the standards of the nineteenth century, the midwestern legislatures were relatively open. Every region of a state had its own representatives, as did the metropolis, the small cities, and the country districts.

Railroad clerks, saloon-keepers, and barbers rubbed shoulders with lumber manufacturers, successful merchants, and corporation lawyers. Catholics sat in the same chamber with Methodists, and Yankees with Germans. New faces, moreover, always outnumbered the familiar ones at the start of each session. The midwestern houses were by no means equal opportunity employers, but their barriers to admission were lower than those of other institutions of comparable size and influence.

Several days after the start of the new year, legislators arrived in Springfield, Des Moines, and Madison to begin the business of lawmaking. Save for rare special sessions, the house chamber would have been empty for nearly two years, without any permanent legislative staff to serve during the interim. Since freshmen predominated among each new delegation, most lawmakers entered the house inexperienced in legislative procedures. Consequently it might be expected that chaos reigned during the opening weeks of the session; yet organizational preliminaries were surprisingly orderly. Enough incumbents were on hand to offer some guidance and continuity, but two other factors provided an even more stabilizing effect. One was the legislature's own set of formal and informal rules, which mandated certain priorities; the other was the political parties, which also served to modulate procedure. Both factors offered organizational guidelines for the assignment of seats, selection of speakers, appointment of committee members and chairmen, and selection of legislative staff.

The legislator's first personal chore in the capital was to find lodgings. Nearly all the delegates in the 1886 Iowa house, whose living arrangements probably were typical of those of other state lawmakers, lodged within convenient walking distance of the capital. Two-thirds shared a dwelling with a colleague: forty-one of these resided at one of three major hotels in downtown Des Moines and twenty-seven others lodged in pairs or threesomes at boardinghouses within easy distance of the statehouse. The remaining one-third roomed alone. The few lawmakers who brought their spouses to Des Moines followed the same general housing patterns as the other men.[16]

Living arrangements revealed partisan preferences in that most Democrats and Republicans in Des Moines in 1886 resided among party colleagues. More than half of the Democrats took up quarters at two hotels. The larger contingent (fifteen) lived at the Aborn, which had housed six of the same guests during the 1884 session. Three Republicans also stayed at the Aborn, two of whom had shared that address in 1884. Most of the G.O.P., however, lived in the company of party colleagues. Twelve Republicans spent the winter of 1886 at the Kirkwood Hotel, along with two Democrats. Common party affiliation was even more characteristic of those who sought out smaller accommodations. Boardinghouse occupants nearly always shared their dwelling with party colleagues. The partisan association in these domestic arrangements occurred too regularly to have been the result of chance, but how such selections were made can only be conjectured. Election by neighboring counties seems to have produced friendships that led some Republicans to share boardinghouse accommodations. Democrats exhibited even more residential fraternity than Republicans: all but seven of the thirty-eight Democratic representatives in 1886 lived in the company of fellow Democrats, while twenty-five of the sixty-two Republicans lodged alone.

These personal associations extended to seating arrangements in the 1886 Iowa house. In that year, unlike the other sessions studied, both Republicans and Democrats occupied desks in all sections of the chamber. But seat selections were not entirely random. Party, incumbency, and common accommodations in Des Moines apparently influenced the seating choices of numerous individuals. Most of the Democratic crowd from the Aborn, for example, clustered together in one corner of the hall. Nine pairs of Democratic seatmates either lived at the same address or had served together in 1884, but only three pairs of Republican seatmates displayed similar associations. The G.O.P., even though its larger delegation increased the probability of adjacent seating, was scattered more widely about the chamber than were the Democrats. In later Iowa houses and in the other two states, seating patterns assumed greater partisan rigidity. Delegates selected their own seats in a sequence determined by lot. Although the order of selection was random, the choice of location was not. And customarily Republicans and Democrats claimed desks on opposite sides of the center aisle.[17]

Party was equally instrumental in the selection of the speaker of the house. Each party customarily united behind its nominee in the voting on the house floor, so this stage of the process was largely a formality. The real contest, which began shortly after the general election of the previous fall, took place within the majority party. Typically a number of aspirants threw their hats into the ring and then initiated rounds of correspondence in search of support. Campaigns reached their peak at party headquarters, located in one of the capital's major hotels, where lawmakers congregated on the eve of the session. Politicking, horse-trading, and rumor-mongering, abetted by the press, highlighted this phase of the proceedings. A clear front-runner usually emerged by the time each legislative party held its first meeting, yet few speaker nominees won a unanimous vote in the caucus balloting.[18]

The quest for the speakership of the 1891 Wisconsin Assembly was typical of these contests. The 1890 vote had barely been tabulated when

Joshua Dodge, a freshman Assemblyman from Racine, placed his name in contention in a letter to Ellis B. Usher, former chairman of the Democratic state party committee. Discounting the qualifications of the other candidates, Dodge focused his attack on James Hogan, whom Usher was backing. Among Hogan's liabilities, he argued, was his Irish background. "One serious danger we labor under," Dodge reasoned, "is that appointments will be too numerously secured by the Irish to the exclusion of the much more deserving Germans." Although he was Lutheran, Usher paid little attention to the advice and worked tirelessly for Hogan. Geography played a greater role than ethnicity in fusing this political marriage, for like the candidate he backed, Usher resided in La Crosse, a small city in western Wisconsin.[19]

Usher saturated the state with letters to Assemblymen on behalf of Hogan, and, when politic, railed against the patronage designs of the "Milwaukee crowd." Horse-trading corralled other backers; some correspondents pledged a vote for Hogan in return for Usher's support of a patronage favor, and Usher's correspondence records that he often kept his part of these bargains. When his own candidacy faltered, Dodge lowered his sights. Pledging his support to Hogan, Dodge asked for Usher's support in his "yearning to be chairman of the judiciary committee." But the Racine Assemblyman failed in this bid too. The prize went instead to another unsuccessful aspirant for the speakership. The chairmanships of major committees were some of the few tangible commodities that political brokers could offer in exchange for support in the speakership race.[20]

Usher contacted various party luminaries on behalf of his protégé. One of these, William F. Vilas, Democratic candidate for United States senator, thought his wisest course was to keep his "hands off" the organization of the legislature. Another, Edward C. Wall, chairman of the state party committee, expressed no such reluctance. A Milwaukeean who had been instrumental in the Democracy's 1890 victory, Wall's influence could be crucial in the speakership contest. When the drift of the campaign became apparent, Wall swung to Hogan, but not before he had solicited Usher's blessings on George Porth and Edward Keogh, both of Milwaukee, whom Wall was plumping for chief clerk of the Assembly and chairman of the railroad committee respectively. Keogh, a long-term Assembly veteran, had hoped for the speakership but settled for the railroad post after Usher had cleared his credentials, as well as Hogan's, with railroad company officials. Two years later geography favored Keogh, who was finally rewarded with the Assembly's top leadership spot. The 1891 session, however, belonged to western Wisconsin. Usher's efforts paid off, and Hogan gained a first-ballot caucus victory despite substantial opposition.[21]

Once the caucus had made its choice, disciplined party lines guided the speaker-to-be to his chair. The tight hold of party on this stage of the proceedings was vividly dramatized in the 1890 Iowa house. Republicans lacked but one seat to form a majority that year, but their shortfall cost them the speakership. Opposing the G.O.P.'s bid for the leadership position were forty-five Democrats, four Independents, and one Union Labor representative. Despite tremendous pressure, the third-party men stayed with the Democratic nominee for speaker through five weeks of negotiations and voting, and party lines remained absolutely rigid through 136 ballots on the house floor. Even the flu that laid its grip on many legislators failed to break the stalemate. The parties arranged pairs for lawmakers too ill to attend, and at least one afflicted Republican arrived on his sickbed when his vote was needed. The deadlock ended in a compromise whereby Democrats received the speakership and Republicans got the post of chief clerk of the house and the chairmanships of important committees.[22]

During the fifteen sessions of the three state legislatures that have been analyzed thirteen men held the speaker's post. Legislative experience distinguished these officers from rank-and-file members. All but one speaker had served previously in the house and eight of the thirteen had sat in two or more sessions. In Iowa this pattern characterized speakers throughout the late nineteenth century: between 1866 and 1900 only one of the eighteen presiding officers was a freshman representative. The speakers were also set apart from the full house by their occupation. Not one farmer became speaker during the fifteen sessions whereas half of the occupants of the chair had legal backgrounds, with the exception that none of the four speakers in Wisconsin was a lawyer. In Iowa lawyers dominated the speakership during the last third of the 1800s. Moreover, most presiding officers were in their forties and all had lived most of their adult life in the states they represented. They made their homes in large cities as well as country communities. Available evidence also shows, with greater bearing on their leadership credentials, that the speakers were all solid party men.

In theory the speaker was expected to act impartially, but his job was eminently political. He appointed committees and their chairmen, referred bills to committee, and presided over floor activities, including the recognition of members who desired to speak. Democrat Clayton E. Crafts, speaker in the 1891 and 1893 Illinois houses, embodied the qualities that apparently enhanced a candidate's eligibility for the position. A middle-aged lawyer, Crafts had served in four sessions prior to his election. In a state where antipathies between the downstate districts and Chicago sometimes disturbed Democratic harmony, Craft's suburban constituency in Cook county represented a compromise. His ties to the city were close enough for him to gain the support of the Chicago delegation yet apparently not so close that the southern Democrats opposed his candidacy, despite their grumbling about it. His Yankee background did not offend downstate Protestants, while his past voting record on social issues offered no cultural threat to Chicago Catholics. Crafts had another quality, moreover, that appealed to all wings of the party—he could stand up under partisan fire. Proof came early in 1891, when Crafts' own vote clinched his election on a straight party-line roll call.[23]

The debts incurred en route to the speakership came due when the victor appointed committee chairmen. This was the speaker's first important business and one of his most delicate. In locating the right man for the right job, the speaker had to mix carefully expertise, geography, and the obligation of bargains struck in the speakership campaign. A prerequisite in any assignment was the avoidance of personal offense to minor party chieftains, men with followings of their own. Understandably, these individuals, some of whom were defeated candidates for speaker, were first in line for the chairs of "important" committees. The policy dispositions of potential chairmen played a role too, but these attitudes were seldom critical criteria. Committees in the midwestern state legislatures exercised far less control over the fate of legislation than Woodrow Wilson observed in Congress during the late nineteenth century.[24]

The Wisconsin Assembly maintained twenty-four standing committees while Illinois and Iowa each had more than fifty permanent house committees. Committee heads were drawn disproportionately from the ranks of experienced lawmakers, with the chairs of the important committees weighted most heavily toward men with prior house service.[25] This relationship occurred consistently in each state and cut across other personal and constituent characteristics. Rural districts and their farmer representatives received at least an equitable share of the chairs. Crafts' appointments in 1893 suggest how a speaker attempted to placate various segments of his party. He assigned chairmanships equitably to northern, central, and southern Illinois, to the metropolis and the countryside, to Yankees and Irish, and to farmers and lawyers, in accordance with their legislative numbers.[26]

The tendency for old incumbents to hold a disproportionate number of chairs was probably not due to their experience or expertise in the legislative process, or to the operation of informal norms of seniority. Tenure was insufficiently institutionalized during these years to support a workable seniority system. Freshmen, moreover, occupied numerous chairs, including those of some important committees, even though former incumbents were on hand to fill these more prestigious spots if the speaker had wanted them. Rather, the connection between incumbency and chair appointments grew out of political considerations. By virtue of prior service, incumbents usually knew the speaker, and their policy dispositions were matters of public record. Both experienced members and chairmen, especially chairmen of important committees, moreover, tended to represent safe electoral districts. This pattern points to the probability that the previous incumbents were the men who were most likely to have developed their own personal power bases, a consideration that weighed heavily in a speaker's selection of chairmen.[27]

Each house also bestowed a number of lesser offices. Aspirants for legislative jobs or some other patronage favor flooded the postal system and the hotel lobbies with their applications at the start of a new session. The crowd of office-seekers left a vivid impression on freshman Assemblyman Charles W. Moore. "There is . . . an army of men here looking for a job," he wrote to his wife in his first letter from Madison; "they button hold each member, and use every argument imaginable to secure influence for them selves [sic]." "Official station is extremely burdensome," complained a state senator, because of "the pressure for place and for [railroad] passes."[28]

But legislators had few places to give. The 1887 Wisconsin Assembly listed only 50 employees, including just 5 committee clerks. In 1893, 77 people were put on the Assembly payroll. In the early nineties Illinois representatives hired 101 people, 22 of whom clerked for committees at three dollars a day. Ethnicity figured in these appointments. In 1887 the names of the young pages in the Assembly were Olson, Best, Willett, Peterson, Norriss, and Whitty; six years later the list of errand boys included the names Shealy, Ballschmider, Burke, McCoy, Andrzejewski, and Monshan. The shift from a Republican to a Democratic majority had altered the ethnic profile not only of the Assemblymen but also of their employees.[29]

Once organized, the houses tackled more substantive matters. The processing of legislative business followed a variety of established precedents. State constitutions outlined basic elements of procedure; more elaborate written guidelines appeared in each legislature's Rules of the House, and these changed little between sessions. Unwritten practices supplemented the formal standards. And no norm had a greater influence on the pace of legislative activity than the custom of the short session.

Unlike the constitutions of most states, those of the three midwestern states did not limit the length of the legislative sessions. Nor did the formal rules specify a maximum number of meeting days. Most legislators and publicists agreed, however, that the session should be brief. In his acceptance speech to Assemblymen in 1887, Speaker Thomas Mills pledged to "expedite the business of the session to the end that we may not remain here a moment longer than the interests of the state demand."[30] Other speakers expressed the same sentiment and so did the rank and file. Deliberations over the date of final adjournment began early in the session and continued intermittently throughout it. The discussions concerned the precise week and day of adjournment, not the principle of keeping the session short.

Past practice more than any other consideration determined the date of adjournment sine die. The legislatures of all three midwestern states convened in the second week of January. By mid-April lawmakers in Iowa and Wisconsin had concluded their business. Illinois legislators stayed in the capital a little longer, usually until mid-June. In each session between 1889 and 1895 the Wisconsin legislature sat for either 101 or 102 days, while the number of days on which business was transacted fluctuated between 62 and 70. Assemblymen had adjourned a week earlier than usual in 1887 but had still held 68 daily meetings.

Short sessions derived from the belief that the functions of government should be limited. The longer the legislatures stayed in session, the more "mischievous" laws they might enact. "This country is cursed with too much legislation," the *Catholic Sentinel* proclaimed when the 1893 Wisconsin General Assembly convened. Governor Horace Boise expressed the same thought in his 1892 inaugural address. Newspaper editors sympathetic to both major parties echoed the theme. "The only function of the legislature is to restrict the freedom of men," the Republican editor of the *Milwaukee Sentinel* reasoned, since the "very essence of law is restriction." Many editors breathed a literary sigh of relief when legislators departed for home. The "best act" of the 1890 Iowa legislature, eulogized the *Davenport Democrat*, "was its last one, that of adjourning."[31]

The disrepute in which state legislatures were held during the late nineteenth and early twentieth centuries fed the demands for expeditious sessions. Excessively local and unneeded legislation, the election of inexperienced and unqualified legislators, the reluctance of the "talented" leaders of business to serve, control by party bosses, corporate pressure and bribery, and a general decline in the moral fiber of lawmakers were the usual charges heaped upon the legislatures.[32] John Moses, first a participant in and then a chronicler of Illinois politics during the late nineteenth century, expressed sentiments common to his times. The performance of the legislature in his state, he scorned, "is not flattering to the progress of the race." One "evil" that needed reform, in his opinion, was the "undue" length of the session.[33] To the suggestion that longer meetings would facilitate more thoughtful consideration of legislation, the *Milwaukee Sentinel* answered that the state's solons would just waste more time and still continue to rush ill-conceived bills through the legislature during the session's final hours.[34] Earlier expressions of similar views apparently were among the reasons that the midwestern legislatures had changed from annual to biennial sessions during the latter half of the century. Illinois went on an alternative year schedule in 1855, as did Iowa in 1858 and Wisconsin in 1883.

The desire for fiscal restraint provided another rationale for short sessions. Cynics reasoned that the longer the legislature sat the more it spent, and the greater financial burden it imposed on taxpayers. "An hour or two wasted in talk" each day, one local Iowa paper sneered, "is an expensive luxury." The legislative reporter of the *Iowa State Register*, the major daily in the state, cited more specific costs of allegedly unnecessary discourse. By his calculation, delivery of a long speech composed of "old material" drained the public treasury of $123. To these watchdogs of the public purse, a brief session promised to be a cheap one.[35]

Lawmaking, of course, cost money, most of which, during those years, went for legislators' salaries. Iowa lawmakers received a biennial stipend of $550 and Wisconsin Assemblymen $500. Fixed salaries, some proponents of the short session contended, prompted lawmakers to favor early adjournment. But when Illinois solons received a salary of five dollars per diem, the *Chicago Tribune* charged that it induced lawmakers to prolong the session. All representatives also received a small stationery fund and mileage compensation for one round trip between their district and the capital. Passes from railroads provided free transportation for other journeys home.[36]

The $300,000 on average that Illinois appropriated every two years to operate its legislature during the late 1880s and early 1890s represented 3 percent of the state's budget. Iowa and Wisconsin spent considerably less on their general assemblies. At these prices, the American state legislatures were bargains in comparison with Congress. The forty-two states allocated a total of $4,000,000 in 1890 to run their legislatures whereas Congress voted itself $6,500,000. When these investments in representative government are expressed as a proportion of combined state and local budgets and of federal outlays, the contrast is accentuated.[37]

Nature cooperated with the advocates of an expeditious session. Newspaper reporters habitually noted in early April that the arrival of robins and "the mercury dancing about the 80 mark" infected legislators with spring fever. Farmers were particularly susceptible to this seasonal disease as their attention turned again to their farms. But lawmaking was a part-time profession for all state legislators during the late nineteenth century, and springtime triggered their desire to return to their private livelihoods.

The short session limited the calendar duration of the legislative meeting. Diversions during the course of meetings further reduced the time available for lawmaking. Temporary adjournments arose out of innumerable pretexts, such as Washington's Birthday, Easter, municipal elections in early April, the funerals of colleagues, a Presidential inauguration, a spring baseball game among legislators. Iowa lawmakers broke away for several days in January to visit state institutions. State encampments of the Grand Army of the Republic, an evening concert, or the annual legislative ball might require the use of the legislative hall at night, while during the day business might have to stop for an address from some honored guest.

The penchant of lawmakers to take long weekends cost more legislative time. Quorums were always difficult to get on Mondays and Fridays, and at some points in the legislative season business was restricted to Tuesdays, Wednesdays, and Thursdays. Many legislators left the capital on Friday morning after a brief session and returned late on Monday, when formalities dictated another short meeting. As the weeks passed, this practice taxed the patience of speakers. More than once Clayton Crafts on Friday mornings ordered the doorkeeper to "arrest" departing members needed for an important vote or to form a quorum.

Lawmakers had a variety of specific reasons to head home early, but the demands of legislative business, which mounted as the session progressed, no doubt fed their eagerness to escape for the weekend. Friday, March 11, 1887, in the Wisconsin Assembly illustrates the tempo of activities in the latter half of the session. The legislative day began at 10:00 A.M. when eighty-three members responded to the clerk's call of the roll. Following the approval of the previous day's journal and the presentation of seven petitions, the Assembly heard reports from four committees. The clerk again called the roll, this time on a motion to recall an Assembly resolution from the Senate. Thirty-four bills on third reading next received consideration and 28 passed, 5 on roll call votes. One bill failed on a sixth roll call. Assemblymen then broke for lunch and reconvened at 2:00 P.M., when the Committee of the Whole heard reports on 129 bills, resolutions, and memorials. The day concluded with a debate over the time of reconvening on the following Monday.

Although each call of the roll took only a few minutes, hundreds of roll calls over the course of the session consumed dozens of hours. The constitutions of Illinois and Iowa required a recorded vote on the passage of all bills, and only five members of the Illinois house and two members of the Iowa house were needed to order a roll call on any motion. Wisconsin's constitution did not mandate roll calls for passage but specified that one-sixth of the members present could request that "the yeas and nays . . . be entered on the journal." As a result of this stringent provision, the Assembly took far fewer roll calls than did the Illinois and Iowa houses. In all three states, however, roll call voting occupied a smaller portion of the business day than did committee meetings and hearings, floor debate, and conversation with constituents, friends, and prominent public figures who visited the chamber.

Pressures to expedite proceedings grew as the date of final adjournment approached. Reluctantly, legislators submitted to afternoon, evening, and Saturday meetings, full business days on Monday and Friday, and time limits on debate. Mass executions of legislation were ordered; a "sifting committee" served death warrants on long lists of ill-fated bills in Iowa. Despite the accelerated pace, much legislation was uncompleted by the last days of the session. The waning hours witnessed a mad scramble of activity, often near chaos, as lawmakers rushed to settle lingering controversies or slip pet bills through the chamber. When the speaker declared the house adjourned sine die, pandemonium erupted. Bills that had failed to get off the ground legally were flung into the air with other heavier objects to celebrate the end of official duties. But these ceremonies were brief. Within thirty-six hours scarcely a lawmaker could be found in the capital.

The last-minute rush in the midwestern legislatures was an endemic feature of American state legislatures. It was the price paid for deference to the short session. Iowa lawmakers, who could enter their sentiments on specific bills in the house journal, frequently complained of the insufficient time to consider legislation. Measured against the obstacle of these tight schedules, several informed observers from other states thought that their own legislatures had not done so badly.[38] Midwestern representatives doomed scores of bills during the final days of the session; yet these wholesale slaughters constituted the process, not the cause, of unfavorable action. Legislation with measurable support had received a fuller hearing earlier.

The interaction of lawmakers day after day, week upon week, on the house floors and in committee rooms created a breeding ground of potential personal conflict. The legislatures developed several mechanisms for upholding standards of parliamentary order and personal etiquette. In addition to the Rules of the House, which outlined formal procedures for conducting business, social conventions induced lawmakers to carry on their business with decorum. Legislators followed a variety of rituals that reinforced the norm of civility.

Customary expressions of personal courtesy began the session. Representatives of long service in Iowa and Wisconsin were invited to claim their old seats. Iowa tradition granted the privilege of convening the first meeting of the session to its oldest member. In all three states bipartisan committees escorted newly elected speakers to their chairs. Throughout the session lawmakers were supposed to "respectfully address" the presiding officer as "Mr. Speaker" and to "avoid personality" in debate. Ritualistic expressions of personal courtesy continued to the closing moments of the session, when speakers received public thanks for their "efficient" and "impartial" manner of presiding over the house. According to custom, a member of the opposition party offered these resolutions of thanks and a representative of the speaker's own party presented a gift to him. Then the speaker dismissed the delegates on a note of social harmony by recalling the friendships formed during the meeting. These symbolic gestures of civility reminded legislators that the transaction of legislative business should conform to rudimentary standards of courtesy.

Genuine friendships had formed during the months at the state-house. "When the gavel fell on the opening day we were mostly strangers. In the intimate association of daily public service we have come to know each other well," Speaker George Burrows eulogized before the departing members of the 1895 Wisconsin Assembly.[39] The limerick writers in Iowa whose custom it was to move final adjournment in verse touched on the same theme. Representative Archibald Hopkins of Illinois confided in his journal that he had "formed many pleasant acquaintances" during his first term in Springfield.[40] The social arrangements of legislators virtually in-sured that friendships would develop. Typically, representatives left their wives at home and arrived as strangers to the city's social circles. During their tenure in the house they were in constant contact with legislative col-leagues, both within the halls of the statehouse and outside them.

The structure of these social networks can only be guessed at, but the housing arrangement of the Iowa representatives in 1886, as well as the seating patterns in all three midwestern houses, suggests that intraparty friendships outnumbered those that developed across party lines. Law-makers formed initial acquaintances at the pre-session party gatherings. Wisconsin State Senator Willet Main noted in his diary early in his maiden term, "I am trying to become acquainted with Senators, especially Re-pubn. Senators."[41] The Illinois and Wisconsin solons who took time off to play baseball on spring afternoons chose sides along party lines. Fraternity among party colleagues strengthened party cohesion and helped to divorce personal from ideological disagreements. Whatever their patterns, close acquaintanceships reinforced the codes of personal civility.

Friendships and the norm of civility ameliorated but did not elimi-nate personal conflict. Resentments resulting from failure to win legisla-tive offices, party disloyalty, and other irritations flared during the ses-sion. And the last-minute rushes occasioned especially unparliamentary behavior. Since the riot of activity at this stage of the proceedings left speakers particularly vulnerable to charges of arbitrariness, the wisest of them would turn the chair over to a temporary replacement. But not "cool, chilly Crafts, the man without nerves." His oversight of floor activ-ities—or lack of it—at these times won him some unkindly epithets. For some "sharp parliamentary practices" during consideration of partisan measures, Republicans labeled the Illinois speaker Czar and Despot. "You could give Tom Reed points," yelled one Republican, equating Crafts' re-fusal to allow the clerk to verify a roll call on the World's Fair appropria-tion with the style of the iron-willed Speaker of the national House of Representatives. Such criticism did not affect Crafts' style, however, for 1893 brought another round of denunciations of his "strong arm work." Crafts' decidedly partisan performance was exceptional. Other speakers avoided arousing such high levels of indignation among the minority.[42]

Strain and tension mounted and tempers sometimes wore thin as the legislative pace accelerated. Fist fights were not unheard of; but when fatigue set in, humor and horseplay often softened the acrimony. Reporters apparently savored a break in the action as much as did lawmakers, for the representatives of the press were fond of recording these lighter moments. Once, in answer to a Republican's inquiry as to whether a bill to suppress obscene literature would prevent the circulation of Democratic newspapers, a Democrat replied that it would, as such papers usually published "facts" in reference to the gentleman's own party.[43]

Many houses had their resident humorist, like Representative F. F. Roe, a farmer by trade, who sat in the 1888 Iowa house. One morning he arrived in the chamber to find his desk decorated with a bouquet of artificial flowers garnishing a skunk's tail. When scheduled business was concluded, Roe took the floor to express his gratitude to his colleagues:

> Mr. Speaker, I can never explain the emotions which are in my bosom at this token of respect . . . nor will my botanical knowledge allow me to diagnose all these beautiful flowers surrounding this magnificent one in the middle . . . This center plume is very common in my county, and is also very fragrant . . . but may not be generally understood by all members of this House.

The house accepted Mr. Roe's gesture of appreciation with "immense hilarity."[44] On the other hand, when blacks or Chinese were smuggled into house seats as a practical joke, the uglier side of the era's social conventions came to view.[45]

Despite breakdowns in decorum, the norm of civility helped to maintain legislative order. The standard of personal courtesy functioned as an institutionalized mechanism to combat the animosities that diverse interests and personalities inevitably spawned. Together with the bonds of fellowship that emerged during the session, the expectations of individual courtesy gave truth to the aphorism that opponents were "our friends the enemy."

Written rules specified the formal procedures of lawmaking but did not tell representatives what substantive considerations to follow in shaping public policy. Formal codes did not instruct legislators when they should put the needs of the whole state before those of their local constituents or how to balance the dictates of conscience against loyalty to party. In theory, lawmakers were free agents in that they could draw on any inspiration they chose in deciding public policy questions. In practice, however, popular sentiment placed a greater premium on some styles of representation than on others.

The most common legislative role that state legislators adopted in the public portrayal of their duties was deference to constituents. The Iowa lawmaker who stated, "I regard it as a duty, in a Representative capacity, to voice the sentiment of my constituents," echoed the public testimony of many legislators. By asserting that they "knew" or "ascertained" the wishes of their constituents and acted accordingly, house members implied that they were behaving as instructed delegates. Some legislators gave explicit appraisals of constituent expectations. "I think I represent the sentiment of 90 percent of the people of my district when I advocate the passage of this bill," announced a delegate from Cook county. The desires of the Germans, the farmers, the miners, and other constituent groups were similarly cited as policy references. In a variety of ways and on numerous occasions, state legislators in Illinois, Iowa, and Wisconsin during the 1880s and 1890s pledged fealty to their constituents. The point is not that the welfare of lawmakers' districts in fact took precedence over all other factors weighing on their policy decisions, but that they so frequently chose to portray their behavior in this way.[46]

Legislators pointed to other influences that affected their policy performance. The delegate who announced, "I am here as a representative of the people—no monopoly, trust or syndicate can control my actions or vote," was expounding in gradiose terms a relatively common motif, one with which lawmakers explained their political stands by announcing publicly that the needs of the state took precedence over special interests. In particular, legislation that affected occupational or entrepreneurial groups or broad economic and fiscal policy prompted lawmakers to defend their positions on such grounds. Loyalty to party, on the other hand, was rarely used to justify legislative behavior publicly, although lawmakers often expressed sympathy with the principles of their own party. A legislator could also draw upon his own convictions to decide his best course of action. But state lawmakers hardly ever explained their actions in these terms. The role of trustee, in which a legislator relies heavily on his own independent judgment in making decisions, was not a popular model of representation.

Lawmakers' fondness for portraying their representational role in constituent terms raises the question whether they knew what the residents of their districts wanted. This inquiry has important implications for the historical analysis of legislative behavior. The impact of constituent policy preferences on the dynamics of decision-making cannot be measured directly. As with any determinant of behavior, constituent influence on legislative performance must be inferred from several sources of information, including correlations between roll call voting and indicators of the socioeconomic demography of legislative districts. Yet circumstantial evidence indicates that representatives were relatively well informed about sentiments in their districts. The fact that few citizens followed legislative deliberations with great care or took interest in more than a handful of issues at any particular time simplified the task of assessing constituent opinion.[47] The pertinent question for lawmakers was which particular issues concerned constituents and how opinion was divided about them.

The structure of state legislative representation facilitated lawmakers' access to constituents. The median house district in Iowa contained between 16,000 and 17,000 inhabitants and in Wisconsin between 14,000 and 15,000 people. The average house member in Iowa represented no more than 4,000 voters while his counterpart in Wisconsin was responsible to about 3,500 adult males. Since a legislator favored mainly the interests of the constituents who voted for him, the number of pertinent opinionmakers should be reduced still more. As for Illinois, its multi-member districts made for larger constituencies, but the general conditions that characterized Iowa and Wisconsin applied to Illinois as well. Official duties, moreover, did not take the representatives of any state away from their districts for long. The short session and the rapid turnover of legislative personnel worked against this and helped to prevent legislative isolation from local concerns. Through their legislative campaigns, their service in local office, and their other political activities, state representatives had numerous occasions to listen to their constituents.

Contact with constituents did not end when legislators entered the house chamber. Letters and petitions flowed into the statehouse. It is impossible to gauge the impact of these communiqués precisely, but legislators did draw attention to them. The testimony, "Personally I am opposed to the bill, but receiving petitions only in favor of it, I vote Aye," was occasionally inserted in the house journal by Iowa lawmakers. Some legislators announced that they had been "instructed" by their county board or some other official body to take a particular position. A stream of visitors to the statehouse brought other messages. Business at the statehouse attracted a variety of occupational and entrepreneurial lobbyists, but delegations of mayors and local public officials, citizen interest groups, state and local party leaders and hangers-on, and of course friends also made the trip to the capitol. Legislators' long weekend trips home, while destructive of house quorums, could serve a constructive purpose if a representative chose to take stock of his constituents. Opinions that did not surface in these conversations may well have been aired in the local newspapers that were published in most counties of the Midwest.

State representatives had little excuse not to be informed about what their constituents wanted. Ritualistic expressions of deference to constituent interest, therefore, embodied more than just hollow rhetoric. The extent to which these constituent signals actually shaped the responses of lawmakers to contested issues, however, is a different question.

4
THE
CONTESTED ISSUES

States made policy on a wide variety of subjects in the late nineteenth century. Education and morals, the authorization and regulation of commercial and professional activity, the maintenance of health, penal, and welfare institutions, the creation of local governments and the specification of their administrative and electoral functions, taxation, civil and criminal law, and the definition of property rights and human liberties all were topics of state action. Despite the substantive scope of their activities, the power of the states was not unlimited, of course, for the Constitution of the United States and the state constitutions, tempered by court interpretations, circumscribed state jurisdiction. These legal-constitutional constraints, however, including the new judicial restrictions on state commercial regulations that came at the end of the century, must be viewed within the framework of all governmental functions. In the nineteenth century, when the role of the national government was far more limited than it has been since 1932, states exercised the primary responsibility for shaping laws on domestic subjects.

The state legislatures were the focal points of such policymaking. And they were busy places. Between 1886 and 1895, during the fifteen regularly scheduled sessions of the Illinois, Iowa, and Wisconsin general assemblies, lawmakers considered more than 17,000 bills and 1,500 resolutions, an average of 1,250 separate items per session. The substance of their agendas was further broadened by amendments on issues that were extraneous to the parent legislation. The reason that legislatures did not become hopelessly backlogged by this load of business was that most of it was noncontroversial, though not necessarily unimportant, and therefore it could be either speedily passed or quickly rejected. Only a fraction of all legislation disturbed the consensus. But these relatively few contested issues consumed a disproportionate amount of legislative time and energy and dominated the public attention given to legislative affairs.

This study concentrates on the contested issues, which have been defined as the most divisive legislation on general public policy in each of the fifteen sessions of the midwestern houses examined. The identification of these issues among the larger universe of legislation represents a sample, and, as with any sampling procedure, its methodological foundation bears an integral relationship to the results of the research. The sampling strategy used in this study satisfied several general requirements. The methodology had to be systematically applicable to all fifteen sessions; it had to produce a data base large enough to support meaningful generalizations about legislative policymaking, yet still reduce a mass of information to manageable proportions for subsequent research; and it had to select data that were suitable for a multivariate analysis of the sources of policy conflict. These several criteria pointed to roll call votes, which are the most uniform and easily obtainable body of information about the policy attitudes of nineteenth-century state legislators.

These general prerequisites governed the way the sampling procedure was implemented. In its operational form, a contested issue was a bill that satisfied each of three tests, which encompassed standards of policy content, parliamentary motion, and yea-nay divisiveness. Since the appendix to this book details the mechanics of the process, each step in collecting the sample needs only a brief summary here.[1]

First, only roll calls on bills that concerned issues of general public policy under state jurisdiction were retained. Second, "unimportant" parliamentary motions were discarded and the minority positions on the remaining roll calls on each bill were averaged, which produced an index of voting conflict for each bill. And third, a threshold value of roll call voting divisiveness was established, which was used as the final criterion for a bill's inclusion in the sample. The conflict-level threshold was set equal to two-thirds of the proportion of the minority party delegates to the full membership of each house session. Use of a standard of conflict that varied with the size of party delegations in the fifteen sessions served two purposes: it could be set high enough to pare thousands of votes down to a manageable number and it was sufficiently flexible to insure that most partisan votes, of particular interest to the study, would be retained.

The sampling process yielded 998 roll calls on 550 bills and resolutions in the fifteen legislatures that met between 1886 and 1895. Roughly 3 percent of all bills and a considerably higher but unknown proportion of all roll calls taken in these sessions are contained in the sample. To this core of data were added 107 supplementary votes, which represent either divisive roll calls on subjects outside the substantive perimeters of the sample (principally resolutions to Congress on selected national issues and apportionment bills) or measures with low voting conflict of particular interest.

Since the contested issues were identified on the basis of roll call voting, it is reasonable to ask whether contemporaries of the late nineteenth century would have concurred that the sample represents the most controversial items of legislative business. A definite answer to the question cannot be given because the information available to corroborate the sample systematically is meager. But extant evidence tends to support its validity. One independent assessment of legislative conflict is an anonymous compilation of the "important actions of members of the House of Representatives" that appeared in the 1892 Iowa *House Journal*.[2] Probably selected by the chief clerk of the house, this list of "votes on contested measures of general interest" contains forty-one bills, resolutions, and committee reports. Twenty-two of these items qualified as contested issues in the sample of votes in the 1892 Iowa house, at least eight others concerned issues embodied in contested legislation in the 1890 and 1894 houses, and eight more items had been chosen as supplementary votes before the house journal compilation was discovered.

The other source that exists for verifying the sample in a relatively systematic fashion consists of newspaper reports. Despite their editorial biases, newspapers provide a fairly comprehensive account of state legislative activities in the late nineteenth century. The picture of policymaking contained in these reports shows that a handful of issues usually emerged as the outstanding controversies of each session. Generally, this legislation also provoked considerable roll call divisiveness. In Iowa, the roll call battles over liquor and school textbooks received extensive press publicity. The legislative fights over compulsory education in Illinois and Wisconsin similarly were headline news. Legislative conflict in Illinois over the construction of a sanitary canal and the appropriation for the World's Fair also attracted much attention from the press.[3]

Exceptions occurred, however, for the press gave generous space to some issues that did not produce substantial roll call dissonance. More commonly, many issues that generated sharp voting conflict received little if any newspaper coverage. This latter pattern, however, may have resulted as much from editorial policy predicated on attracting readers as from a commitment to report legislative events comprehensively. Still, press reports suggest that the sample of contested issues contain most of the highly divisive subjects of public policy debated at the statehouse.

A review of these issues is facilitated by classifying them by their policy content. The 550 bills on contested issues were placed into one of five broad policy spheres: Community Mores, Commerce, Fiscal Policy, Government, and Public Services. These categories form the basic substantive framework of the analysis of legislative voting in this study. The policy spheres were then subdivided into more specialized content categories, which produced a total of seventeen policy topics.

Community Mores contains legislation on liquor policy, the schools, standards of personal social behavior and the status of social minorities, the rights of the criminally accused and the indigent, and expressions of American nationalism.[4] The dominant characteristic of these policy deliberations was debate over cultural norms. Embodying social rules for society, Community Mores reflects struggles over the legitimization of values, and thus references issues of a highly symbolic nature. Most public policy contains a symbolic dimension, for every authoritative decision of government ultimately reflects a philosophic choice. What distinguishes Community Mores from the other policy spheres is the extent to which it legislated symbolic social choices and normative cultural assumptions.[5]

The legislation of the four other policy spheres, by contrast, had more tangible, practical consequences. This is particularly true of Commerce, which allocated scarce economic resources among particular economic groups. Legislation on Commerce has been subdivided into four categories: business (railroads, manufacturing, merchandising, and other commercial activities), private finance (banks, securities, interest rates, and insurance), agriculture and labor, and property rights. The third sphere, Fiscal Policy, embraces bills that raised and dispensed public monies, legislation classified as either taxation or expenditure. Government, the fourth sphere, involves the procedural functions of state and local government and includes three main topics: election procedures, political structure (the judiciary, state agencies and institutions, and the oversight of local government), and policy regarding officeholders. Finally, Public Services contains legislation on specific administrative functions that were performed by states or delegated to local government: public health and safety, roads, and a residual category of legislation on miscellaneous subjects.[6]

The classification of the contested-issue roll calls by policy sphere (table 4.1) shows that each of these broad substantive categories holds a substantial portion of the total sample of votes, but that Community Mores and Commerce proved the most contentious subjects.[7] Voting disputes over Fiscal Policy and Public Services not only contain the fewest roll calls, but the incidence of these disputes fluctuated more widely from session to session, especially in Illinois and Iowa, than did controversies over other types of legislation. Since the five separate policy spheres were created in part on the basis of the actual pattern of roll call fights and not simply out of an abstract conceptualization of policy content, the more specialized policy topics indicated substantive modalities in voting conflict with greater precision (table 4.2). Lawmakers in each of the three states divided most frequently over Liquor, Business, Expenditures, Political

Table 4.1. Number of roll call votes on contested issues by policy sphere and session in the Illinois, Iowa, and Wisconsin houses, 1886 to 1895.

State and year	Community Mores	Commerce	Fiscal Policy	Government	Public Services	Session total
Illinois						
1887	32	12	18	13	6	81
1889	12	25	8	13	15	73
1891	16	9	25	16	3	69
1893	15	13	6	19	20	73
1895	10	22	2	15	13	62
Total	85	81	59	76	57	358
Iowa						
1886	28	17	20	17	1	83
1888	32	18	12	15	23	100
1890	15	4	13	2	15	49
1892	10	24	5	11	7	57
1894	23	12	12	10	21	78
Total	108	75	62	55	67	367
Wisconsin						
1887	6	17	10	14	8	55
1889	6	16	10	13	7	52
1891	18	16	10	6	4	54
1893	12	19	7	8	2	48
1895	21	12	11	12	8	64
Total	63	80	48	53	29	273
Total for three states	256	236	169	184	153	998

Structure, and Personnel, policy topics that held 51 percent of the contested roll calls. This clustering was most apparent in Wisconsin, where 63 percent of the votes on contested issues concerned these five topics. By contrast, legislation on Nationalism, Property, Taxation, Elections, and Roads generated a much lower rate of conflict and accounted for only 14 percent of the total number of roll calls sampled. One particular policy topic, moreover, tended to attract a disproportionate amount of controversy in each state: Liquor in Iowa, Business in Wisconsin, and Expenditures in Illinois. Prairie State representatives, however, distributed their disagreements more equally among the seventeen policy topics than did their colleagues in the other two states.

Table 4.2. Percentage distribution of roll call votes and bills on contested issues by policy sphere and policy topic in the Illinois, Iowa, and Wisconsin houses, fifteen sessions.[a]

Policy classification	Roll calls			All three states	
	Illinois	Iowa	Wisconsin	Roll calls	Bills
Policy Sphere					
Community Mores	24	29	23	26	22
Commerce	23	20	29	24	23
Fiscal Policy	16	17	18	17	15
Government	21	15	19	18	22
Public Services	16	18	11	15	18
Policy Topic					
Liquor	7	17	11	12	8
Schools	4	3	4	4	3
Social behavior	4	6	7	5	5
Rights	7	2	1	3	3
Nationalism	2	1	1	1	2
Business	7	5	21	10	11
Private finance	5	8	2	5	5
Agriculture and labor	6	5	4	5	4
Property	4	2	2	3	4
Taxation	3	4	4	4	4
Expenditure	13	13	14	13	11
Elections	3	2	1	2	3
Political structure	11	5	8	8	8
Personnel	8	8	10	9	11
Public health and safety	9	3	5	6	7
Roads	4	5	2	4	4
Miscellany	3	10	3	6	6

a. Percentages are rounded and are based on the cumulative totals of roll call votes and bills for five sessions of each state, and on the cumulative totals of roll calls and bills in the fifteen sessions.

The quantitative profiles shown in tables 4.1 and 4.2 record the broad substantive distribution of roll call disputes and index their relative frequency among the states and between sessions. Although lawmakers themselves may have classified individual legislative proposals into generalized policy categories similar to the ones discussed in this chapter, they could have done so only after appraising the content of each item. Analysis of the contested issues and their connection with patterns of legislative voting behavior therefore requires a closer description of legislative content. This discussion does not review every contested issue. Rather, the objective has been to summarize the characteristic elements of legislation within each topical classification and to sketch its historical and statutory policy context.

Community Mores

If the frequency of contested roll calls is a valid barometer of controversy at state capitals, then liquor was the hottest topic in town. Almost one-half of the votes in the Mores sphere concerned this volatile subject. In this respect the late-nineteenth-century Midwest was not unique; the liquor problem enjoyed one of the longest runs of any substantive issue on the stage of American political history, analoguous to the hold of the tariff issue on national politics. Public concern with prohibition, saloons, and individual consumption of alcoholic beverages surfaced and resurfaced in state and local government during the last two-thirds of the nineteenth century and entered the federal arena in the twentieth century. Liquor, however, was probably more widely divisive on the local scene than was the tariff because jurisdiction over prohibition lay with the states until ratification of the Eighteenth Amendment.[8]

The three midwestern states had already legislated solutions to the liquor problem by the time their general assemblies convened in 1886 or 1887. Iowa had prohibited the manufacture and sale of liquor by statute in 1855, modified this restriction shortly thereafter, and returned again to prohibition in 1884 with a law that contained sweeping enforcement provisions. Illinois and Wisconsin had updated their saloon laws in the 1870s. Both were "local option" states, which meant that local officials could authorize the operation of "dram shops" in their community and collect fees when they granted licenses. But these legal arrangements did not end controversy over the issue. In the first place, liquor law was frequently violated, particularly in the Hawkeye State, which had highly restrictive antisaloon statutes. Equally important, adamant foes of the demon rum were not satisfied with anything less than absolute prohibition. Such ideological rigidity inevitably invited a political fight.[9]

Increased pressure in the 1880s to curtail saloons and the availability of alcoholic beverages produced similar legislative proposals in the three states. The most sweeping of such initiatives, often embodied in proposed constitutional amendments, prohibited the manufacture and sale of alcoholic beverages throughout the state. Three such contested measures appeared in Illinois, four in Iowa, and one in Wisconsin. Less drastic legislation allowed voters to decide whether to license saloons in their own county or city. Bills based on this idea divided Illinois legislators in each session between 1887 and 1895, and a proposal to double license fees, while less severe than local prohibition, threatened to close many saloons in the state. In 1889 the opponents of prohibition in the Wisconsin Assembly failed to prevent the amendment of the 1874 municipal local option law whereby licensing required popular approval, and though they worked unsuccessfully in the next two sessions to rescind the new policy, they marshaled enough votes to reduce some license fees. In Iowa, where licensing meant a retreat from prohibition, local option measures divided lawmakers in each session studied.

Since local option could legalize as well as prohibit saloons in a community, temperance advocates proposed additional methods of combating the "liquor traffic." In 1887, Wisconsin lawmakers banned state aid to county agricultural fairs where liquor was available. Debate was renewed on this question in 1893 when foes of dry fairs sought to repeal the law. Two years later, Assemblymen battled over legislation that made it "unlawful for any person to sell or give away any ale, beer, cider, wine or other intoxicating liquors to any inmate of any soldiers' home, retreat or asylum for disabled veteran soldiers and sailors within two miles of the boundary lines of such homes . . . "[10] It was the "most sensational" floor fight of the session, according to the *Milwaukee Sentinel.* Legislative conflict over spirits revolved around various other questions, such as whether the state should require schools to teach the effects of alcohol on the "human system," whether to punish saloon-keepers, parents, or children when minors illegally acquired liquor, and whether to forbid the collection of debts from the estates of deceased persons for liabilities incurred in taverns. How localities should spend license monies split Illinois lawmakers, while the drys in Wisconsin sought to forbid the collection of taxes at places where liquor was sold, a proposal that was actually prohibition in weak disguise. In Iowa, opposition reflexes were so sensitive to "sumptuary legislation" (which regulated personal social habits) that considerable dissent materialized against a bill to prohibit habitual drunkards from practicing medicine.

The old saw, "You can't legislate morality," epitomizes the struggle over prohibition in Iowa. The largest body of liquor votes in the state developed over legislation to enforce the existing prohibition law. Despite the stringent Act of 1884, violations—in some counties, total disregard—of the liquor statutes persisted. In 1886 antisaloon proponents mobilized behind the Clark bill, which strengthened the 1884 law by providing a broader definition of "nuisances." To draw the noose more tightly around these illicit liquor dens, a major provision of the bill stipulated that "evidence of the general reputation of the place . . . shall be admissible for the purpose of proving the existence of such nuisance." During this struggle foes of prohibition were unable to remove from the 1884 statute a clause allowing those who gave information about illegal liquor operations to receive one-half of the fine levied against violators.

An equally protracted struggle developed in the same session over legislation aimed at imposing stricter community control over the regulation of pharmacists. Given the sole right to sell alcoholic products for medicinal, mechanical, culinary, and sacramental purposes, some pharmacists were exceeding their authority by illicitly dispensing alcohol or by fronting for backroom whiskey parlors. The primary intent of the 1886 bill and of later legislation on pharmacies was elimination of these "blind pigs." One senate amendment to the 1888 bill, for example, increased the number of petitioners required to attest to the "good moral character" of an individual applying for a pharmacist's permit. The amendment substituted a majority for one-third of the freehold voters of the locality issuing the license. Harsher features of the pharmacist statute were removed in 1890 amid further voting disagreement.

Demands for effective prohibition persisted in Iowa during the early 1890s, but the tempo of the legislative battle over liquor subsided in the 1890 and 1892 meetings of the house (though not in the senate), when a Democrat sat in the governor's mansion. In 1894, however, the issue became the session's major preoccupation. Many supporters of prohibition concluded, from political necessity if not moral conviction, that the current policy was neither socially nor politically workable. Relief from this dilemma emerged as the premier item on the agenda for 1894 long before lawmakers assembled in Des Moines.[11] The solution enacted left prohibition technically on the statute books, but added a proviso that permitted circumvention of the law when a sufficient number of local residents concurred. Saloons then had to pay a penalty fee for the privilege of operation. The mulct law, as this unorthodox local option was termed, climaxed a generation of conflict over liquor in the Hawkeye State.

The flap over prohibition in Iowa was equaled in intensity, though not in duration, by disputes over school policy in Illinois and Wisconsin. In 1889 the two states enacted similar compulsory education laws without substantial dissent. The Edwards law in Illinois, which amended the state's original compulsory school statute of 1883, and the Bennett law in Wisconsin stipulated that basic subjects should be taught in the English language and that school attendance should conform to certain regulations. Both provisions became controversial questions at the next session. Wisconsin Democrats, beneficiaries of the popular outcry against the Bennett law, scheduled repeal of the statute as the first item of legislation in 1891. In the same year legislators in Illinois reached a deadlock over a bill to replace the Edwards law and failed to resolve the English language issue. In 1893 Illinois lawmakers returned to the education question, but this time the principle of compulsory attendance and its enforcement by truant officers became a key obstacle to hammering out a new school law.

Iowa legislators had wrestled with the topic of education several years earlier. There, however, the main issue at controversy had been compulsory schooling itself, though disagreements had also developed over provisos requiring the state to provide free text books and clothing to needy children. Too volatile for consensus during the 1890s, compulsory education did not come to Iowa until 1902.

Other items of school policy, by comparison, were tame affairs, consuming little floor time and press attention. These measures proposed a review of school law, specified qualifications for county superintendents of schools, created a state superintendent of education in Wisconsin, determined the manner of altering school district boundaries, and established the times of and compensation for attendance at teachers' institutes.

Legislative disagreement over social norms, such as those embodied in prohibition and school language requirements, was likely when no universal cultural standard existed to mold consensus. Controversy over Social Behavior, the third policy topic of Community Mores, derived from the same clash of normative outlooks. Representatives in Illinois and Iowa, for example, differed over whether baseball games desecrated Sunday, a day of strict religious observance for many nineteenth-century Protestants. Perhaps for parliamentary rather than philosophic reasons, a Democratic lawmaker in each house offered an amendment to these bills that added draw-poker to the list of prohibited Sunday activities. House passage of the Sunday baseball bill in Illinois stirred the *Chicago Times* to console its readers with the news that this legislation did not affect "town-ball, old-cat, hand-ball, mumble-the-peg, marbles, shinny, or seven-up."[12] Sarcasm did not deter the house majority; they also resolved to close stores and certain factories on Sunday.

Related legislation forbade the sale of tobacco to minors. A minority of Assemblymen wanted to broaden this restriction by making the use of cigarettes illegal for everyone. Social proscriptions, not medical evidence, underlay these proposals. Other legislation that sacrificed individual freedom to cultural conformity included an anti-lottery proposal in Illinois and a measure in Wisconsin forbidding the marriage of first cousins. Religion was seldom the explicit object of contested legislation, but one exception was an amendment to a bill establishing a new reformatory in Illinois, which rotated annually the denomination of chaplains servicing the institution. Equally divisive was a further amendment to the bill that instructed reformatory officials to "keep the inmates at hard labor."

Social Behavior also covers legislation affecting social minorities such as women, foreign language groups, blacks, and children. The women's movement, which focused at this time on the right to vote, produced the largest single bloc of these roll calls. Female suffrage proposals arose in six sessions of the three state legislatures, but the issue seldom caused protracted fights. Most such measures conferred suffrage only in municipal or school elections, and the two that were enacted (Illinois in 1891 and Iowa in 1894) granted voting privileges on this limited basis. Equality between the sexes was also at issue in bills outlawing salary discrimination against female teachers and granting married female attorneys certain property rights formerly enjoyed only by male attorneys.

Those unable to read English or preferring another tongue fell into another minority group. Some Iowa lawmakers regularly cited the linguistic diversity of their constituents to justify the printing of official publications in foreign languages. An analogous dispute in Wisconsin concerned the use of Polish in official publications in Milwaukee, a city with a substantial Polish constituency. The American Protective Association (APA) viewed the Poles as one of several groups that threatened the traditional cultural fabric of the country. Its members entertained the paranoid fear that Catholics were plotting a violent conspiracy against Protestants. The Association's anti-immigrant, anti-Catholic campaign prompted an effort in the 1895 Wisconsin Assembly to prevent secret societies from bearing arms, a measure reportedly directed at the Catholic Knights.[13]

Despite the fact that few blacks lived in the upper Midwest in the late nineteenth century, racial inequality was entrenched there. Testimony that "equal protection of the laws" stopped at the color line is found in the content of the 550 contested issues: only one concerned Negro rights. This measure, designed to insure equal access to public accommodation for "all persons," grew out of a civil rights convention in Milwaukee in 1889; it met defeat on a divided vote in 1891 but was finally enacted in 1895.[14] Protection of the young, still another minority group, seldom provoked dissension. Illinois's famous child labor law of 1893 passed without sharp roll call divisions, although a proposal to strengthen the statute did produce one contested vote in 1895. Wisconsin's 1891 child labor law also passed after only one contested vote.

Legislative deliberation over criminal Rights reflected the ageless struggle to balance the rights of the accused against responsibility to society. Representatives in Illinois registered the sharpest division of opinion over this question. The hazard of an unfair trial by locally prejudiced juries was at issue there (and also in Wisconsin) in 1887 during the consideration of change of venue procedures. Whether juries should be required in certain criminal cases provoked conflict in both Illinois and Iowa. Illinois lawmakers also disagreed over a bill providing for court-appointed counsel for indigent defendants. Legislation requiring mandatory penalties for an individual convicted of more than one crime as well as a life sentence for a third offense divided the Illinois house in two successive sessions in the late 1880s. In the early 1890s members of that legislature advocated the covering of police wagons in order to shield prisoners from public view; the measure met a roadblock until it was amended to apply to Chicago only.

Capital punishment symbolizes the gravity of the stakes in the search for equity between defendant and society. Illinois Senate Bill 425 of 1895, the harshest of three measures on this subject, inflicted the death penalty on persons convicted of assaulting railroad personnel or passengers in connection with train robberies. The murder of an engineer during a train robbery while the legislature was in session focused attention on the proposal.[15] Prairie State lawmakers disagreed too over the definition of rape in their 1887 deliberations and, eight years later, over whether to make that crime punishable by death.

The individual rights of the indigent, unlike those of criminals, were an infrequent source of controversy. The four votes on this topic variously concerned control of financial assets of the insane, definition of that affliction and procedures of commitment, restraints on the assignment of children to the poor house, and procedures governing the incarceration of tramps.

Participants in the war between the states had sheathed their weapons a generation before the legislatures of the late 1880s convened, but the passion kindled by that fratricidal struggle lingered as long as they survived. This sentiment lay behind the determination to legislate remembrances to Union veterans. All but two bills on Nationalism honored these patriots in some way, providing for their burial, building monuments and halls in their honor, housing their aged widows and mothers, exempting them from road taxes, publishing their names, or reimbursing those who had paid a draft exemption fee and then enlisted. The case made for the veterans in the midwestern houses attests to the legacy of the sectional conflict, but this legislation also could disguise boondoggles, since it enriched private contractors at public expense. Nonetheless, the emotive quality of the veterans' bills, as well as of two measures requiring the American flag to be displayed on school grounds, manifests the social symbolism characteristic of Community Mores.

Commerce

Railroads were the major long distance carriers of inland freight and the country's largest nonagricultural business during the late nineteenth century. Their impact on economic activity was paralleled by the controversy they produced in legislative halls: bills concerning railroads accounted for 5 percent of all the contested roll calls in the fifteen sessions and one-half of the votes on the topic of Business. Regulation of rates and other practices, liability to employees, and free passes were the three general subjects that came under legislative review.

One set of regulatory bills reduced passenger fares in specific instances: for passengers boarding trains without tickets, for those on sleeping cars, and for those on certain round trip and one-way fares. Proposals in Iowa to give rate-making powers to the state railroad commission and legislation in Wisconsin to increase railroad taxes, which would include the power to appraise railroad property, represented greater governmental challenges to the entrepreneurial autonomy of these corporations. Lawmakers disagreed over other propositions that would have interfered with railroad activities: requiring that railroads construct switches at terminals, delaying the deadline for universal installation of automatic safety couplers, maintaining stations, regulating the sale of railroad bonds, and outlawing discrimination between long haul and short haul. The few contested railroad measures in Illinois mainly concerned street railways in Chicago. This legislation included a bill to regulate passenger fares and, in 1895, two bills that according to opponents bestowed monopolies on existing municipal lines. Governor Altgeld's veto of the two 1895 bills prompted further disagreement on the floor.

Two aspects of railroad company behavior came under particular attack, especially in Wisconsin. The first was the practice of issuing free train passes to governmental officials in order to curry favor with them. Legislators in each lower house sought abolition of this practice. The second reform sought a statutory definition of railroad liability to employees injured on the job. The risk was high for the hundreds of thousands of men who worked for the railroads during the late nineteenth century, for many of them were hurt, hundreds fatally, each year. Under prevailing common law, however, court judgments favored railroads more than workers. During the sessions between 1887 and 1893 Wisconsin Assemblymen divided over proposals to remove the "fellow servant" principle of the common law, under which injured employees had to prove that other workers were not responsible for the accident, from the railroad defense against plaintiffs. Enactment of a restricted version of the proposal in 1889 failed to satisfy workers, and a stronger liability measure, covering employees engaged in train operations but not maintenance crews who worked in the shops, won passage in 1893. Lawmakers, however, first struck out a provision stipulating that proof of equipment defects was "presumptive evidence" of company negligence.[16]

Most commercial enterprise was subject to state action. States licensed and incorporated manufacturing, merchandising, and other commercial ventures, permissions that customarily contained tax and regulatory provisions. In addition to the railroad legislation, contested measures on Business concerned the taxation of express and mining companies; the licensing of detectives, department stores, and out-of-state corporations; and the regulation of business consolidations, corporate indebtedness, and receiverships. In Wisconsin, legislators met substantial opposition when they endeavored to outlaw the buying and selling of commodity options (called "gambling" in the bill). Similar obstructions greeted Assemblymen who sought to empower the attorney general to determine who held stocks in corporations negligent in meeting debts. In Illinois, discord surrounded legislation that allowed city councils to regulate telephone and electric rates. Discontent with the practices of private utility companies spawned proposals in each state that would permit cities and towns to construct and maintain their own facilities. Resentment against the power of utility companies, however, vied with community interest in developing municipal services. The fusion of these sentiments is reflected in a Wisconsin bill that authorized towns to issue bonds to aid the private construction of telephone lines.[17]

Two enfranchising measures in Wisconsin developed into unusually prolonged floor fights. The peddler law, passed in 1889, revised the regulation of traveling salesmen, increasing their license fees and stipulating other special requirements. The issue was complicated by questions about who should collect the fees and whether the law should embrace "transient merchants," and two years later debate was resumed on the issue by opponents seeking to repeal the law. Equally troublesome was the so-called pipeline bill of 1893, permitting a private water company from Illinois to lay its pipes on state property in Waukesha, Wisconsin, for the purpose of transporting water from Waukesha to Chicago and possibly to Milwaukee. Although superficially this was a routine request for state authorization, the matter occasioned extended floor debate, close votes over amendments, and assorted parliamentary tactics. Two issues lay at the heart of the conflict: whether it was proper for the state to assist a private commercial venture, and whether the state was usurping local policymaking prerogatives. Waukesha residents who lobbied against the legislation argued that the pipeline application was a matter of town, not state, jurisdiction. The Milwaukee Sentinel's legislative reporter described the imbroglio as "the most intensely exciting legislative struggle of the season," a remark analogous to the Sentinel's assessment of the commotion over the peddler bill four years earlier.[18] The comparatively large number of roll calls on Business in Wisconsin is largely attributable to these two issues.

If peddlers and pipelines were prosaic topics to warrant major investments of legislative time, the Assembly did tackle legislation of wider symbolic, if not much more effective, application. Concurrent with Congressional consideration of antitrust legislation, lawmakers in both Wisconsin and Illinois debated the merits of bills "to declare unlawful, combinations in restraint of trade, production and manufacture . . . and to prevent monopoly." State senators, not representatives, manned the roadblocks to these measures, several of which advanced successfully through the lower house.

The second topic in the Commerce sphere, Finance, contains legislation on banks and other financial institutions, on promissory notes and securities, on interest rates, and on insurance. Banking legislation was not a divisive issue in the midwestern legislatures. Illinois, for example, enacted three important banking laws in 1887 without notable voting conflict. But one of these, a measure incorporating savings banks, was declared unconstitutional shortly thereafter, and a new bill on the subject, along with one to incorporate building and loan associations, did incur voting opposition in the next session. In the Hawkeye State, lawmakers clashed over legislation that defined fraud in the transaction of loan agreements, and also disagreed about a proposal to make silver dollars the standard circulating medium of exchange. In Illinois, dissent arose over the specification of penalties for the fraudulent sale of promissory notes. Another financial matter, interest rates, became a volatile subject in the Iowa house during the late 1880s when floor controversy surrounded bills to reduce the legal rate of interest from 10 to 8 percent and to define and punish usury. A kindred bill in Illinois incorporated pawn shops and raised the maximum rate of interest they could charge.

Voting divisions over insurance policy, like those over promissory notes and interest rates, occurred frequently in Iowa. Hawkeye State delegates disagreed on the appropriate way to regulate insurance companies, dividing over questions such as the extent of company liability to claimants and the provisions of fire insurance policies. Bills regulating and incorporating mutual and fraternal insurance societies met opposition in all three states, but none of them became a major controversy. Neither was there much dissent over the creation of offices to monitor the operation of insurance laws in Iowa and Wisconsin.

Farmers formed the largest occupational group in the Midwest; yet legislation that dealt explicitly with Agriculture seldom fell within the category of contested issues. This observation, however, must be qualified by the recognition that the services provided by railroads, insurance companies, and lending institutions affected farmers. Among the few measures that centered sufficiently on farmers' roles as producers to warrant separate categorization were the bills regulating the practices of stockyard companies. Cattle and hog raisers were the primary beneficiaries of this legislation. In Illinois, such bills limited the charges for "yardage, freight, grain, hay and other articles furnished," and forbade discrimination in the provision of these services. Iowa's "herd law," which allowed counties to choose between fenced enclosures of stock or the use of common grazing lands, and which defined fencing requirements when enclosure was adopted, erupted into controversy during the late 1880s. Other measures on Agriculture provided for the publication of agricultural statistics, exempted fruit trees from taxation, and offered bounties to manufacturers of beet sugar.

Industrial workers, like many farmers, aired economic grievances in the years after the Civil War, but as with Agriculture, bills concerning Labor seldom upset legislative consensus. Yet disagreement did accompany some proposed remedies for the abuses in factory and mine work. Lawmakers in Illinois and Wisconsin divided over bills that required the regular payment of wages, and delegates in Iowa disagreed about strengthening the law that compelled mine owners to pay money wages to miners, thereby reducing employee dependence on company truck stores. The coal miners' dissatisfication with the procedures of weighing and screening used to determine their wages was debated in several sessions of the Iowa house, but the issue did not qualify for this study's roll call sample until the session of 1892. Substantial opposition developed during the same meeting over legislation that forbade employers to disqualify union members as employees. Another controversial subject in both Wisconsin and Illinois during the mid-1890s was the proposed creation of a state board of arbitration. A handful of other bills pertinent to the welfare of workers provoked voting dissonance: proposals to limit the working day on government projects to eight hours, improve mine inspection, require safer working conditions for railroad employees, and forbid prisoners to perform work that competed with private employment.

Legislation concerning Property, the last policy topic within the broader sphere of Commerce, rarely incited a major controversy, although the subject engendered a larger number of contested bills than did either Agriculture or Labor. The common denominator of this collection of measures was adjustment of the intricate details that had evolved in real estate law. Proposals to revise prevailing legal practices ranged from methods of recording cemetery deeds to procedures for disposing of tax-delinquent property, including its attachment and repossession. The remedies available to a co-owner aggrieved in the conveyance of real estate held jointly typifies the kind of specific legal relations that legislators reviewed. The premise that the private ownership of property protected a broad range of usages was implicit in these deliberations. Hence it is not surprising that the majority of Illinois lawmakers balked at an attempt to limit inheritance bequests to $500,000 or 1,500 acres for any one beneficiary.

Legislators showed greater sympathy for complaints about the expense of relying on commercial abstracting firms to search and verify property titles. Efforts to adopt the so-called Torrens (or Australian) system of transferring property, which eliminated dependence on private abstracts, was the only legislation on Property that sustained more than a brief roll call skirmish. Following narrow defeats in both the Wisconsin and Illinois houses in 1893, the reform received resounding support from Prairie State representatives in the next session and was enacted in 1895.

Fiscal Policy

Legislation on Taxation seldom addressed the fundamental imperfections in the revenue system that critics cited.[19] Most state and local revenue derived from the property tax, which placed a very heavy burden on real estate, especially rural land, while undertaxing urban, corporate, and intangible property. To alter the method of property assessment and valuation was a troublesome task, as Illinois lawmakers found in 1887. The new revenue scheme introduced in that legislature substituted county assessors for township-level officials, replaced the State Board of Equalization with a new Board of Tax Commissioners possessing greater powers, and improved the means of identifying taxable property. Hailed as an important reform, an amended version passed the house but failed in the senate. Interest in tapping new revenue sources increased by the middle of the next decade, however, and in 1895 Prairie State delegates enacted an inheritance tax against considerable opposition. This law placed a 1 percent tax on estates over $10,000 left to immediate family members and imposed a higher rate on inheritance conveyed to other relatives. In 1893 Wisconsin Assemblymen disagreed over a change in the law that would have permitted taxation of logs in the area where they were felled. Proponents argued that assessment at the mills, which were sometimes outside Wisconsin and usually outside the timber counties, deprived localities and the state of just revenue. At their next session Assemblymen also divided over bills that taxed mortgages and created a tax commission charged with recommending ways to equalize the tax burden.

The other tax issues concerned minor alterations to the tax code, for example: exempting certain properties from assessment, such as graveyards, school land, and family portraits; limiting the indebtedness permitted to local government; and legalizing county tax levies that exceeded the prescribed maximum. A contested bill in the 1891 Illinois house authorized cities to levy an extra tax of three mills, with the primary intent of providing Chicago with sufficient funds to dress up public facilities in anticipation of the 1893 World's Fair. A variety of revisions of the tax code dealt with assessments and other fiscal alterations for road construction and maintenance, but these have been classified under the policy topic Roads. Most divided votes on Taxation in Iowa concerned the property tax rate, which the legislature fixed at each biennial session. Argument over the appropriations for state institutions frequently delayed completion of that task. Methods of handling trust fund monies and the federal refund of Civil War income taxes produced several other contested votes.

Legislators engaged in far more disputes over the spending of public money than they did over its collection. Expenditures constituted a large portion of the contested issues in each state. Controversy over funding centered on state support of two types of organizations: state agencies, and associations of a quasi-public character. General appropriation bills "to provide for the ordinary and contingent expenses of the State" caused frequent floor dissension in Illinois between 1887 and 1891. Specific appropriations, not the general level of state spending, usually sparked the dissent registered during consideration of these long itemized documents. Such objections frequently surrounded expenditures for the State Board of Health and its activist secretary, John Rauch, a leader of the public health movement. Rauch's campaign to eradicate smallpox and other infectious diseases through vaccination programs, quarantines, and inspection of new immigrants to the state incurred suspicion and resentment.[20]

Support for state charitable institutions occasioned other disputes over expenditures, especially in Iowa where the construction and improvement of insance asylums was at issue. Further, legislators in every state, but notably in Illinois, feuded over appropriations for the state militia. Specific and more random funding requests, such as those for improvement of the capitol grounds and adjacent streets and for publication of geological surveys, also brought dissension.

Whereas local government financed most common school costs, it was the responsibility of the state to support the institutions of higher learning. Every two years the lawmakers of Iowa denounced the appropriations for the University of Iowa as extravagant and misguided. Representative William Redman, a future house speaker, charged in 1886 that the University bill "was a grab at the State Treasury for the education of lawyers and doctors," a view expressed by numerous colleagues in later sessions.[21] The universities of Illinois and Wisconsin, in contrast, had many more legislative friends. Brief squabbles over financing university gymnasiums in these two states were the closest equivalent to the anti-university sentiment manifested in Iowa. The establishment of normal schools, on the other hand, led to significant controversies in all three states. Although the need for professional teachers certainly grew with the expansion of population and educational perspectives, such legislation also promised infusions of state money into the fortunate communities that won the contest to host these institutions. Hence regional and local boosterism was rife, and interested constituents and their legislative representatives clashed with one another in the races to secure these plums.

The late nineteenth century also saw the growth of many occupational associations representing various agricultural and trade groups. Organized at both the state and local level, these societies served as informational and pressure groups. Arguing that they were perfoi ming public services, legislators approved subsidies for some of their activities, such as the publication of reports and the holding of fairs and expositions. Although these appropriations were usually small, legislators still questioned the amount as well as the purpose. Some from each state, for example, objected to granting state aid to dairy associations.

The bill appropriating one million dollars to underwrite Illinois' contribution to the 1893 World's Fair in Chicago was a different matter. The expenditure was extraordinary not only in purpose but also in amount; it represented a tenth of the state's biennial budget. The argument that the state and its metropolis would be on display to the nation did not sway most Illinois representatives, many of whom wanted a 50 percent reduction in the initial request. In the end lawmakers settled on the house and senate conference committee recommendation of $800,000. Meanwhile, officials of Iowa and Wisconsin, with fewer resources and no fair within their own borders, quibbled over more modest sums to finance their exhibits at the Fair.

Government

Lawmakers had a special interest in legislation on the political process. Arrangements regarding elections and officeholding affected their roles as elected officials and trustees of political parties. Personal and partisan interests alone did not provoke controversy over this legislation, but sometimes these considerations were a root cause of the disputes.

Elections made up the smallest category of roll calls on Government. One group of issues dealt with voter qualifications: the registration of urban voters, the definition of the powers of poll inspectors, and, in Wisconsin, the disfranchisement of aliens. The other group concerned procedures to be followed during elections. Illinois and Iowa legislators fought over the details of the secret (Australian) ballot; most of them agreed with the principle of the reform, or at least decided it was politic not to oppose it. Division over the bill in Illinois focused primarily on the provision regarding the postelection preservation of ballots. Still other procedures under consideration were the scheduling of elections, the duration of polling periods, and the reporting of campaign costs. A bill in Wisconsin in 1895 that required the disclosure of expenses by all candidates in state elections, including those for U.S. senator, was the only contested proposal of its kind.

Bills assigned to Political Structure concerned the judiciary, the state administration, and the oversight of local government. To relieve crowded court dockets and solve other judicial problems in Illinois and especially in

Chicago, lawmakers proposed the substitution of a county superior court for circuit and county courts, the replacement of justices of the peace with regular judges, and the creation of district courts in Chicago. Voting divisions accompanied reorganization of the district courts in Iowa and the creation of a new circuit district in northern Wisconsin that included Chippewa county. Some delegates saw the inclusion of this county, a center of lumber milling, as a move to expedite the adjudication of suits against lumber corporations, which allegedly favored the delays inherent in the old court arrangement.[22] But court reorganization was only one of several judicial reforms that led to legislative contests in the late 1880s. A kindred struggle occurred over the creation of special commissions to select jurors. Charges that Chicago "boodlers" improperly influenced jury selections in the city reportedly drew supporters behind the Illinois measure.[23] The bill cleared both houses, but similar legislation in Wisconsin was killed by the Assembly. Other contested issues on the judiciary dealt with miscellaneous administrative matters, such as the location of Iowa's supreme court and the number of its judges.

Frustration with the old court system was one reason that reformers in Illinois frequently called for a constitutional convention. The constitution of 1870 needed rewriting, proponents argued, because it failed to meet current revenue and judicial needs. But between 1889 and 1895 every resolution on constitutional revision went down to defeat. Illinois did not hold a constitutional convention until the early 1920s and did not get a new constitution until 1970. The constitutional revision that occupied Wisconsin lawmakers was more limited in scope. Following the passage of identical resolutions in two successive legislatures—the amendment procedure required in Wisconsin—voters in 1892 ratified a change that prohibited the enactment of special laws for cities. (Towns and villages were already so proscribed.) The issue remained alive in both the 1893 and 1895 sessions as critics sought repeal of the amendment.

Most proposals to revise governmental organization and procedures could be achieved through legislation and did not require constitutional changes. Bills of this sort established new state agencies, such as a boys' reformatory in Illinois, a bureau of railway statistics and a board of charities in Iowa, and an omnibus board in Wisconsin to administer reformatory, charitable, and penal functions. Other measures set up routine administrative procedures, such as those for determining the fees charged for incorporating businesses and providing certificates to notaries public.

The states also oversaw the organization of local governments. In Illinois, measures that established incorporation procedures for villages whose boundaries were contiguous to existing towns and villages were seen by some opponents as schemes to allow saloons to take root near communities under prohibition.[24] Plans to alter ward, town, and county boundaries regularly divided Wisconsin Assemblymen, and representatives in Iowa disagreed in several sessions over legislation governing the publication of proceedings of county government in local newspapers.

Policy concerning public office was a highly politicized subject during the late nineteenth century. Formal enabling authority does not run government; people do. Political parties during these years clearly understood this fact. By controlling the appointment process, parties blended the staffing requirements of government with their own need to encourage support and reward loyalty. Many critics, on the other hand, saw patronage as the bane of partisan politics, devoid of any legitimate public function. It is not surprising, therefore, that legislation on Personnel, the third policy topic within the larger sphere of Government, generated frequent voting conflicts. Contested issues on the subject arose in all fifteen sessions of the three midwestern legislatures.

Each legislature created and abolished various offices and defined the criteria for their occupancy, either through bills that legislated directly on the subject or through provisos to other measures, such as the 1895 labor arbitration bill in Illinois and the peddler bill in Wisconsin. During consideration of the Illinois measure, the matter of appointing arbitration board members evoked most of the contested votes, while in Wisconsin the proposed abolition of the office of treasury agent developed into a major point of contention during debate on the peddler bill. Several proposals to make certain officials elective rather than appointive and a provision for additional judges and court clerks caused further disputes over personnel policy, although other objectives were also at stake in these bills. State control over the structure of local governments added another tier of offices over which several conflicts developed.

Legislators disagreed not only about the creation and dissolution of particular positions but also about the conditions of officeholding, including salaries as well as the fees received by such local officials as justices of the peace and sheriffs. Criticism of the fee system to compensate local law enforcement officials stimulated legislative efforts to abolish the practice. Measures that fixed the term for particular offices, specified their duties, and set qualifications for applicants also caused dissension.

Designation of the official state newspaper was an appointment of a different sort. Winning this printing contract did not make publishers public employees, but their services were financed with public money and their tenure was subject to the vicissitudes of political fortune. Armed with their newly won majority status in 1891, Wisconsin Democrats overrode Republican obstruction and made the *Milwaukee Journal* the official state organ. Two sessions later this action was undone after the electoral pendulum swung back to the Republican side.

The blatant partisanship underlying numerous appointment practices was used as a prime argument by those who pressed for civil service reform. The Chicago Civic Federation and like-minded advocates of governmental efficiency, for example, lobbied for a municipal civil service law, intended primarily for Chicago.[25] House passage of the bill in 1895 encountered only mild opposition, but an amendment to exempt policemen with five or more years tenure from the provisions of the act engendered a higher level of conflict. Hailed as reform legislation when it was enacted, the bill was one of the leading issues of the session.

Public Services

As social organization and technology grew more complex during the latter half of the nineteenth century, the state increasingly exercised its police powers to protect Public Health and Safety. The advent of steam technology brought public dangers as well as economic progress. The fear of steam boiler explosion underlay legislation that mandated inspection of stationary steam engines and licensed their operators. The appearance of steam-powered machines on public roads aroused other anxieties, which led a bloc of Illinois representatives to sponsor a bill requiring an engine to stop one hundred yards in front of approaching horses and the operator to keep a "good trusty man" well ahead of the machine to assist in controlling the animals. Iowa solons split over legislation that imposed harsh penalties on railroad officials for hiring engineers to drive passenger trains who had less than a year's experience in operating locomotives. Some Illinois delegates found fault with bills that forced railroads to elevate their tracks over city streets and that increased the amount of damage awards to relatives whose kin were killed by railroads found guilty of negligence. Railroad traffic on Chicago's busy streets was the primary stimulus behind these two bills.

Danger from mobs and rioters, a concern heightened by the Haymarket and Bay View riots of 1886, stimulated other legislation to protect public safety. Lawmakers submitted a variety of proposals to contain future confrontations. Most of the "law and order" measures in the 1887 Illinois legislature won easy passage, but a section of one such bill that stipulated state citizenship requirements for individuals deputized to quell riots caused opposition. A minority of Wisconsin Assemblymen opposed the importation of a "squad of armed or unarmed men" from another state to perform police duty, a restriction aimed at Pinkerton private detectives.[26] Divisive too was a proposal to loan state trust funds to the Kosciusko Guards of Milwaukee, a group that had been instrumental in suppressing rioting workers in Bay View, for the purpose of constructing an arsenal and armory.[27] This bill allowed state use of the structure "for the purpose of military defense in case of war, insurrection, rebellion, riot, or invasion." An Illinois bill that prohibited minors under sixteen from possessing and using deadly weapons in public places reflected the widespread violence of daily street life.

The public was at risk too from lax standards for physicians, though the movement to outlaw herb doctors and "Indian medicine men" was not universally embraced. Consensus collapsed in all three midwestern houses over legislation mandating licensing requirements for the practice of medicine and dentistry, and efforts to impose equivalent standards for veterinarians met comparable resistance. In Iowa the majority of representatives did not like a proposed revision of the statutes whereby coroners would be required to deliver unclaimed cadavers to a requesting medical school or physician for study, nor did they favor legislation that increased the authority of the State Board of Health to implement quarantines. Quarantines were a touchy subject in Illinois too. The campaign for public health also incorporated the preparation, sale, and transportation of foods. Several bills on this subject were broad in scope, such as the legislation to prevent adulteration of food and to provide for the inspection of meat intended for human consumption. Other measures had a more limited application, including the one that regulated the cutting of ice in sections of Milwaukee.

The biggest fight over public health in the midwestern legislatures occurred in 1889 and concerned the Illinois sanitary canal. At issue was a proposal to construct a waterway connecting the Illinois River with Chicago in order to carry sewage wastes away from the city. The idea was more than a quarter of a century old, but the growth of Chicago's population and the correlative increase of sewage heightened concern among public health advocates. But ridding Chicago of one problem could deliver another to downstate residents, who were warned of playing host to Chicago's filth. These admonitions included a legislative exhibit of vials allegedly containing Chicago's future offering to its neighbors downstream. The possibility that the canal would also serve as a major water artery between Chicago and the Mississippi brought opposition from railroad officials, who envisioned new competition. The canal bill eventually surmounted these obstacles after months of politicking, both on and off the floor of the house.[28]

Road maintenance was a major function of local government during the late nineteenth century. The state established general road policy but local government administered it. In rural areas the township trustees laid out roads, levied road taxes (with most rural residents choosing the option of paying them with labor), and customarily appointed untrained overseers to supervise road work in the several highway districts of each township. As a result, country folk made do with roads that were poorly coordinated and frequently impassable. Rural residents, nevertheless, jealously guarded their prerogative to pay road taxes in either labor or money and to perpetuate decentralized control over road maintenance. Even minor proposals to change the scheme encountered resistance. An Illinois bill, for example, that allowed townships to employ a road superintendent "outside their own body" to direct work met fatal opposition. Controversial too were proposals that required rural road abutters to trim "growing fences," such as the Osage orange hedge, and that concerned the construction of sidewalks and road drainage ditches. Unlike rural communities, cities in the late nineteenth century increasingly laid hard paving, usually requested and financed by street abutters, who paid the assessments in money. Several contested measures reflected variants of this procedure, such as the bill allowing city residents in Iowa to deduct from their general road tax the amount they had paid for special street assessments.[29]

A "good roads" movement emerged in the Midwest in the mid-1880s, and by the mid-1890s road reform legislation appeared with greater frequency. The most advanced of these initiatives, which required road taxes to be paid only in money and created an integrated system of roads under county supervision, ran ahead of legislative opinion and suffered either defeat or emasculation. In the 1894 Iowa house, for example, legislative guardians of the traditional system diluted the scope of a bill that required the whole of the combined town and county road tax (five mills) to be paid in money; the amended form of the law retained the mandatory cash payment only for the allotment to the county (one mill). Wisconsin's timid road reform act of 1893, which assessed road taxes in money unless a town voted to retain the labor system, and which provided for the appointment of road superintendents with three-year terms, proved so offensive to a number of Assemblymen that they nearly succeeded in repealing the law in the next session. A decade passed before legislative opinion in the Midwest gathered behind effective rural road reform.[30]

A final category of legislation on Public Services, labeled Miscellany, merged several sets of roll calls, each too small to warrant separate categorization, that concerned specific governmental functions. For example, twenty-one roll calls were taken on fish and game legislation, with fishing stimulating a higher level of conflict than hunting. Opponents nearly disbanded Illinois' board of fish commissioners in 1893, and in Iowa and Wisconsin the legislators also attacked such bodies. In 1887, sharp voting differences developed over restrictions on methods of fishing in Iowa and Illinois and over the establishment of game wardens and seasonal hunting periods in Wisconsin. A running legislative battle was fought in Iowa over the regulation of trespass. This bill, which prohibited hunting on enclosed farm lands without permission of the owner, failed in 1888 and 1892, but it survived several potentially debilitating amendments to become law in 1894.

Bills to provide free school books were among the most contentious policy questions in the Iowa General Assembly between 1886 and 1894. While the basic issue was whether government should provide free texts to school children, the legislation floundered on procedural questions. Lawmakers debated at length whether the state or local government should determine textbook policy, whether cities should be exempt from the law, whether school books should be uniform, whether the plan was fiscally viable, and whether the "book trusts" overcharged. The last issue reflected allegations that book companies had bribed legislators to oppose state control of book prices. More than a dozen roll calls failed to resolve these issues in 1888; so the floor fight resumed in 1890 until a compromise was reached. As with the remedies proposed for liquor, roads, and several other questions, lawmakers resolved to allow county option on text uniformity and free books. Anxious to explain their votes, numerous delegates inserted statements in the house journal, a practice unique to Iowa. Only the mulct liquor law of 1894 motivated so many lawmakers to justify their behavior in this fashion.[31] In Illinois and Wisconsin free textbook legislation provoked only a fraction of the discord it aroused in Iowa.

Finally, miscellaneous contested issues affected the powers of local government. One piece of legislation passed in Illinois in 1895 permitted cities to license and regulate bicycle firms. The representative from Chicago who filed this bill explained that he acted at the behest of the "wheelmen," who were displeased with "bicycle repairers and dealers in second-hand wheels."[32] Another type of legislation extended the scope of other jurisdictions, granting certain taxing and acquisition authority to the Chicago park commissioners, and designating certain officials as overseers of paupers. One apparent source of division over such bills, as over road and textbook legislation, was the wisdom of delegating new authority to local administration.

Contested legislation touched numerous areas of public policy. Review of these voting disagreements belies the notion that politics was issueless during the late nineteenth century and that politicians avoided substantive problems in the legislative arena. Legislators debated and voted on a broad array of matters, too many, in fact, for most issues to receive adequate consideration during the short session. Despite these rushed conditions, legislators decided thousands of questions of public policy during the course of the fifteen sessions under consideration. Most of this legislation concerned routine affairs of state, but some proposals represented responses to more fundamental issues that arose with social and economic change. Lawmakers may not have shown particular enlightenment in their remedies to these problems, but they did act upon many of them. Under the prevailing conceptions of federalism, which assigned the lion's share of domestic functions to the states, it was their province to do so.

5

PARTY VOTING

To cynics, Republicans and Democrats in the late nineteenth century offered a choice between Tweedledum and Tweedledee, which was no real choice at all. In terms of policy, such critics have indicted party politicians for avoiding substantive issues and placing self-interested struggles for organizational aggrandizement ahead of solutions to society's problems. They have viewed parties, in short, as encumbrances on the polity. But the American party system has its defenders too. Some of these admirers have said that by pursuing a politics of accommodation rather than divisive ideologies, the parties have helped to sustain democratic processes. Seldom, however, have either critics or defenders submitted legislative evidence, particularly from the state level, to substantiate their case. The neglect is understandable, for party activity in state legislatures has not been systematically reconstructed for most periods of American history. Yet close inspection of the legislative record is indispensable in evaluating the impact of party on policy.[1]

It is instructive to keep in mind the distinction between the concept of "responsible parties" and voting disagreements between party legislative delegations when assessing party performance. The model of a responsible party, popularized by political scientists in the 1950s, encompasses the enunciation of an explicit party program, the recruitment of nominees loyal to these principles, the education and mobilization of voters behind these proposals, and the endeavor to insure cohesive party action in legislatures consistent with preannounced party goals. Regardless of whether American parties have ever achieved this ideal, their failure to fulfill the criteria of responsible party government does not preclude their influence on policy. Party disagreement on legislation, however random such conflict may appear, affects the content of statute books. Moreover, parties may display elements of responsible behavior, in terms of the model of party government, and yet not fully satisfy it. Final judgments, of course, rest on actual performances. This chapter looks at the record of the parties in the midwestern state legislatures by observing the frequency of party voting disagreement on contested-issue roll calls and by reviewing the party positions on the questions that divided them.

For the purposes of this study a legislative party is defined as an aggregate of lawmakers with common partisan designations, as listed in legislative manuals. With few exceptions, the midwestern legislators claimed Republican or Democratic associations. State legislative factions had a dichotomous relationship to the larger party organizations: they were simultaneously semiautonomous units and parts of a more general partisan collectivity.

The political scientist Frank Sorauf has provided a useful conceptualization of partisan structures. "The major American political parties are . . . tripartite systems of interaction," he says, which consist of the electoral organizations, the partisans in office, and the "party in the electorate."[2] The electoral component of this system concentrates on placing party affiliates in office, sometimes by appointment but usually by election. Its campaign units are essentially state and local organizations, which vary according to the local political tradition and socioeconomic environment. Unpaid "professionals," not the mass public, are the core of this element of party life. But because substantial numbers of citizens develop long-standing sympathies for a particular party and vote regularly on the basis of these attachments, party identifiers "in the electorate," Sorauf's third component, constitute a distinct partisan grouping. The relative stability of party electoral strength in the late nineteenth century appears to be largely attributable to these routinized political habits. Finally, officeholders form the remaining component of the party system. Through open association with the party and by acting in concert with its objectives, occupants of official positions comprise the party "in office," to use Sorauf's phrase. The partisan associations of office holders suggest several reasons why lawmakers act in partisan ways, but they do not predict the extent of such behavior. That question can only be answered empirically.

Party voting on roll call votes provides a suggestive index of partisan behavior. The term party vote denotes a roll call alignment on which at least the majority of one legislative party voted differently from the majority of the other party, in a two-party legislature. One cannot assume, however, that partisan motives prompted each legislator to join with his party on such divisions. A party vote is an empirical tabulation, based on a sorting of yeas and nays according to legislators' party affiliations. The motivational wellsprings of individual behavior are not self-evident from quantitative indicators of collective action. It is reasonable to infer, however, that the higher the level of interparty voting disagreement, the higher the probability that partisan considerations underlie individual voting decisions.

Conversely, a roll call vote that does not reach a given threshold of partisan divisiveness does not eliminate possible partisan influences in the voting. Sorauf's conception of party structure helps to explain this logic. Republican and Democratic legislators maintained various kinds of ties with their parties. Some participated in electoral organizations outside the legislature while others were members of the party leadership structure within the chamber. And, since lawmakers, like the general public, identify with their party with varying degrees of intensity, the strength of these internalized attitudes is related to the way that party colors an individual's policy decisions. Since no single measurement technique can record all of these behavioral subtleties, three indicators, each of which sets a different threshold of disagreement, have been used here to index party voting.

How often did the midwestern legislators vote along party lines? Not often, if a stringent definition of a party vote is used. Measured by A. Lawrence Lowell's criterion, which requires that each party maintain at least 90 percent unity in voting in opposition to the other party, only 11 percent of the 998 contested issue roll calls from the fifteen sessions were party votes.[3] By Lowell's criterion party voting ranged from a high of 25 percent in the 1893 Illinois house to a low of 2 percent in the 1889 Wisconsin Assembly (see figure 1). In his terms, the parties in the three statehouses rarely formed two tightly knit phalanxes on contested issues during the 1880s and 1890s.

The requirement that both delegations display near unanimity in order to make a roll call qualify as a party vote is a demanding standard. In a delegation of not more than fifty members, five defectors from one party could cause a vote to fail the Lowell test. But minor splintering in a party does not rule out the possibility that most Republicans usually voted differently from most Democrats. This was frequently the case in the late-nineteenth-century Midwest. When a party vote is defined as instances when a simple majority of Democrats opposed the majority of Republicans, two-thirds (66 percent) of the contested issues manifested partisan contrasts. In Illinois in 1891 and in Wisconsin in 1893, five out of every six roll calls (84 and 85 percent) qualified as party votes by this definition. In only two of the fifteen sessions (Iowa 1894 and Wisconsin 1889) did the majorities of the two major parties fail to disagree on at least 50 percent of the contested issue votes. On some of these divisions, one or both parties failed to achieve a high degree of unity, a situation permitted by such a lenient definition of a party vote. Nevertheless, this index suggests the tendency of members of the two parties to vote differently, and it is widely used in analyzing legislative behavior.[4]

The third criterion, an index based on a 60 percent disagreement

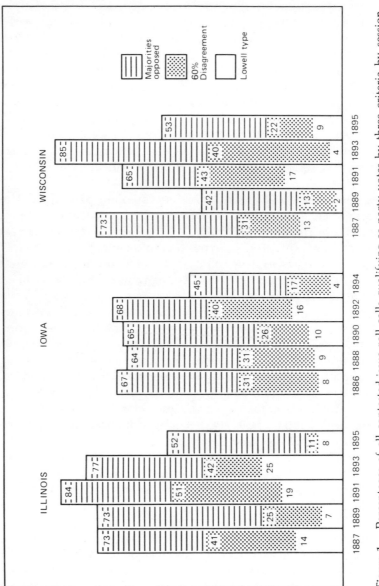

Figure 1. Percentages of all contested-issue roll calls qualifying as party votes by three criteria by session, Illinois, Iowa, and Wisconsin.

threshold (the obverse of 40 percent on the index of likeness) is in several ways the most realistic test of party voting. This definition, which specifies that 80 percent of one party voted against 80 percent of the other (or proportional variants of this relationship) does not require that the parties mutually display near-maximum cohesion, nor does it count essentially nonpartisan divisions as party votes.[5] Measured this way, party voting occurred on slightly less than one-third (31 percent) of all the contested roll calls. Although only one session (Illinois 1891) recorded party disagreement on more than one-half of the votes, five other sessions tallied a party vote on four out of every ten roll calls (see figure 1). Illinois showed the greatest fluctuation in party disagreement, from a high of 51 percent in 1891 to a low of 11 percent in 1895. Despite this variation, party voting occurred more frequently in Illinois than in the other two states, judged by all three indices. Even more significant, however, is the relatively similar level of party disagreement among the three states.

Rates of partisan conflict did fluctuate in relation to the relative sizes of party delegations. Although the correlation is not perfect, particularly for Wisconsin, the highest rates of party voting generally occurred in the early 1890s when a close balance existed between Republicans and Democrats, while the lowest rates appeared in 1894 and 1895 when the G.O.P. held large majorities. Although party voting is not simply the product of the ratio of party delegation size, the data suggest that the massive Democratic losses in the elections of 1893 and 1894 contributed to the substantial reductions of partisan dissonance in the subsequent legislative meetings.

Because rates of party voting vary according to the measurement criterion used and also because no argument unequivocally favors one index over the others, the extent of legislative party discord in the late-nineteenth-century Midwest still remains partially undetermined. A review of the levels of party voting that occurred in other state legislatures and in Congress provides comparative benchmarks with which to assess the data obtained for this study. The comparisons can be only approximate because the method of selecting roll calls differs from one study to the next.

The first systematic review of party voting in nineteenth-century legislatures was A. Lawrence Lowell's 1902 study.[6] Lowell analyzed all non-unanimous roll calls in numerous legislatures, including seven sessions of five northern states (Massachusetts, New York, Pennsylvania, Ohio, and Illinois) during the late 1890s. He found first that on a simple majority basis the parties opposed each other on 42 to 56 percent of all non-unanimous votes taken in six of the seven state houses; in the seventh session (Massachusetts 1899) the rate reached 92 percent. When he pared down his sample to include only roll calls on which 10 percent or more of the minority party voted on the losing side, Lowell reported that party voting ranged between 66 percent (Illinois) and 94 percent (Massachusetts). And then, when he applied his own stringent definition of a party vote (90 percent unity in each party) to this smaller sample, he recorded a rate of party voting that was roughly analogous to the level in the fifteen midwestern sessions between 1886 and 1895, with the exception that his data showed a much greater fluctuation from state to state.

Lowell's study of the 1899 Illinois house made it possible to examine party voting in that state both before and after the political turmoil of the early 1890s. The identification of contested issues among the roll calls in the 1899 session yielded a sample of votes roughly equivalent in character to that used for the sessions of 1887-1895. In terms of simple majorities the parties cast opposing votes on 77 percent of the fifty-seven contested roll calls. Indexed on the basis of the 90 percent unity standard, party conflict shrank to 14 percent. Both measures, in short, record levels of party voting that resemble the averages obtained for the five earlier sessions of the Illinois house.[7]

The only other investigation of state party voting during the late nineteenth century that is presented in a form suitable for comparison is James Wright's study of Colorado politics.[8] In the 1887 session of the Colorado house the majority of Republicans opposed the majority of Democrats on 45 percent of the twenty roll calls on "significant issues" that Wright selected, but none of these votes reached a 60 percent threshold of party disagreement. A higher rate of party conflict occurred in both 1893 and 1894 when slim majorities of Republicans faced Populists as their chief legislative adversaries. Wright's analysis of forty votes in these sessions shows that the majorities of Republicans and Populists were opposed on two-thirds of the roll calls, while slightly more than one-third of the roll calls qualified as party votes by the 60 percent disagreement criterion. Although the 1887 Colorado house did not display the level of partisan voting manifested in the midwestern legislatures, a little later, in the early 1890s, the rate of Republican-Populist disagreements did approximate those observed in the upper Midwest.

The Lowell and Wright studies suggest that the incidence of party dissidence in the three midwestern houses during the late nineteenth century was similar to that in other northern states during the same period. In Congress, however, the frequency of party cleavages during these years exceeded the state rates. Brady and Althoff's study of the House of Representatives between 1890 and 1910 uncovered relatively high rates of party division, particularly after 1893.[9] And since these authors included every roll call in their index and measured party voting by Lowell's stringent 90 percent unity criterion, even higher levels of party conflict would probably have been discovered if low-conflict votes had been excluded and a more liberal definition of party voting had been used. Similarly, a systematic study of voting in the United States Senate during the last third of the nineteenth century made by Shade and his associates documented rates of party voting considerably in excess of those in the Midwest statehouses. These researchers found that the majorities of the two parties were opposed on approximately nine out of every ten high-conflict roll calls.[10]

A review of several studies of voting in midwestern legislatures during the twentieth century puts the late-nineteenth-century findings into chronological perspective. Five studies of the post-1945 Illinois and Iowa houses show that party voting approximated the levels of the 1880s and early 1890s.[11] Although precise comparison is hampered by the differences in roll call samples, the data from the two time periods are sufficiently compatible to permit one to draw instructive inferences. In both eras a large portion of roll calls in Illinois and Iowa were unanimous or nearly so; highly cohesive party voting occurred infrequently (even when low-conflict votes were excluded), but the frequency of party divisions increased significantly when less stringent thresholds of conflict were used. In contrast to the highly cohesive party voting typical of the British Parliament and, to a lesser extent, of Congress during the late nineteenth century, the major parties in the Midwest seldom disagreed as solid blocs. But midwestern Republicans and Democrats differed on some issues and did so about as often as other state legislative parties in comparable settings.

Although partisanship was greater in Congress than in the Midwest during the late nineteenth century, the legislative role of the state parties gains significance from another set of comparisons. Urban-rural conflict is often cited as a prominent feature of political life during the decades after the Civil War. A variant of this theme pictures farmers-legislators at odds with the representatives of the city. Were legislative disagreements between these two groups as common as divisions between Republicans and Democrats? In the midwestern houses, during the late nineteenth century at least, delegates from the city and from the country rarely opposed one another en bloc on contested issues. Only 15 roll calls in the fifteen sessions examined evidenced urban-rural dissidence at the 60 percent disagreement threshold, whereas these legislatures split 310 times along party lines by the same measurement standard. Since 12 of the 15 urban-rural votes occurred in one session (Iowa 1888), sharp conflict between city and country legislators was even more sparsely distributed among the other fourteen sessions.

If a distinctive urban policy orientation existed, it should have been most evident among the delegations from Chicago and Milwaukee. The substitution of these metropolitan lawmakers for urban delegates generally, therefore, gives additional power to tests for urban-rural conflict. In fact, however, metropolitan-rural disagreements were infrequent. Such splits appeared on only fifteen roll calls in the five sessions of the Illinois house and on only four votes in two sessions (1893 and 1895) of the Wisconsin Assembly. Party voting conflict between metropolitan Republicans and Democrats in each city, by contrast, occurred as frequently as between the full partisan delegations. The lawmakers from the big cities, moreover, voted as a cohesive unit (80 percent or higher on the Rice index of cohesion) as frequently as did all Democrats and Republicans, but the metropolitan representatives also split along partisan lines twice as often as they unified to form a single urban bloc.[12] In short, Chicago and Milwaukee legislators cooperated on numerous policy questions, yet they were much more likely to agree with their fellow partisans from the city and from the countryside.[13]

Lawmakers from rural constituencies displayed greater voting disarray than did their urban colleagues. On only twelve contested roll calls did 90 percent or more of the rural representatives vote on the same side of the question. When the definition of cohesion was lowered to 80 percent (equivalent to 60 percent on the Rice index) eighty unity votes were found, a substantial increase over the more stringent threshold. But the country delegates achieved far less cohesiveness than did either party delegations or urban lawmakers. Thus the absence of sharp urban-rural conflict in the state legislatures during the late 1800s stemmed primarily from the disunity of rural representatives.

Delegates from country districts, of course, came from many different backgrounds and embraced a variety of occupations. One can reasonably posit that farmers were at least as responsive to rural and agricultural interests as any other occupational group, and that when legislators differed over contested legislation along urban-rural lines, that conflict was most pronounced between farmers and metropolitan lawmakers. In the sessions studied, however, farmers did not battle representatives from Chicago and Milwaukee, nor did they mass their forces against lawmakers from Iowa's cities. Few issues brought farmers together in a solid nonpartisan phalanx on the house floor. On the other hand, farmers often did behave as partisans. Horticulturists and stock raisers voted cohesively as party men as often as did the full party delegations. And farmers disagreed along party lines as frequently as and sometimes more frequently than each partisan group.[14]

One should not conclude from these observations that urban and rural differences had no effect on legislative behavior. In the form just summarized, the data simply show that urban and rural lawmakers seldom opposed each other in relatively cohesive blocs. Just as partisan considerations may affect legislative behavior in ways not recorded by tests of individual roll calls, so may constituency or occupational factors influence voting decisions even though sharp urban-rural or metropolitan-farmer disagreement is absent. The issue here is partly one of degree.

The use of roll call "scales" offers a way to tackle this problem. A scale brings together roll calls (by means of statistical techniques discussed in the appendix), usually on issues of related content, on which blocs of legislators voted in relatively similar fashion. The "scoring" of each lawmaker's responses to these clusters of roll calls produces a frequency distribution of voting scores. With such indices in hand, the researcher can proceed in conventional statistical fashion to determine the independent variables that best correspond to the ordering of lawmaker scores contained on each continuum. The greater the correlation between any one variable and the voting scores, the greater the probability that the variable reflects a factor instrumental in producing the voting pattern. Like any other quantitative technique, scale analysis does not neatly divulge the motivations that prompted the voting decisions. Rather, it offers empirical clues to the factors that influenced legislative behavior.[15]

Scale analysis of twelve sessions produced a total of seventy-four acceptable scales.[16] Examination of legislators' scale scores in relation to party affiliation and urban-rural constituent differences puts the comparative impact of these two factors into clearer perspective. Party, not population density, describes the dominant voting alignment on the scaled legislation. Party yielded the highest correlation of all the variables used in this study on two-thirds of the scales, with the urban-rural correlation exceeding the party coefficient on a quarter of the scales.[17] Since scales contain varying numbers of roll calls and since some urban-rural coefficients exceeded the party correlation only because party bore little relation to some votes, the analysis was refined to sharpen these comparisons. When a threshold value was used to denote a "significant" correlation and when each scale was weighted by its number of roll calls, the prominence of party was accentuated. Party reached a correlation (gamma) threshold of 0.75 and was the highest correlate on 61 percent of the scaled roll calls. The urban correlation, by contrast, exceeded that rendered by party and met a 0.5 threshold on only 11 percent of the scaled votes. Most of these urban-rural correlations occured in Illinois, the state with the largest urban population.

An alternate method of analyzing scale scores permits the relative impact of the two factors to be stated more succinctly. Party affiliation accounted statistically for more than 50 percent of the fluctuation (variance) in scale scores in six sessions whereas the urban factor explained a paltry 7 percent.[18] The impact of party varied from session to session, as the data below demonstrate, but the strength of its correlation with the

Session	Roll calls scaled (N)	Party variance (%)	Urban-rural variance (%)
Illinois 1893	45	77	4
Iowa 1888	55	54	5
Iowa 1894	24	47	12
Wisconsin 1891	34	65	4
Wisconsin 1893	44	54	8
Wisconsin 1895	48	34	9

voting vastly exceeded the influence of urban-rural constituency differences. One can estimate on the basis of these calculations that, on average, party affiliation was seven times more successful than urbanization in explaining the variations in the responses to scaled legislation.[19] Regardless of the measurement strategy employed, party provides a far better description of voting patterns in the midwestern houses than does population concentration.

Despite its comparative prominence, party voting occurred selectively on contested issues. It is reasonable to assume that lawmakers rely on different decision-making referents when they consider different kinds of policy. Extension of this logic holds that the salience of partisan factors will vary with the content of legislation. Review of the party voting data (see table 5.1) shows this to have been the case. Party divisions fluctuated widely among the five policy spheres, but in a similar pattern among the

Table 5.1. Percentage of party votes by policy sphere and session in three midwestern houses, 1886 to 1895.[a]

State and year	Community Mores	Commerce	Fiscal Policy	Government	Public Services
Illinois					
1887	47	50	28	54	0
1889	58	8	62	31	0
1891	62	22	44	75	0
1893	87	8	50	58	15
1895	10	9	0	27	0
Iowa					
1886	64	0	15	23	100
1888	72	11	17	20	4
1890	73	0	8	50	0
1892	70	25	20	64	29
1894	48	8	0	10	0
Wisconsin					
1887	50	23	10	50	25
1889	83	6	0	0	14
1891	50	25	30	67	75
1893	67	21	29	50	50
1895	29	0	27	42	0

a. Party vote defined as 60% disagreement.

three states. Party conflict occurred most regularly on Community Mores, with Government ranking second. Commerce and Public Services, by contrast, evoked few party votes; and Fiscal Policy occupied a middle position. On average for the three states, party voting (at the 60 percent disagreement threshold) occurred on 57 percent of the votes on Mores and 40 percent of the roll calls on Government; and the rates for Fiscal Policy, Commerce, and Public Services were 24, 15, and 9 percent respectively. Differences between the states modify but do not materially alter this pattern. Only Community Mores among the five policy spheres generated party disagreement on half of the votes in each state, and Government held consistently to its second rank in all three legislatures.

The seventeen policy topics etch the connection between party and subject more vividly. Liquor headed the list of partisan topics (see table 5.2); over one-half of the roll calls on this subject provoked a party vote in each state. The partisan character of Community Mores was due largely to the liquor issue, which accounted for one-half of the party divisions on cultural legislation and for one-fourth of all party votes, regardless of subject, in the fifteen midwestern sessions. In Iowa, the liquor question had no rival in its capacity to animate party battle: prohibition and other legislation concerning alcoholic beverages totaled two-fifths of all party votes in the state. Policy regarding alcohol also was Wisconsin's most partisan subject, both in relative and absolute terms. School and veterans' legislation led the list of partisan topics in Illinois, yet one out of every two roll calls on liquor in this state qualified as a party vote. With some exceptions, social policy in general and liquor in particular were the most consistently partisan subjects in the three midwestern state legislatures.

Party disagreement over the issues of Government varied among the states. In Illinois, party voting reached a 50 percent plateau on both Elections and Political Structure; in Iowa only Elections exceeded that rate. None of the three governmental policy topics achieved the 50 percent plateau in Wisconsin. Still, Badger State Republicans and Democrats disagreed more often on these subjects than on others, except for taxation and four of the topics in the Mores sphere. Legislation on Business, Private Finance, Agriculture and Labor, Property, and Miscellany, by contrast, were conspicuously absent from the list of frequently partisan topics. Taxation, Expenditures, Public Health and Safety, and Roads also scored low on this index in Illinois and Iowa. With some exceptions (see tables 5.1 and 5.2), midwestern lawmakers seldom voted along party lines on legislation that, broadly speaking, contained an economic content.

Time brought some changes in this pattern. The rate of party voting on Community Mores and Government, the leading partisan subjects in the sessions between 1886 and 1893, declined in 1894 and 1895. Although the reduction in partisan conflict cut across all issue classifications in the

Table 5.2. Average percentage of party votes by policy classification for fifteen sessions of three midwestern houses.[a]

Policy classification	Illinois	Iowa	Wisconsin
Policy sphere			
Community Mores	54	65	49
Commerce	16	12	16
Fiscal Policy	41	11	19
Government	50	29	38
Public Services	5	6	24
Policy topic			
Liquor	54	74	62
Schools	87	38	45
Social behavior	15	68	37
Rights	50	29	0
Nationalism	71	50	50
Business	11	5	17
Private finance	32	7	0
Agriculture and Labor	20	28	17
Property	0	11	20
Taxation	9	20	50
Expenditure	48	8	10
Elections	50	71	25
Political structure	53	22	45
Personnel	46	23	33
Public health and Safety	3	0	29
Roads	0	11	33
Miscellany	18	5	11

a. Party vote defined as 60% disagreement. Percentages are rounded and are based on the cumulative totals of party votes among all roll calls in each category for five sessions of each legislature.

mid-1890s, the decline is most striking in relation to social and political subjects. Issues concerning Community Mores were largely nonpartisan questions in Illinois in 1895. By contrast, Democrats and Republicans in Iowa and Wisconsin still divided on Mores with some regularity during the mid-nineties, though at lower rates than in earlier sessions. Longitudinal analysis would be needed to determine whether the mid-1890s inaugurated a new pattern of voting on social policy or whether the depression years marked only a temporary lull in the traditional partisan reaction to these questions.

This decline should not be overstated, however. Community Mores still claimed the largest proportion of party votes in the 1894 Iowa house and in the 1895 Wisconsin house, and in Illinois in 1895 no policy topic was an especially partisan issue. Community Mores and Government accounted for at least 50 percent of the party votes in each of the fifteen sessions, including those of 1894 and 1895; the lowest proportion occurred in Wisconsin in 1887. The depression years of 1894 and 1895, moreover, did not usher in higher levels of partisanship on economic questions; party voting subsided on these issues too.

Although the Republican and Democratic parties dominated the midwestern legislatures of the late 1800s, a third party, labor, made some showing in the Illinois and Wisconsin houses during the 1887 session. Because they were small in size and the Republicans held substantial majorities in both houses, the labor parties could not affect the course of legislation unless they maintained absolute unity and the other blocs divided. Even if this situation did not occur, the labor men could at least symbolize their point of view through cohesive voting.

The tiny delegation of the Wisconsin People's party, all six of whom represented districts in Milwaukee, usually voted as a unified bloc, although poor attendence on roll calls marred this consensus. The United Labor party of Illinois showed much greater disarray, failing to match the unity displayed by the major parties. On another point, agreement with one of the major parties, the two labor delegations also differed. The Wisconsin People's party supported the Democrats on all party votes in the 1887 Assembly, but the United Labor men evidenced no consistency on party votes: they variously joined the Republicans or the Democrats, divided among themselves, or failed to muster a quorum. This vacillation is partly attributable to their attitude toward the roll calls on Community Mores, which attracted a substantial share of the party votes in the session of 1887. Unlike the Republicans and Democrats, who showed unity on Mores, Illinois' United Labor men split or abstained on most such issues. Social questions did not trigger predictable partisanship from the Illinois labor representatives.

The labor parties, however, did unite on some contested issues that were of interest to working class populations. Both of these third parties supported bills requiring the regular payment of money wages. The Wisconsin People's party also favored anti-Pinkerton legislation, the exemption of personal items from tax assessment, and increased railroad liability for injuries to employees; they opposed bills facilitating the garnishment of property and establishing jury commissions. United Labor representatives voted cohesively for legislation that limited the amount of untaxed inheritance, reformed tax assessment procedures, broadened the law on financial swindling, and licensed operators of stationary steam engines. They opposed a state citizenship requirement for the deputization of civilians in civil emergencies. Some issues of presumed interest to labor constituencies, on the other hand, did not receive full support from the labor delegations. They variously opposed, split, or abstained on bills that regulated Chicago pawn shops, protected trainmen from overwork, prohibited state aid to national guard armories, restricted the power of justices of the peace in incarcerating tramps, and created jury commissions in Illinois.

The labor parties' voting record on contested issues does not fully describe their legislative performance. They may, for example, have offered proposals that failed to clear committees or to receive substantial voting support from other legislators. But the evidence surveyed for this study shows that the American labor contingent of 1887 bore little resemblance to the labor and socialist parties of modern Europe. These European counterparts, ideological organizations with relatively well-developed programs and historical continuity, customarily displayed a disciplined unity in legislative voting.[20] The worker representatives in the Midwest evidenced none of these characteristics. Rather, the 1887 labor parties were essentially short-lived political reactions to local economic and political upheavals. They failed, as did the wider worker and socialist movements in America of which they were a part, to sustain broad voter support and thus to challenge effectively the political hegemony of the partisan establishment.

Where did the major parties stand on the issues that divided them? Answers to this question flesh out the substantive character of the Republican and Democratic legislative responses and suggest the extent to which distinctive policy orientations differentiated these two organizations.

On liquor, the issue that most frequently separated them, the parties were uniformly consistent: Republicans always favored a restrictive policy and Democrats always supported a more lenient position. Not one roll call on the subject found the parties reversing this posture, although a few liquor votes that concerned issues peripheral to the general principle of prohibition did not qualify as party votes. But on the basic questions of prohibition and the status of the saloon, the Republicans predictably voted dry and the Democrats wet.

Prohibition was the most prominent of numerous proposals, usually advanced by Republicans, for wider control of social behavior. Democrats customarily fought these proscriptions. In Illinois and Wisconsin they opposed the stringent regulation of school attendance and the mandatory use of English during the controversies over the Edwards and Bennett laws in

1891 and 1893. Iowa Democrats voted against compulsory education altogether. Illinois Democrats favored the rotation of the denominations of chaplains assigned to the proposed boys' reformatory. Their colleagues in Iowa and Wisconsin disliked restrictions on the sale of tobacco to minors and on the publication of government proceedings in foreign languages. Hawkeye Democrats did not agree to prohibiting baseball and other sports on Sunday, and party colleagues in the Badger State voted against the secret society bill that was intended to embarrass Catholic fraternal orders. The Democratic opposition to female suffrage is difficult to reconcile with the party's libertarian posture on most social issues; but to the extent that Democrats viewed female suffrage as a tactic to advance prohibition, their response to women's rights was consistent with their stance on other Community Mores.

The individual rights of the accused evoked repeated party conflict only in Illinois. There, Democrats objected to revisions of criminal procedure that favored the state over the accused. They refused, for example, to support bills that revised the change of trial venue rules, lowered the age of criminal liability for rape, imposed harsh penalties for convictions of a third crime and for train robbery, and eliminated jury trials when indictments carried jail sentences. On a similar ideological plane, Illinois Democrats approved the bill that required enclosed wagons for the conveying of prisoners. Symbolic expressions of patriotism also found the parties in opposition. Democrats in each midwestern house opposed numerous bills honoring or materially assisting Union war veterans. Iowa Democrats even showed the surprising ability to unite against legislation that required schoolhouses to fly the United States flag.

Democratic and Republican attitudes toward commercial legislation, which claimed comparatively few party votes, were less distinctive than their views on Community Mores. Nevertheless, one faint tendency is discernible: Democrats more than Republicans were friends of the workers. Democrats in Illinois, for example, favored the protection of trainmen from overwork and a reduction of pawn shop interest rates. In Iowa they opposed a Republican measure that hampered the recruitment efforts of labor unions, and supported stricter regulation of the weighing of coal, which would give fairer compensation of miners. Party colleagues in Wisconsin favored the requirement that wages be paid weekly and that the types of products manufactured by prison labor be limited. They also supported the railroad liability bills of 1887 and 1893, although similar legislation in 1889 and 1891 did not result in party votes. To the extent that the prohibition of commercial traffic from a portion of Grand Avenue in Milwaukee promised hardship to teamsters and small businessmen, Democrats sided with the interests of workers rather than of the affluent residents who lived along the thoroughfare.

The other areas of commercial policy showed fewer signs of partisanship. Democrats in Illinois supported the regulation of chattel mortgages, the taxation of certain out-of-state companies, and appropriations to provide for the collection of agricultural statistics. Iowa Democrats wanted to make silver dollars legal tender in their state, but they refused to grant cities the power to tax streetcar companies or to provide subsidies to beet sugar producers. Despite the tendency for workers to find Democrats more receptive than Republicans to their economic interests, the voting analysis sustains an important conclusion: that the relation between state and estate was essentially nonpartisan in the late-nineteenth-century Midwest, with neither party taking an unabashed class-oriented posture or promoting a unique economic program.

An analogous consensus prevailed over fiscal policy in two of the three states. Only in Illinois, where the Democrats were more parsimonious than the Republicans, was the issue of expenditure treated in a consistently partisan way. The Illinois Democracy voted to cut expenditures in the following legislation: the general appropriation bill of 1889; specific items of other omnibus funding legislation; and the proposals to finance a new reformatory, a northern national guard camp, and the Prairie State's share of the World's Fair. In Iowa and Wisconsin public spending rarely aroused partisan animosity. The most notable exception was the greater generosity of Iowa Democrats toward state educational institutions, especially the University of Iowa.

By contrast, legislation that dealt with the structures and procedures of government occasioned numerous party splits. Critics of late nineteenth-century politics have frequently cited these battles as evidence that the party system promoted a scramble for personal gain rather than concern for the public interest. That the two parties looked after their own organizational affairs is beyond dispute, but the reasons they did so may not be so one-dimensional as their detractors imply.

If one concedes that some voters experienced real difficulty in satisfying voting requirements and finding time to vote, it follows that partisan responses to legislation on elections expressed genuine policy differences. Democratic support of legislation to expedite voter registration and polling procedures benefited not only party electoral interests but also potential voters. And if it can be assumed that cultural factors helped to distinguish the accused from those who sat in judgment on them, Democratic opposition to the jury commission bills in Illinois and Wisconsin may have derived in part from the ethnic competition in society. Policy that benefited partisan interests did not necessarily harm the public.

Party conflict over Political Structure and Personnel requires a different interpretation. In such legislation as the awarding of printing contracts, the creation and dissolution of governmental agencies and local jurisdictions, the appointment of new judges and other officials, the guarantees of minority party representation on governing boards and commissions, and the apportionment of legislative districts the desire for party aggrandizement is very evident. Illinois Democrats, for example, voted to increase the fees received by election officials and the secretary of state when the party was in power, but favored the abolition of the fee system for justices of the peace when the party returned to minority status in 1895. In 1893 Democrats in Wisconsin opposed new procedures for rendering annual school accounts, but in the next session they favored the proposal that county officers submit financial reports to their county boards annually. Both Democrats and Republicans supported popular referenda to solve certain policy questions on some occasions, but at other times they preferred to let officeholders decide similar issues. No doubt several considerations prompted the actions of politicos on legislation of this sort, but organizational housekeeping appears to have been their primary motive. Yet in a broader sense, legislative conflict over the details of governmental operations was an extension of the more general competition between the major parties. In a time of acute partisanship in many sectors of society, team psychology had much to do with the game the parties played.

If the concept of responsible parties means the promotion of broadly developed programs, the mobilization of voters behind these ideas, and concerted legislative efforts to enact them, then the midwestern Republicans and Democrats in the late nineteenth century did not meet this standard. But it does not follow that these parties were impotent where policy was concerned or insensitive to their constituents' interests.

Not until the twentieth century did a broadly based consensus develop in the United States that government had a responsibility to attack an array of socioeconomic problems. The role of both state and national government was comparatively limited throughout the 1800s. As late as 1902, for example, all governmental expenditures accounted for only 8 percent of the gross national product whereas in the early 1970s public outlays constituted a third of the GNP.[21] As these budgetary comparisons imply, the managerial-social service state dates from the 1930s, not the 1880s. This perspective on the scale of governance and the impact of public policy puts legislative parties of the nineteenth century into their proper historical context. The low programmatic profile of the midwestern legislative parties is consistent with the tradition of limited government characteristic of the decades following the Civil War. Many late-nineteenth-century editorialists, in fact, criticized lawmakers for legislating too much, not too little.

But the point must not be overstated. Government, especially state government (in concert with its local administrative arms) did expand its involvement in social and economic affairs in the late nineteenth century.[22] Both parties provided votes for these new policies, though neither took the lead by calling for a more activist state or promoting comprehensive policy alternatives to cope with the new industrial order. Yet the claim that party officials should have developed integrated policy solutions to the problems of a modernizing society sets an unrealistically high standard for American political parties in the late nineteenth century. Neither party, the evidence suggests, received strong signals from their partisan constituents urging them to adopt specific governmental innovations on numerous policy fronts.

The failure of both Democrats and Republicans in the Midwest to develop a programmatic posture during the 1880s and 1890s was typical of American parties generally.[23] The midwestern parties disagreed over much legislation, particularly at lower thresholds of conflict, but like their sister organizations at other times and places, they did not seek to implement elaborate designs of governing. Party leaders did not interpret their role as emphasizing doctrinaire commitment to distinctive and integrated policy schemes. Policymaking was only one of the lifelines sustaining party existence, and not the most important one. Theodore Lowi's interpretation of the constituent function of American parties expresses this idea. "Party in a democracy," he argued, "institutionalizes, channels, and socializes conflict over control of the regime." Historically, American parties typically have emphasized this single function. The primary role of a party in America, Lowi wrote, has been to act as a "conduit," as a "more or less passive channel for regular expression without influencing much along the route."[24] The midwestern parties did not compile comprehensive legislative records, particularly regarding economic affairs, largely because there was no consensus that they should do so. Given their delicate coalition structure, it might even have been politically dysfunctional for them to embark on such a course.

But their lack of a programmatic function does not mean that the parties were devoid of substantive character or that they played no role in enacting public policy. The midwestern parties in the late nineteenth century stood for certain generalized ideals, which explains why officeholders, party activists in the electoral organizations, and loyalist voters could join together in common cause season after season. Frank Sorauf, a close student of party life in America, has made this point: "American legislative parties are tied to the rest of their parties by some agreement on an inarticulate ideology of common interests, attitudes, and loyalties."[25] Sorauf made his comment with the twentieth century in mind, but his observation fits the late nineteenth century as well. Although highly cohesive party opposition, a mark of ideologically oriented and programmatic parties, occurred rarely in the fifteen houses studied, most Republicans did vote differently from most Democrats on two out of every three roll calls on contested issues. An informal commonality of interests and attitudes played as large a role in producing this voting disagreement as did concerted party strategy to enact a program.

The voting behavior of Republicans and Democrats in the midwestern houses reflects several differences of philosophy, or elements of a "silent ideology," to borrow Frank Sorauf's phrase. The most pronounced partisan disagreements occurred over definitions of social behavior. Republicans assumed a restrictive posture on a variety of questions that reflected the cultural diversity of the times, such as the differing attitudes toward liquor and saloons, foreign languages, and the use of Sundays. On these and other issues related to cultural norms, Republicans were willing to use the coercive power of the state to fashion their version of social order and moral rectitude. Democrats usually resisted such legislation as violations of personal liberty or oppressive instrusions of governmental paternalism.

Strains of antistatism appear in Democratic opposition to other measures as well. Their anti-inspection sentiments and their other objections to some of the public health laws illustrate this theme, as do their objections to the imposition of greater road costs on local communities and the requirement that townships trim hedges that bordered roads. Muted apprehension that larger governmental units would usurp local jurisdiction also fed their opposition to these issues, although this alarm was more a tactic than a distinctive partisan principle. A different element of party contrast shows up on issues affecting nonagricultural workers. Democrats more than Republicans stood behind labor, as well as behind the renter and the borrower. On these and other issues Democrats exhibited a measured resistance to the encroachment of government and large economic organizations on the autonomy of individuals.

The conflict over Community Mores epitomized these contradictory outlooks. Surely the parties could have gained much by avoiding cultural issues, which had a volatile impact on politics in the post war era. Yet they closed ranks on these questions more readily than on others. Thus, the factors that prompted these contrasting responses to sociocultural legislation go far toward explaining the basis of partisan behavior and political philosophy generally at the statehouse during the late nineteenth century.

6
LEGISLATING COMMUNITY MORES

If sweeping change breeds sociopolitical pathology, then the United States in the late nineteenth century was ripe for discord. Industrialization, increasing urban density and size, erosion of local isolation, the growth of corporate size and power and of economic interest organizations (including labor), attacks on conventional scientific and religious understanding, and more healthy living conditions all contributed to the reshaping of the world Americans had once known. Not everyone was equally touched by these developments, but even the specter of change could appear threatening to traditional social relationships.

Immigration, which brought a record number of newcomers into the United States during the 1880s, fueled such concerns. More than earlier foreign migrations, this new influx included a higher proportion of Catholics and Jews, peasants, and central and southern Europeans. The *Chicago Tribune*, the *Iowa State Register* in Des Moines, and the *Milwaukee Sentinel*, centerpieces of midwestern Republican journalism, worried publicly about the meaning of the trend. Anti-Catholicism permeated an 1891 *Tribune* editorial lamenting "foreign Papal immigration." The tendency of Italians, Hungarians, Poles, and Bohemians "to hang about the cities" meant that these cities were "becoming un-American"—in danger "of becoming great European colonies with all their passions and prejudices against our institutions and forever alien to American civilization and thought." The only "hopeful spots" in the current immigration figures were the small numbers of "sturdy Germans" and "self-sustaining" Scandinavians.[1]

The *Iowa State Register* had no misgivings about the immigration of Finns, which the paper welcomed as a "thrifty class of people," but it took a less sympathetic view of the arrival in the United States of larger numbers of Poles and Russians, "many of them of an inferior class." At home in Iowa, the *Register* found fault with the state's German and "Bohemian" language press for its alleged penchant for arousing a "spirit of lawlessness, and mobs and riots," and its appeal to "race prejudices" in its position on certain issues such as prohibition. The use of German in the public schools was also unacceptable because it retarded assimilation. "This country can never be a polyglot country," declared *Register* editorialists: "America is for Americans." Similarly, the *Milwaukee Sentinel* wrote critically of the preference of many Catholics and Lutherans for religious, not public, schools. Citing the religious backgrounds of the inmates in the Milwaukee house of correction, the *Sentinel* saw proof that sectarian education lowered morality.[2]

Despite their cultural biases, the midwestern Republican editors had hit upon a fundamental social truth: the peopling of America was undergoing a massive change. And many of the newcomers were different. The earlocks of the Russian Jews, the physical features of the Asians, and the itinerant habits of many Italians, Poles, and Greeks, all of whom spoke in tongues incomprehensible to most native Americans, were only the most visible signs of the new social collage. But Germans, Scandinavians, and Irishmen, as well as other groups from the British Isles and northern Europe also broadened the new ethnic pluralism. Although the Yankee may not have been aware that his own behavior was ethnocentric, he was quick to recognize the ethnocentricity of others. And the signs of ethnicity were all about him. Many ethnic groups tended to settle in residential clusters after their arrival in America, but firmer evidence of social clannishness appeared in such ethnically enclosed institutions as clubs, schools, and churches. Foreign language and religious newspapers kept their readers abreast of events in their wider ethnic communities. Most newcomers clung to some of the cultural traditions in which they had been raised. The Irish demonstrated a fierce devotion to the Catholic church and showed particular reverence for the priesthood. Germans had special attachments to their language, Sunday recreational activities, and beer. And nearly everyone tended to choose a marriage partner from his or her own ethnic group, which gave rise to suspicions, especially among older Americans, that separate cultural enclaves would be perpetuated indefinitely.

This flowering of cultural diversity in the late nineteenth century occurred at a time when various segments of American society exhibited a zealous determination to cleanse the world of supposed mortal sins. Dancing, card playing, gambling, smoking, indulging in cheap fiction and "obscene" literature, violations of the Sabbath, and general idleness all entered this list of social evils, but the use of alcoholic beverages and its partner in crime, saloon life, held first place. Adherents of pietistic Protestant congregations, denominations that had evolved during the evangelical revolution of the nineteenth century, kept the closest watch on violations of community mores and found Catholic and non-English-speaking groups to be the most frequent offenders. The presence of the new ethnic groups did not alone create the concern for social purity, for the history of the suppression of social deviancy predates nineteenth-century immigration. The social laxity of fall-away Protestants in the 1800s was equally condemned. But the behavioral divergencies, supposed and real, of the new ethnic pluralism appear to have exacerbated social pharisaism. Some crusaders for social conformity, however, may have acted more out of status rivalries and anxieties produced by the changing cultural order than out of a genuine commitment to religious values or particular social practices.

Motives, of course, usually remain obscure. Yet the presence of the newer Americans appears to have been the overt stimulus of some public conflicts. The attacks on foreign languages, the defense of the public schools, the demands for the public use of the Protestant version of the Bible, the conflict over the religious denomination of chaplains serving public institutions, and anti-Catholicism in various forms, which culminated in the activities of the American Protective Association, were all expressions of social intolerance of the habits of newcomers. Suffrage rights for women and aliens, the rights afforded to the criminally accused, and the general regard for "law and order" and "character" also had linkages to ethnocultural loyalties and perspectives. Expressions of nationalistic sentiment, as displayed in ceremonial remembrances of the Civil War and its veterans, bore less explicit ties to ethnic roots. Yet this defense of national cohesion sprang in part from Yankee Protestant uneasiness about the erosion of community homogeneity and its threat to Yankee hegemony.

Demands for binding codes of community mores flowed to the statehouse. The legislature had the authority to legitimize particular cultural standards and toward this end supporters and opponents of various causes coordinated propaganda and pressure campaigns. Social groups usually formed the backbone of these bodies. Some maintained extensive organizational networks throughout each state. Because of their frequent visits to the state capital and their persistent proselytizing in the community, these organizations had an important role in the policymaking process.

The most formidable coalition of these interest groups joined forces in the effort to suppress "the liquor traffic." The Protestant churches, with the exception of German Lutherans and some smaller German groups, formed one column of the attack. With the Methodists in the lead, the Congregational, Baptist, Presbyterian, United Brethren, and Christian churches all passed resolutions in support of the restriction of alcoholic beverages. The Women's Christian Temperance Union (WCTU), largely a political adjunct of Protestant denominations committed to prohibition, was a close ally. WCTU followers customarily held their meetings in some friendly church, and particularly in Methodist sanctuaries. Invariably they sent a delegation to the state capitol to plead the dry cause when an important liquor bill came up for consideration. Women suffragists often cooperated with their sister reformers. The Good Templars, a fraternal organization, was a less visible advocate of prohibition. In Iowa, where the passion against drink surpassed the cadences of drys in Illinois and Wisconsin, a State Temperance Alliance embraced a coalition of organizations united against the saloon. The Alliance welcomed the lawmakers who addressed and attended their biennial meetings, held strategically in Des Moines during the opening phase of the legislative season.[3]

The prohibition movement attracted a variety of fellow travelers. Newspapers lent a hand, with the powerful *Iowa State Register* providing the most shrill and dogmatic demand for prohibition among the Midwest's major dailies. Farmer and labor organizations on occasion endorsed the principle of prohibition. During the height of labor politics in Illinois in the late 1880s, several legislative candidates ran on joint prohibition-labor tickets. Prohibitionists usually mounted their own campaign, but with little chance of electoral victory, the party functioned primarily as a pressure group whose message was aimed mainly at Republicans. The Prohibition party's gubernatorial vote in Iowa during the 1880s and early 1890s varied inversely to Republican efforts to enforce prohibition. In Illinois and Wisconsin the ability of the temperance men to field legislative candidates reminded Republicans of their presence.[4]

Antiprohibitionists launched an organized resistance to the "fanatical" liquor reformers. Personal Liberty Leagues appeared in each state, but they never matched the scale of the WCTU and other temperance bodies. Liquor wholesalers and saloon-keepers made their position on liquor legislation known to legislators, for obvious reasons. The Iowa State Pharmaceutical Association pressured its state legislature for relief from the harsh restrictions on the sale and use of alcohol in drugstores. Brewers and distillers assumed a lower public profile at the statehouse, but undoubtedly they watched its deliberations carefully and probably worked behind the scenes to protect their economic interest. The manufacture of beer and liquor were major industries in Wisconsin and Illinois. Distilled liquor in Illinois, for example, ranked second in the gross value of manufactured products in 1890 and first in net value, and by 1914 the four distilleries in Peoria were turning out one-fifth of the nation's whiskey. In contrast to the Protestant churches, the Catholic hierarchy seldom took a public stand on the liquor issue, although the bulk of its congregation presumably opposed prohibition. But under the leadership of Irish Catholic clergy, the Catholic Total Abstinence Union (CTAU) preached moderation in the use of intoxicants even though the group did not join prohibitionist ranks in the legislative lobbies. The editors of Wisconsin's major Irish Catholic newspapers, which regularly covered CTAU activities, took a similar position. Collectively, the antiprohibitionists did not muster the organizational strength of their opponents. Instead, they relied on the Democratic party to protect their "personal liberties."[5]

Community activists in the struggle over liquor policy also brought pressure to bear on other cultural issues. Protestant clergy petitioned the legislature for official condemnation of gambling, restricted use of Sundays, and other matters. The WCTU sought legislative action against prostitution "dens" in northern Wisconsin and for a stricter definition of rape in Illinois. State Prohibition party platforms advocated numerous social policies, including female suffrage, strict observance of the Sabbath, and absolute prohibition of public funding of "parochial and sectarian" schools, in addition to the party's pet project. Illinois Prohibitionists favored a compulsory education law that required some instruction in the English language. The Catholic and German Lutheran churches in Illinois and Wisconsin played an active political role in the effort to repeal the Edwards and Bennett laws. Clergymen from these churches also lobbied in opposition to bills that prohibited the marriage of first cousins, provided free textbooks, and conducted a census of private schools. Newspapers constituted a somewhat different instrument of pressure. Through editorial advocacy and reporting practices, the large urban dailies, the county weeklies, and the ethnic press all offered particular viewpoints on community mores.[6]

Far from being isolated from constituent demands, midwestern legislators received numerous signals, both formal and informal, on currents of public opinion. The patterning of constituent expectation was probably as clear on questions of community mores as on any other collection of subjects. But precisely how constituents viewed most matters that came under legislative review remains largely speculative; the reconstruction of public opinion is one of the most intractable historical problems. The activities of community groups and the views of articulate citizens suggest likely directions of general public opinion but cannot be strictly equated with it. Nor can one deduce popular sentiment simply from the basis of legislative behavior. Yet the patterning of legislative responses to social issues implies that lawmakers based their voting decisions on stable and recognized referents.

Analysis of roll call scales offers a convenient method of locating the dominant voting alignments in a legislative session. Scales bring together the roll calls (within the topical restrictions imposed by the researcher) in which each legislator responded in relatively consistent fashion in comparison with the positions of his colleagues. The technique both indicates which issues fit into a common behavioral framework and provides an index of scores (a scale) that arrays lawmakers in accordance with underlying voting determinants. Votes on the liquor issue, the most frequently contested topic of Community Mores in the late-nineteenth-century Midwest, predominated in most of the Mores scales (see table 6.1). Compulsory education (schools) attracted a major share of the votes in the Mores scales in the sessions that met around 1890. But legislators responded in similar, though not necessarily exactly the same, patterns to other social subjects: restrictions on Sunday activities, the use of tobacco, the distribution of official publications in foreign languages, the civil rights of the

Table 6.1. Association (gamma coefficients) between Community Mores scales and selected variables, three states, thirteen sessions.

State and year	Number of votes	Major issues	Party	Catholic	German	Yankee	Urban
Illinois							
1887	11	Liquor; Sundays	0.90	−0.30	−0.28	0.29	−0.15
1889	10	Liquor	0.92	−0.32	−0.25	0.21	−0.27
1891	11	Liquor; schools	0.95	−0.29	a	a	−0.22
1893	11	Schools; child labor	1.00	−0.17	−0.10	0.17	−0.14
Iowa							
1886	20	Liquor	0.98	−0.39	−0.54	0.51	−0.23
1888	24	Liquor; tobacco; schools; women	0.99	−0.59	−0.27	0.42	−0.16
1890	10	Liquor	1.00	−0.45	−0.45	0.31	−0.23
1892	11	Liquor; foreign languages	1.00	−0.59	−0.55	0.45	−0.22
1894	14	Liquor; women; U.S. flag	0.99	−0.71	−0.54	0.50	−0.18
Wisconsin							
1889	8	Liquor	0.96	−0.44	a	a	−0.34
1891	10	Schools; tobacco; civil rights	0.96	−0.41	a	a	−0.14
1893	11	Liquor	0.99	−0.53	−0.55	0.67	−0.34
1895	12	Liquor	0.74	−0.26	−0.69	0.56	−0.44

a. Not calculated.

criminally accused and the indigent, orphans and child labor, and with lesser consistency, the status of women and capital punishment.[7]

With striking regularity, party affiliation described the basic pattern of these voting alignments (table 6.1).[8] Only in the 1895 Wisconsin Assembly, where Republicans greatly outnumbered Democrats, did the association between party affiliation and scale scores on Community Mores fall below a correlation (gamma) of 0.9. Party voting, of course, declined in all depression-year sessions. By contrast, legislators usually did not divide sharply along urban-rural lines over this legislation. But responses to Community Mores did vary in accordance with some other constituent characteristics in Iowa and Wisconsin, where substantial correlations between district ethnicity and scale scores occurred. In these two states, the cultural contrast in the constituent affiliations of the two parties carried over somewhat mechanistically into the correlations with legislative voting; the sharp partisan division automatically arrayed many representatives of German and Catholic populations against colleagues who had won election in Yankee and Scandinavian districts. Yet these ethnic differences also were related to the way Republicans and Democrats voted on Community Mores. The constituent epicenters of the parties lay in different social worlds, both demographically and philosophically, and this sociopolitical context affected party disagreement over the highly symbolic questions of community stability and moral order.

But party and culture were not uniformly complementary. The two factors sometimes worked at cross purposes, particularly among a minority of legislators in each party. Separate analysis of the voting scores of Republicans and of Democrats shows that defections from each party occurred along the lines of constituent ethnicity. In Illinois, where the ethnic contrast in the constituent basis of the party legislative delegations was less pronounced than in Iowa and Wisconsin, these voting cleavages were greater within each party than among the fully assembled house. In the other two states, voting conflicts related to constituent ethnicity tended to be sharpest among the whole body of legislators, although the imprint of culture left traces on the voting of Republicans and Democrats too. Policy-making on Community Mores usually pulled members of each party together in common cause, and in Iowa and Wisconsin especially this tendency was reinforced by the cultural settings in which the parties found their electoral strength.

Party and constituent culture (ethnicity) were the predominant but not the exclusive determinants of voting behavior on Community Mores. Care is needed, when mapping out the broadest patterns in legislative voting, not to overemphasize the central tendencies. Generalizations are homogenizers: they tend to follow main currents at the expense of back eddies and tributary streams. This elementary statistical caveat has significant implications for research that relies heavily on numeric analysis of overt activity, such as roll call voting, to locate the determinants of decision-making. The motivational underpinning of group behavior is usually complex and is seldom disclosed completely by quantitative overviews. Close inspection of roll call voting in the midwestern houses shows that beneath the larger behavioral uniformities lay instructive deviations from state to state, from year to year, and from issue to issue. Community Mores, for example, contained common thematic threads, and yet its component items retained substantive distinctions. A detailed examination of the responses to these subjects is required to clarify these individual properties and to document more finely the connection between party and culture.

Prohibition

The debate over liquor in the midwestern houses echoed the arguments voiced in the community. Legislative proponents of stringent controls over alcohol recited the imperatives found in Prohibition party platforms and in WCTU resolutions. To the most strident of these legislative advocates of prohibition, liquor and the saloon were twin "evils." Eradication of these social cancers was necessary to preserve the community's fundamental institutions—home, family, and even "civilization" and "free institutions." "If we do not wipe out this saloon," ran a common motif, "it will soon wipe out your home and mine." In Iowa, where prohibition was the law but not always the practice, Republican governor William Larrabee argued that lax enforcement of the liquor statutes bred disrespect for "law and order." With unwitting contradiction, he urged Hawkeye lawmakers in 1886 to tighten public control over the prohibited substance with the exhortation: "True Americans are law-abiding." Allegations that insobriety imposed extra fiscal burdens on local communities supplemented arguments that saloon life undermined public morality. Advocates of dry legislation linked the liquor "evil" with all sorts of social deviancy. A Wisconsin Assemblyman, for example, opposed the sale of beer at agricultural fairs because it "would be the mother of a long line of paupers, lunatics, and criminals." To legitimize these contentions, prohibitionist lawmakers asserted that "the better class of people" demanded the reform.[9]

Opponents parried with various rebuttals. Democrats customarily responded that prohibition violated "personal liberty." Men had an inalienable right to follow their own tastes and habits so long as the rights of others were not infringed. These spokesmen acknowledged that human nature inevitably led to some excesses, but they resisted the proposition that "you can make a man good or righteous by statute." Prohibition was not moral reform in this view, but governmental "paternalism" and a pas-

sion of "fanatics." Lawmakers added a practical dimension to these philosophic defenses. Experience, some debaters observed, had proved prohibition unenforceable. Other legislators announced that their constituents did
not want it, a rationale that Republicans who defected from party ranks
on liquor votes often found expedient.[10]

The Democratic solution to the liquor problem varied between states,
and depended upon legal and political circumstances. Iowa Democrats
attempted to loosen the grip of statewide prohibition with local option.
This plan, argued Democratic Governor Horace Boise, conceded "the
right of self-government to citizens capable of deciding for themselves
what is best for their own localities . . ." Wisconsin, on the other hand,
was a local option state and there Democrats sought repeal of the existing
policy in 1893 on the grounds that the law allowed the majority to subvert
the rights of the minority. Sounding very much like Iowa Democrats, Wisconsin Assembly Republicans defended the prevailing statute as "local
home rule, in its best sense."[11]

Speeches from the floor of the house probably changed few votes on
the subject. The struggle over prohibition had a long history in the Midwest, and at least since the 1870s legislative battle lines on the topic had
remained relatively constant.[12] Most lawmakers in the late 1880s and early
1890s apparently entered the house predisposed on the issue, or at least,
willing to follow the lead of their party on liquor roll calls. Ninety percent
of the contested issue votes on liquor in the fifteen house sessions between
1886 and 1895 found the majorities of the two major parties opposed. Invariably, Republicans supported a restrictive liquor policy and Democrats
favored a lenient standard. On average among the three states, 79 percent
of Republican votes favored a stringent policy on liquor and only 16 percent of the Democratic responses took this position.

Voting on liquor is brought into sharper focus by examining the
scores on a prohibition index. Constructed for the nine sessions in which
numerous contested votes on liquor occurred, these scales indicate the relative frequency with which individual lawmakers supported prohibition,
thus facilitating comparative analysis of the factors that shaped these responses.[13] Party affiliation accounted for at least one-half of the variation
in prohibition index scores in eight of the nine sessions, with the 1895 Wisconsin Assembly constituting the single exception (see table 6.2). Party
had its greatest hold over responses to temperance in Iowa. Only in 1894
did the grip of party loosen in the Hawkeye State, and then the defections
came exclusively from the G.O.P. Assessing the party's recent reverses,
due largely to the liquor issue, many Iowa Republicans concluded that re-
juvenation of their electoral chances depended on moderating the party's
rigid stand on prohibition. Some Republicans in the 1894 house asserted
that they owed their election to promises to support such a revision,

Table 6.2. Percentage of variation explained in prohibition index scores by selected variables, three states, nine sessions.

Group affiliation	Illinois			Iowa				Wisconsin	
	1887	1889	1886	1888	1890	1892	1894	1893	1895
All legislators									
Party	55	56	81	72	94	100	50	61	25
Ethnic District	10	11	32	44	37	37	43	49	32
German	5	7	27	28	22	24	28	23	24
Urban	4	9	6	17	16	10	12	20	16
Mean score	48	45	56	65	56	53	50	44	67
Republicans									
Ethnic District	38	28	60	38	15	0	27	53	36
German	31	14	40	20	4	0	11	30	30
Urban	10	19	1	15	1	0	11	44	16
Mean score	72	79	83	91	97	100	67	83	76
Standard deviation	30	31	20	23	6	0	29	28	32
Democrats									
Ethnic District	33	14	28	35	12	0	0	26	a
German	17	12	14	10	4	0	0	4	a
Urban	4	9	13	6	5	0	0	14	a
Mean score	11	18	12	14	11	0	0	14	25
Standard deviation	15	23	10	12	8	0	0	27	29
Roll calls (N)	10	9	20	11	8	5	14	7	12

a. Not calculated. The 1895 Assembly did not contain enough Democrats to permit intraparty analysis.

pledges subsequently honored with antiprohibition votes.[14] In Illinois and Wisconsin, party had comparatively less impact on voting decisions; yet party affiliation still correlated more closely with the voting on prohibition legislation than did any of the other factors.

Despite the impression left by some historical accounts, urban-rural cleavage was not the principle legislative fault line over liquor legislation. On average, urban lawmakers and particularly the metropolitian delegations opposed prohibition. But urban Republicans were considerably more supportive of prohibition than were rural Democrats. Delegates from rural constituencies showed less consensus on liquor than did their colleagues from urban locales. In some sessions, in fact, lawmakers from small city districts, and particularly Democratic legislators, gave prohibition greater support than did fellow partisans from rural constituencies. These details notwithstanding, urbanization explained only a modest proportion of the variation in prohibition index scores.

The ethnic composition of legislative districts corresponded more closely to voting responses on temperance. Lawmakers' prohibition scores varied markedly among the various ethnic classifications of constituencies (see table 6.3). Representatives of Yankee and Scandinavian constituencies in all three states rallied behind prohibition while delegates from districts with numerous Catholics and Germans showed substantially less enthusiasm for the reform. The social basis of party electoral success explains a portion of this pattern. But the relationship between ethnic district types and voting tendencies on prohibition persists within each party delegation. Republicans from German districts defected more frequently from their party on the liquor issue than did colleagues from Scandinavian and Yankee districts, who were prohibition's most reliable legislative supporters, An obverse relation held for Democrats, although their voting showed less sensitively to constituency types than did Republican responses. Being well unified politically if not philosophically in defense of "personal liberty," Democrats maintained greater party cohesion on the issue than did their opponents.

If constituent sentiment influenced legislative behavior on the liquor issue, as the data imply, then the pattern of these constituent links should remain visible even when districts changed party representation. Several assumptions underlay the way the proposition was tested. Legislators from politically stable districts should have displayed more extreme positions on prohibition than did delegates from districts that experienced partisan turnovers. Representatives from secure districts perceived their constituents to be in greater accord with the party's position on prohibition than lawmakers whose districts had recently changed parties. Lawmakers from the latter class of districts thus would have experienced greater cross pressures between party loyalty and constituent expectations than would

Table 6.3. Support for prohibition (percent) by Ethnic District and legislator Party, three states, nine sessions.[a]

Ethnic District	All representatives			Republicans			Democrats		
	Ill.	Iowa	Wis.	Ill.	Iowa	Wis.	Ill.	Iowa	Wis.
Mixed Catholic	32	18	39	64	97	89	4	10	4
German Catholic	28	7	27	48	19	38	5	9	19
German Lutheran	—	10	45	—	25	75	—	9	35
Mixed German	29	7	—	42	30	—	14	7	—
Mixed Lutheran and Catholic	26	65	22	39	70	47	4	23	8
German Protestant	—	—	36	—	—	45	—	—	0
Scandinavian	76	92	89	100	84	89	32	—	—
Mixed	—	—	61	—	—	82	—	—	15
Low Yankee	49	63	75	80	81	84	9	18	51
Southern	49	—	—	81	—	—	25	—	—
Middle Yankee	55	66	98	81	83	98	17	10	—
High Yankee	58	79	—	92	91	—	21	18	—

a. Data are rounded mean percentages, weighted by the number of legislators from each district classification but unweighted by the number of roll calls on liquor each session. Higher scores indicate greater support for prohibition. Data years: Illinois, 1887, 1889; Iowa, 1886-1894 (intraparty scores for Republicans, 1892, and Democrats, 1892, 1894, are excluded because of zero variation); Wisconsin, 1893, 1895.

representatives from electorally secure districts. These specifications rest on the assumption that party electoral support was partially the function of public attitudes toward liquor and, more generally, toward community mores, a contention that is consistent with several studies of popular politics in the Midwest. One must be mindful, however, that methodological obstacles prevent precise historical reconstruction of public opinion.[15] The general thrust of the hypothesis, nonetheless, has theoretical consistency.

The Democrats' loss of thirty-six Assembly seats to Republicans in Wisconsin between 1893 and 1895 provides an opportunity to examine this contention. Both the Democrats in 1893 and the Republicans in 1895 responded in general conformity with the prediction. Democratic lawmakers whose districts stayed with their party between the two elections averaged a prohibition score of 8 percent in 1893, whereas their party colleagues in this session whose constituents would switch to Republican Assemblymen in the next election scored 22 percent. The newly elected Republicans who filled these formerly Democratic seats provided their party with less support on temperance in 1895 than did members of the G.O.P. from secure districts. The first group of Republicans averaged 70 percent on the prohibition index, compared with an 80 percent score among colleagues from secure constituencies. Although this margin of difference is small, the relationship between the responses is consistent with the hypothesis. This gap is widened, moreover, when the analysis centers on turnover districts with substantial German populations, whose aversion to prohibition is widely documented.[16] Republicans from the fourteen German turnover constituencies averaged 51 percent on the prohibition index in 1895. Support for antisaloon legislation declined still further among Republicans who both represented German turnover districts and had German backgrounds themselves. These seven lawmakers registered 33 percent on the liquor index, whereas the average prohibition support score of all Republicans was 76 percent.

Voting patterns in the 1893 and 1895 Assemblies imply that constituent sentiment usually reinforced but sometimes disrupted the customary partisan responses on liquor roll calls. The analysis suggests that lawmakers' personal ethnic background accentuated these tendencies. To document the interaction between culture and party on temperance legislation more fully, the voting performances of legislators, classified both by their personal ethnic background and by their constituency type, were inspected. For convenience, this analysis is restricted to a comparison of the voting of German legislators with that of Yankees, British, and Scandinavians, subclassified into three broad ethnic groupings of constituencies in the 1893 and 1895 Wisconsin Assemblies. In general, the arrangement of the voting data by these two subdivisions shows that support for prohibition related to both constituent and legislators' personal core culture backgrounds within each party (see table 6.4). Within most classifications, for example, the contingent of Yankees, British, and Scandinavians (designated collectively as Yankees in table 6.4) scored higher on the prohibition index than did German lawmakers. That both constituent and personal background combined to influence temperance voting is evidenced further in the German Protestant and ethnically mixed set of districts. Within this classification, Yankees outscored Germans on each of the three intraparty observations. The average prohibition score for these middling districts fell midway between the extremes registered by delegates from the polar constituency types.

National background alone did not modulate differences in party support on the prohibition issue, however. In 1893, for example, the four Yankee Democrats from the Catholic and German districts and the lone German Republican from the Yankee districts stood shoulder to shoulder with the majority in their parties. The small number of legislators in some categories and the imperfect information about the strength of ethnic identity inhibit attempts to separate personal influences from constituent and partisan effects on voting. Yet this evidence implies that the dual pull of party and constituency could override decision-making references derived from a lawmaker's own social origins. Among some legislators, however, personal background appeared to play a greater role. The three German

Table 6.4.   Support for prohibition (percent) by Wisconsin Assemblymen by district and personal ethnic classifications, 1893 and 1895.[a]

Legislators' districts and ethnic backgrounds	1893		1895
	Republicans	Democrats	Republicans
Catholic and German districts	45 (4)	9 (32)	63 (13)
Germans	14 (1)	5 (18)	39 (8)
Yankees	62 (2)	3 (4)	100 (5)
German Protestant and mixed districts	82 (13)	11 (13)	69 (15)
Germans	74 (4)	0 (7)	38 (4)
Yankees	90 (7)	33 (2)	78 (10)
Scandinavian and Yankee districts	93 (22)	47 (7)	89 (19)
Germans	100 (1)	0 (1)	61 (3)
Yankees	93 (20)	54 (6)	89 (16)

a. Yankees include Britishers and Scandinavians. Higher scores indicate greater support for prohibition. Figures in parentheses indicate number of legislators voting.

Republicans from Yankee districts in 1895, for example, showed less commitment to liquor restrictions than did Yankee colleagues from the same grouping of constituencies. Moreover, both Republicans and Democrats from constituencies atypical of the majority of their parties recorded the highest rates of party defection on the liquor issue. Together, constituent and personal affiliations uncharacteristic of each party acted in tandem to undermine party cohesion on prohibition. The six Yankee Democrats from the Scandinavian and Yankee districts in 1893, for example, stood out clearly as party apostates. Collectively, this small bloc of Democrats voted more often for prohibition (54 percent) than against it.

Party and culture combined with similar effect in Iowa's liquor wars. Here, party ranks held together especially tightly on the issue, which dominated the political stage in the state in certain years. Still, some Republicans guarded the prohibition ideal more zealously than others. Although Democrats were more unified on the issue, they had a few mavericks in their midst during the sessions of the late 1880s. Constituency factors left their imprint on the pattern of these deviations. Party defectors on liquor roll calls represented districts more closely resembling the opposition party's than their own in terms of ethnic composition, public opinion on saloons, and electoral patterns.[17]

An analogous interaction among factors marked the voting on the saloon question in the Prairie State. Both Republicans and Democrats from Chicago, the antithesis of a core culture community, assumed a more antiprohibition stance than did most of their party colleagues. But the connection between constituency and liquor policy was not confined to the contrast in voting between the metropolitan and downstate delegations. In fact, ethnic factors explained a greater proportion of the variation in prohibition scores when metropolitan legislators were removed from the analysis.

The sharpest intraparty cleavage over liquor legislation in the Illinois house occurred among Republicans from southern Illinois. Of the thirty-one southern G.O.P. members who voted on liquor roll calls in the 1887 session, eight sided with the prohibition position on less than one-half of their votes, while ten Republicans cast, on average, 90 percent or more of their votes for prohibition. The Republican deviants represented relatively large Catholic and German populations; only one defector counted a majority of Yankees among his constituents. The ten Republicans who were most supportive of the antisaloon crusade resided in a cultural milieu where Yankees predominated. The number of urban dwellers moderately differentiated those two extreme blocs of Republicans; yet only one deviant represented an urban district (Adams county) and two defectors won election in completely rural localities. Illinois' multi-member districts permit an additional test that testifies to the likely impact of constituent factors on these voting sequences: none of the Republican deviants *shared* a constituency with a prohibition loyalist.

Ethnic culture played an instrumental role in policymaking on prohibition. Through time and between states, legislators from similar constituent and personal ethnic backgrounds exhibited a rough consensus on liquor policy. These cultural influences usually complemented partisan cues. Because the major parties represented relatively distinct collections of ethnic groups, whose attitudes toward alcoholic beverages in particular and cultural uniformity in general differed, and because legislative party positions on prohibition evolved into a staple item of policy conflict by the 1880s, party served as the dominant framework in which disagreement over liquor unfolded. Owing to the vicissitudes of electoral politics, however, some delegates in each party won seats in districts that were atypical of the majority of their colleagues. A legislator's personal background could similarly class him as an ethnic minority in his party. To the extent that quantitative indicators of political behavior and social condition offer clues to individual motivation, these atypical legislators experienced the greatest dissonance between partisan and cultural loyalties on prohibition.

Ethnicity influenced but did not dictate voting positions on liquor. Legislators did not act as socially programmed automatons on this or any other issue. Group political behavior usually derives from numerous factors. On prohibition legislation, party was the channel through which most of these influences flowed. Had constituency rather than party functioned as the chief voting dimension on liquor, the Illinois United Labor party would have demonstrated solid opposition to prohibition; all the labor men represented urban constituencies, all but one of which lay in Chicago. Yet the Labor party registered less opposition to prohibition than did Democrats, who represented all types of constituencies.

Rather, culture used in a broader sense than individual ethnicity helps to explain the partisan dispute over liquor. In this larger meaning, culture embraces the totality of a society's social norms and customary mores. Ethnic pluralism infused diversity into American culture, but ways of life in the United States were not the exclusive product of ancestral, religious, and regional differences. Social styles were partially independent of these influences. Party disagreement over liquor and kindred Community Mores symbolized these competing cultural outlooks and represented a legislative manifestation of contrasting cultural ideologies that attracted adherents of various social backgrounds. The popular referendum on prohibition in Iowa in 1882 provides evidence in support of this argument. Ethnic factors accounted for a considerable share of the intercounty fluctuation in the vote for statewide prohibition, but even when ethnic, urban, and economic factors were controlled, partisan preferences still explained a substantial portion of the variation in the referendum.[18] Legislators' prohibition scores in Iowa exhibited an analogous configuration when subjected to similar statistical analysis. Competing cultural ideologies that included but transcended ethnic differences informed party philosophy in the late nineteenth century and served as a directive for policymaking.

Prohibition generated the archetypical interaction between party and culture, but other issues tapped the same behavioral dimension. Still, each legislative subject possessed a distinctive though not wholly unique content and context, which affected legislative decision-making. These variations are very evident in the responses to compulsory education and use of the English language.

Compulsory Education and the English Language

School policy evoked fewer legislative quarrels than did proposals to shape liquor law. Whereas at least one liquor bill triggered substantial voting disagreement in each of the fifteen houses, school legislation failed to qualify as a contested issue in numerous meetings. The ultimate objective of each of the two policy areas accounts for this contrast. Much of society tended to hold an uncompromising position about liquor policy. To its foes, Demon Rum was an evil, pure and simple, with no rightful place in society, and therefore prohibition was essential. To others, prohibition was an unconscionable restriction of individual freedom. The question of schooling drew forth no equivalent dogmas. No legislator indicated opposition to the *principle* of education, nor did the concept of public schools incur any measurable legislative hostility in the late-nineteenth-century Midwest. But when state-mandated *standards* of education were seen as an infringement of private rights and cultural norms, school legislation encountered a different reception. Such issues could unleash a hornet's nest of controversy.

Compulsory education became common in the states in the late nineteenth century; Wisconsin joined the movement in 1879, and Illinois followed four years later. In 1889 both states amended these codes. In Illinois the Edwards law and in Wisconsin the Bennett law (as the revisions were known) required that children within specified ages attend a school in the district in which they resided for a minimum number of weeks each year. Illinois parents who were found negligent in their "duty" to send their children to "some public day school" were liable to fines of "not less than twenty dollars," unless they showed "to the satisfaction of the board of education" that the child attended "a private day school approved by the board . . ." Locally appointed truant officers were instructed to arrest youthful offenders whose behavior suggested truancy. And in virtually identical language, each law stipulated that "no school shall be regarded as a school under this act unless there shall be taught therein in the English language, reading, writing, arithmetic, history of the United States, and geography." Though a "quiet attempt" was made to strike the English language proviso from the Illinois bill, neither law aroused notable dissent on its way to passage.[19]

The revised school policy sparked a tidal wave of popular protest. The English language provision received the greatest criticism, particularly from Germans, who denounced the requirement as an attack on their cultural integrity. But supporters of parochial schools disliked the requirement concerning school districts as well. Alert to the political ramifications of these dissatisfactions, Democrats pledged to expunge the statutes. Republicans proceeded more cautiously: both the Illinois and Wisconsin branches of the G.O.P. promised in their platforms to modify the laws but simultaneously reaffirmed a commitment to compulsory education. Wisconsin Republicans, moreover, continued to assert that the state had a duty to "guarantee to all children sufficient instruction in the legal languages of the state . . ." The majority of voters went Democratic in the election of 1890, and the school issue was responsible for many defections from the Republicans.[20]

Their election victories were tied so closely to the school issue that Democrats in the two states found it imperative to honor their platforms. In Wisconsin, Assembly Democrats unanimously approved the repeal of the Bennett law and, to a man, opposed Republican attempts to enact a revised bill retaining the English language feature. Republicans matched Democratic unity on their substitute proposal but divided over the repeal measure. The minority of G.O.P. delegates, who refused to abandon the Bennett law, represented the most Yankee constituencies in the state and were themselves of core ethnic backgrounds.

Party lines in Illinois held more firmly in the voting on the school issue. Prairie State Democrats rallied behind a revised attendance plan and withstood cohesive Republican maneuvers to graft an English proviso onto the bill. House Democrats passed their own version of compulsory education, but the issue became deadlocked for the remainder of the session when the senate, under Republican control, refused to budge from its insistence on inclusion of the language requirement. With the Edwards law still on the statute books during the election of 1892, Illinois Democrats consolidated their previous gains by winning control of both legislative houses and elevating John Altgeld to the governor's chair. The repetition of Democratic electoral success cooled the Republican ardor for the English language provision, but the party stubbornly resisted the Democratic proposal for lenient enforcement of school attendance. The Democratic version of compulsory education levied no fines, did not require parents to petition for permission to use private schools, and avoided the use of the term truant officer. Instead, school boards had the discretion to appoint "proper persons" to report violations of the law to school officials, who notified parents in writing of the complaint. Finding these provisions too permissive, Republicans abstained from voting on the motion to pass the bill.[21]

The controversy over school attendance in Illinois and Wisconsin derived fundamentally from competing philosophies about the proper relationship between government and community mores. Lawmakers articulated these varied outlooks in numerous impassioned speeches in the Illinois house. Republicans viewed the "little red schoolhouse" as an agent of socialization that promoted civic responsibility and cultural homogeneity. Democrats disliked the sociopolitical implications of both these goals and refused to empower the state to "invade the sanctity of the home and usurp parental power." But the political context of the issue exacerbated the partisanship of the conflict. The legislative histories of the repeal activities illustrate the impact that an issue of high public salience can have on the behavior of legislative parties. Unlike prohibition, which leaders of the two major parties in Illinois and Wisconsin had learned from experience to handle gingerly or, if possible, to avoid, the school issue burst on the scene suddenly and unexpectedly. Once the parties had committed themselves on the question, extensive public attention monitored their subsequent performance. That legislative party leaders were aware of the political visibility of their actions is manifest in the frequent party caucuses on the subject. In Illinois, where Democratic margins were razor thin, house leaders of both parties strained to keep all colleagues in the fold. The combination of these organizational activities and ideology explains the tight party cohesion on the school issue in the two states.[22]

Iowa Republicans and Democrats also sparred over compulsory education but without the unity exhibited in Illinois and Wisconsin. The merits of compulsory schooling itself, moreover, not linguistic or school district requirements, were in dispute in the Hawkeye State. Here most legislators resisted rigorous enforcement of school attendance. The majority of each party, for example, opposed the provision of the 1886 bill that made violation of compulsory attendance a misdemeanor, and rejected the section of the 1888 measure that empowered constables and policemen to act as truant officers. In Iowa, as in Illinois and Wisconsin, the greatest legislative support for mandatory schooling came from Republicans, but they lacked sufficient unity on the issue to enact a compulsory education statute during these years. Liquor, not schooling, galvanized party bloc action in Hawkeye legislative politics.

Sponsors of compulsory education in Iowa may have purposely eschewed an English proviso in order to maximize support for mandatory school attendance. There were numerous indications that language could be a touchy subject. The state was linguistically diverse, foreign languages were spoken in some public schools, and some editorialists decried the babble of tongues spoken in the state. Language controversy, moreover, had surfaced in the legislature. In 1886 several Iowa Democrats charged that the house had been misled into a hasty repeal of the law allowing the proceedings of county boards of supervisors to be published in foreign languages. The action, critics protested, did "a great injustice to a large class of the most thrifty, upright and honorable citizens of the state," who "can neither read not understand the English language." Republicans defeated Democratic attempts in 1888 and 1892 to reinstate the option, however. Sharp party voting greeted motions in 1890 and 1892 to make available multilingual copies of the governor's inaugural address.[23]

The fights over language policy and saloons demonstrated an axiom of political behavior in the late-nineteenth-century Midwest: issues that pinched the cultural sensitivities of partisan electorates could put considerable pressure on legislators to vote with their parties on these subjects. But whatever the variety of mechanisms that contributed to party disagreements on such occasions, the result of these responses placed the parties in conformity with the normative preferences of their electorates. Responsiveness to constituent demands did not exclude responsiveness to other considerations. Party patronage was also at stake, as, for example, in the contest over the publication of local governmental proceedings. Nor did all subjects that appeared to contain the seeds of cultural conflict uniformly blossom into sharp partisan discord. When lawmakers perceived an issue as extraneous to partisan ideology and as neutral in its impact on the partisan loyalties of their electorates, they lacked important inducements to act as representatives of their party on the issue. The question of free school textbooks was such a subject.

Legislation to provide state aid to local school districts for textbooks appeared repeatedly in Illinois, but it produced significant voting disagreement on only one roll call. Wisconsin enacted a free-textbook law in 1887, largely on the strength of Republican support but with Democratic votes as well. Representatives in Iowa recorded more than a score of roll calls on the subject in 1888 and 1890. Since the Iowa and Illinois bills specified textbook uniformity, the question seemingly contained ingredients likely to trigger party voting. But other considerations, such as widespread public support for free or cheap school books and the propriety of employing convicts to manufacture them, diluted preoccupation with the possible sociopolitical implications of uniformity.

Debate over textbook uniformity in Iowa did raise some themes heard in debates on community mores. In answer to the proposition that standarized texts would instruct all children in the state about the evils of liquor, came the rebuttal that the scheme violated democratic home rule. Yet legislators more commonly emphasized economic motifs in their commentaries on the textbook question. Charges that the "school book syndicate" lobbied "unethically" and set "extortionate" prices constituted one rationale for legislative action. Both cost and educational benefits would be realized, some advocates said, from uniformly classifying texts by grade level. Voting responses in the Iowa house indicate that delegates from rural constituencies found this argument especially persuasive.[24]

On balance, Republicans in Iowa, Illinois, and Wisconsin showed greater favor than did Democrats for free and uniform textbooks; yet neither party affiliation nor ethnic factors correlate closely with voting behavior on the issue. The patterning of votes recorded in the Iowa textbook scales of 1888 and 1890 bore no relation to the alignment of lawmakers on mores in these sessions. In contrast to the rigidity of party lines on liquor in Iowa, symbolized by the 1887 Republican platform statement that "Iowa has no compromise to hold with the saloon," accommodation was the key to the passage of the state's textbook bill. In its amended form, the law exempted cities and permitted county option on uniformity and free books.

Female Suffrage

Legislation on women's suffrage represented another variant of the basic pattern of voting on Community Mores. The parties differed over the merits of the reform, but without the sharp disagreement displayed on prohibition, compulsory education, and the use of foreign languages. In Illinois, Republicans offered moderate support for women's rights, but in Iowa and Wisconsin the party was divided over these proposals, as their average scores (expressed as a percentage in favor of female suffrage) indicate:

State	Republicans	Democrats
Illinois	74	45
Iowa	58	6
Wisconsin	43	5

A slight majority of G.O.P. Assemblymen in the Badger State opposed the enfranchisement of women. Democrats in Wisconsin and in Iowa showed uniform distaste for sharing the ballot with women, whereas colleagues in Illinois were of two minds on the issue.

The fight over female suffrage may appear to parallel the struggle over prohibition. Although legislative reaction to the two issues places them in the same kinship group, the relationship was closer to that of kissing cousins than twin sisters. A legislative vote for prohibition did not automatically predict a ballot for women's rights, nor did opposition to liquor restrictions preclude receptivity to female suffrage. Still, both the most consistent supporters and opponents of women's political rights arose from the same legislative blocs that assumed rigid positions on anti-saloon proposals. Solid Democratic rejection of these "foolish measures" in Iowa and Wisconsin suggests that the Democracy may have viewed female suffrage as a tactic to advance prohibition, or at least as the expression of the same cultural ethos. Republicans in these two states could muster no equivalent party cooperation on the issue, despite arguments about its equity and its mitigation of political vice. This fragmentation shows some connection with the ethnic background of the legislators' constituents, but that relationship was neither strong nor consistent across the three states.

A legislator's own ethnic background seems to have exerted greater influence on these voting decisions. This factor and constituents' ethnic modalities were the two attributes that best describe advocates of women's voting rights in the Wisconsin Assembly. Of the thirteen Republicans who supported the reform in 1893, eight were Yankees and two were British Protestants, with a German Methodist, a Norwegian Lutheran, and a Swiss Catholic rounding out the feminist phalanx. This small bloc gave slightly greater support to prohibition and represented considerably fewer German constituencies than did their twenty-six colleagues on the negative side of the female suffrage question. Two years later, when the G.O.P. delegation drew more heavily from German and Catholic districts, personal background again showed a more intimate relation to the voting than did constituency. Thirty-three Republicans in the 1895 Assembly favored an end to sex discrimination in suffrage; of the twenty whose national ancestry is known, seventeen had roots in British or Yankee families. They were joined by only two of the sixteen known German Republicans. Attitudes toward curtailment of saloons significantly differentiated the two groups of the G.O.P., with the female suffrage bloc scoring 89 percent on the prohibition index, as compared with 66 percent for their colleagues who defended the status quo.

Legislators' cultural background had an analogous though weaker correlation with the voting in Iowa and Illinois. Iowa Republicans in 1894 narrowly passed a bill "conferring upon women the right to vote in municipal and school elections," with much greater help from the Methodists and Congregationalists in the delegation than from the Baptists, Presbyterians, Episcopalians, and Lutherans. Ethnic background made little apparent difference in the way Illinois Democrats divided in 1893 over a proposal to repeal the law allowing women to vote in school elections, although Germans were the members of the party most willing to rescind the privilege. Only eight Republicans shared this position. Chicago constituencies or personal German ancestries, or both, characterized these opponents, who also diverged from their party on other cultural questions.

The champions of universal suffrage usually were found among Republicans of core cultural associations, and its staunchest opponents were Democrats of German origins. But despite these cultural modalities, ethnicity functioned as a less reliable predictor of policy decisions on female rights than on prohibition. And the women's question made nothing like the impact on party cohesion that compulsory education did. Whatever their party and ethnicity, a large majority of lawmakers resolved to keep politics a male domain.

Prohibition, compulsory education, and female suffrage engendered the basic patterns of interaction between party and culture in the voting on Community Mores. Party affiliation usually was the dominant factor in these divisions; five out of every six roll calls on Community Mores arrayed the majority of Republicans against the majority of Democrats. Some of these disagreements, and especially those on Rights and Nationalism, evidenced little connection with constituent or personal ethnic factors. Contested legislation on criminal rights and veterans, most of which occurred in Illinois, provides one illustration. Virtually all of the roll calls (thirty out of thirty-two) on these two subjects in the Prairie State house separated the party majorities. Ethnicity had little overt impact on the voting, as analysis of the criminal rights and judicial procedure scale in the 1887 Illinois house attests. Party described the basic alignment of lawmakers on this collection of legislation, which included proposed changes in the definition of rape, in court venue, in jury selection, and in the financial rights of the mentally deficient. Aside from a bipartisan tendency for delegates from southern districts to oppose these reforms, no substantial correlation with constituent factors materialized.

Illinois' petition to Congress in protest of the Sunday closing of the Chicago World's Fair, an issue classified as Social Behavior, activated a different set of perspectives. The two parties registered their customary opinions on a question of this kind but their unity sagged, due partly, analysis suggests, to constituency factors. A virtually solid bloc of Republicans from Chicago and from districts with large German and Catholic populations (many of whom lived within a day's excursion of the Exposition) disagreed with the majority of the G.O.P., who supported the Congressional Sunday ban. Most Democrats opposed the Sunday closing, yet the division in the party resembled the Republican pattern, with the exception that urbanization was not a pronounced correlate. A similar link to constituents' policy expectations appears to have helped shape legislative responses to other issues of Social Behavior, such as the prohibition of Sunday baseball and the regulation of child labor in the Prairie State.

Yet legislation offered in the interest of good morals or that threatened social precedent did not always provoke analogous partisan and cultural cleavage. The 1894 Iowa bill to eliminate capital punishment, for example, evoked neither sharp partisan discord nor a patterning of yeas and nays along the lines of any personal or constituent factor tested. Division over similar legislation in the 1888 Iowa house did not replicate the voting alignment recorded in the Mores scale of the session. These analyses of voting, along with the testimony of several lawmakers, imply that personal philosophical opposition to the death penalty superseded partisan and ethnic considerations as a reference for decisions about capital punishment.[25]

An attempt to prohibit the marriage of first cousins in Wisconsin resembled capital punishment in that idiosyncratic personal attitudes appeared to play a major role in the voting. Ostensibly, the marriage bill harbored the seeds of partisan and ethnic conflict in that the measure proposed a change in social custom and law, German Lutheran pastors lobbied against it, and nine of the ten Democratic German Lutherans voted against it. But the Catholics, the other Germans, and the Yankees in the party all split over the measure. To one Irish Catholic, Michael Burke, the bill represented "a radical reorganization of social policy," but to another, John Gaynor, the measure had scientific merit. Conceding that "man's highest development is made possible by giving the highest limit of individual liberty," Gaynor concluded that in this instance "the infraction of a slight measure of individual liberty" must "give way to the welfare of the whole." But Democrat John Smith, a Yankee who had broken with his party over the liquor issue, was not persuaded by Gaynor's statistical and medical brief. "If we are to listen to what physicians tell us about marriage," Smith responded, "none of us would ever get married."[26]

Smith's vote against the marriage bill, which ran contrary to prediction, symbolizes a recurrent phenomenon in the midwestern legislatures and probably in all deliberative bodies. Legislators brought their own prejudices and predilections to the statehouse and these individual predispositions affected their policy decisions. Failure to acknowledge such individual variations distorts the complexity of political behavior as much as does negligence in abstracting its modalities. In a broader context, the voting on the marriage and death penalty bills reinforces another lesson made explicit by the analysis: patterns of legislative behavior varied with the content of issues. The widest of these divergencies occurred between broad spheres of policy, but more homogeneous policy topics and specific issues within them contained variations too.

7

ETHNICITY AND DIMENSIONS OF LEGISLATIVE VOTING

Just after New Year's Day 1891, Jay G. Lamberson and C. Hugo Jacobi arrived in Madison to begin their maiden terms in the Assembly. Each man was forty-four years old and had resided in Wisconsin all his adult life—Lamberson in Richland county, which lay in southwestern Wisconsin, and Jacobi in Jefferson county, thirty miles west of Milwaukee. Once a merchant, Lamberson had turned to livestock and dairy farming, but tenants worked most of his one thousand acres. Jacobi had put his college education to use in the insurance and importing business, although he also served as an officer of the bank in Watertown, the small city where he lived. The two freshmen lawmakers apparently satisfied their constituents, for both were returned to the Assembly in 1893 and Lamberson was given a third term.

Although they were alike in many ways, the two legislators differed in others. Lamberson, a Yankee, could trace his paternal lineage back to the early Dutch settlement of New York. Jacobi, German by birth, had come to the United States with his parents in 1855. He belonged to the German Lutheran church in Watertown; Lamberson attended a nondenominational liberal Protestant congregation in rural Richland county. The residents of Jefferson and Richland counties, like the lawmakers they elected, represented contrasting ethnic worlds. Jacobi's district contained one of the state's highest proportions of Germans, most of whom were Lutherans. Lamberson's constituents were largely descendants of old-line American families, with only a handful of Germans or Catholics in their midst. As their social profiles suggest, the two Assemblymen claimed different political affiliations. Lamberson had narrowly won election as a Republican in 1890 and 1892 (Democratic years in Wisconsin), but he received a healthier share of the vote in the Republican landslide of 1894. By contrast, Jacobi, a Democrat in a traditionally Democratic district, had coasted to victory in 1890 with 81 percent of the vote and again won handily in 1892. But, although the majority of his constituents stayed Democratic through 1894, Jacobi did not return to the Assembly in 1895.

The legislative performances of the two men also followed a pattern of contrasts and similarities. Each lawmaker was a staunch party loyalist. On the issues of Community Mores, for example, the two were in complete disagreement. Lamberson's commitment to "moral reform" exceeded even that of his Republican colleagues. In 1893 he stood with the small band of G.O.P. lawmakers who refused either to repeal the Bennett law or to bury the issue of female suffrage, and in 1895, unlike many of his party brethren, he did not relax his opposition to saloons. The proposals to restrict the sale of tobacco and narcotics to minors and prohibit the marriage of first cousins, the regulation of child labor, and the subsidies to Union veterans also found Lamberson and Jacobi on opposite sides of the ledger. Yet on numerous aspects of economic policy the two lawmakers shared common outlooks. They voted in relative accord, for example, on fiscal legislation in 1891 and on the bill that provided state aid to a private water company in 1893. They disagreed, however, on the merits of antitrust legislation. Across the array of commercial and fiscal legislation of 1891 and 1893 Assemblymen Lamberson and Jacobi recorded a variety of similarities and differences.

In numerous respects, Lamberson and Jacobi were archetypical lawmakers of the late-nineteenth-century Midwest. Their particular constituent and personal associations epitomized the connection between ethnicity and party, and their responses to Community Mores and other party-line legislation assumed a consistent partisan course. On other issues, however, they displayed no such regularity. Their performances provoke some intriguing questions about legislative behavior in the late nineteenth century. What was the relative importance of party, personal ethnic background, and constituent attitudes in determining responses to cultural policy? Although all these influences may have mutually interacted in the cases of Lamberson and Jacobi, not all legislators so neatly embodied the complementary attributes of these two men. What effect did ethnicity have on responses to other, noncultural issues? How did ethnicity compare with other potential determinants of legislative behavior?

The proposition that ethnicity affects attitudes and actions, including political behavior, is supported by theory and by a great deal of evidence. Ethnicity is an experiential phenomenon that denotes one of the cultural dimensions of a person's social and psychological past. Individual experiences vary, but in the late nineteenth century, when cultural styles were less nationally homogenized than in the mid-twentieth century, people clung more closely to their cultural kin for their important personal contacts. The only life-style many ever knew or understood was one submerged in the traditional folkways and the social networks of their own cultural group, in its religious practices and values, and in its educational, health, and recreational institutions.[1]

Yet ethnic identity is not uniform or static. It is a dynamic expression that varies among individuals as well as ethnic groups, and it changes over time and from one generation to the next. Its manifestations may depend upon a variety of contextual relationships, including the proximity of other ethnic groups. Some individuals have only dim recollections and little interest in their ethnic background, and others may even disavow their "old world" origins; but the lack of ethnic awareness does not eliminate the possibility of ethnic effects on behavior. Family nurturant styles common to various ethnic groups may instill cultural habits and normative values that persist into later life. The choice of marriage partners often manifests these unarticulated predispositions and may, in turn, perpetuate them. Although individuals may not be aware of these influences or identify closely with any ethnic subculture, the socialization process shapes their cognitive orientation toward the world and helps to mold their personality traits.

Ethnic distinctions, moreover, lead many individuals to type others culturally. Distorted ethnic stereotypes are the most vicious expressions of the status ranks that some groups have assigned to others. The existence of such status ascriptions can affect how an individual feels and acts. Even if the real, substantive differences between certain cultural groups are slight, the simple belief that such differences exist or the irrational dislike of ethnic "others" may be sufficient to trigger negative reference-group behavior. There is no reason to assume that state legislators in the nineteenth century were free of such prejudices.

Ethnicity can cue behavior through a variety of mechanisms, but the disentanglement of these channels is not essential to the hypothesis that ethnicity can affect legislative voting decisions. Since ethnicity is a cultural phenomenon, it can be expected that its political manifestations will be more pronounced in relation to cultural than noncultural issues. A corollary to this assumption holds that when ethnic contrasts in roll call voting occur, lawmakers should display policy positions consentient with the attitudes of their own ethnic group. This expectation does not mean, however, that legislators will invariably mirror the cultural choices of their group. As politicians, lawmakers play a variety of roles and may consider a wide set of factors in selecting each policy position. According to these two expectations, legislators of "core" backgrounds (for example, Yankees, Britishers, Scandinavians) should show greater support for uniform standards of Community Mores than do delegates with "peripheral" ties.

If ethnicity does have an independent effect on voting, such contrasts should be visible in the voting analysis when party affiliation is controlled.

The examination of these speculations began with the 1893 Wisconsin Assembly. A nearly complete file of ethnic information was gathered for the members of this legislature, and Republicans and Democrats each had sizable delegations in the session. Their voting tendencies were indexed by five roll call scales, which incorporate the basic voting alignments on contested issues found in the 1893 session. The data in table 7.1 are mean (average) scale scores for various ethnic groupings of legislators.

The voting of the Wisconsin Assembly on Mores conformed most closely to the predictions. Among Republicans, Catholics and Lutherans offered decidedly less support for "moral reform" than did other ethnic groups in the party. The British, Scandinavians, and Continental Protestants, all of whom were either immigrants or the sons of foreign-born par-

Table 7.1. Voting scores (average percentages) in five roll call scales by legislators' ethnic background, Wisconsin Assembly, 1893.[a]

Party and ethnic background	Mores	Pipeline	Commerce	RR/Silver	Government
Republicans					
Yankee	79	64	78	76	72
Britisher	88	39	83	83	72
Scandinavian	93	71	72	87	57
Continental Protestant	90	44	70	77	62
Catholic, German Lutheran	52	65	59	76	71
Party mean[b]	79	59	74	79	68
Democrats					
Yankee, Britisher, Scandinavian	27	24	65	12	14
Irish Catholic	22	33	48	5	11
German Catholic	8	58	52	3	10
German Lutheran	7	62	56	4	13
Continental Protestant	9	15	64	2	18
Party mean[b]	15	36	54	6	13
Roll calls (N)	11	9	7	8	9

a. Percentages are rounded to nearest whole number.
b. Party averages include legislators whose ethnicity is unknown.

ents, stood solidly behind the G.O.P.'s position on Mores, and even outscored the Yankees. Democrats exhibited an analogous pattern of party
support and defection on social policy issues. Their ethnic "minority,"
Yankees, Britishers, and Scandinavians, deviated considerably from the
remainder of their colleagues. The Irish response to Mores closely resembled the voting of the party's minority and did not match the cohesiveness
of the German Catholics, German Lutherans, and Continental Protestants. Since most of the votes in the 1893 Mores scale concerned liquor,
the unity of Democratic Germans is intuitively reasonable and parallels
the presumed sentiments of most Germans in the community at large.
Nevertheless, despite these apparent ethnic influences on the voting on
Community Mores, it should be noted that the effect of party affiliation
was even greater. The score of each ethnic group settled around the party
average (mean), and no one group displayed a voting profile that placed it
in the general policy orbit of the rival party.

On the noncultural policy issues, ethnic background accounted for
little variation in Republican voting scores. Contrary to expectations,
however, it did account for substantial variation among Democrats on
some economic questions. This cleavage is especially noticeable on the
Pipeline scale, constructed from legislation granting a right-of-way easement on state land to a private water company. The majority of German
Catholics and German Lutherans in the Democratic party opposed the
authorization and adopted a voting position much closer to that of the
Yankee Republicans than to the remainder of their own party. Unlike cultural issues, which prompted a cohesive response from German Democrats, the pipeline matter separated Continental Protestants (most of
whom were non-Lutheran Germans) from their German colleagues of
Catholic and Lutheran affiliations. Religion evidently did not drive a policy barrier between these Catholics and Lutherans, for their voting performances indicate essential agreement on the issues indexed by all five of the
scales.[2]

Although overshadowed by the impact of party, ethnicity showed
some association with voting behavior, most notably on cultural issues
but also, for Democrats, on the pipeline bill. Yet these apparent ethnic effects could have been the product of other factors, such as the legislator's
constituency. Community Mores, for example, embodied the kinds of issues likely to arouse the cultural sensitivities not only of lawmakers but
also of the voters in their districts, and Wisconsin Assemblymen may have
deferred to these constituent cues. The relative impacts of these various
influences were estimated by means of multiple correlation and regression
analysis, which employed four explanatory variables: legislators' party
affiliation and personal ethnic background, and constituent-level indicators of ethnic composition and urbanization. Since party explained nearly

all of the variance in the voting scores on the Government and RR/Silver scales (see table 7.1), discussion will focus on the remaining three scales.[3]

The results of this analysis (not shown tabularly) confirm the dominance of party in comparison with other determinants of the voting on Community Mores. Yet neither Democrats nor Republicans were totally unified on these roll calls. Defections in both parties, however, showed a closer tie to the ethnic composition of constituencies than to lawmakers' personal ethnic backgrounds. When the two constituent indicators, urbanization and constituent ethnicity, were first factored into the regression equations, legislator ethnicity offered little additional information about the sources of deviation in Democratic and Republican voting (adding 5 percent to the explained variance for each party). In combination, the three variables accounted for 22 percent of the differences in Democratic scores. Republican voting, on the other hand, varied in closer accord with these three factors (which explained 53 percent of the variance), and especially in relation to the number of Germans and Catholics among constituents. Personal ethnicity cannot be totally discounted as a decision-making referent on social issues, but regression analysis does suggest that some of the voting differences that occurred along the lines of legislators' own backgrounds were partially the result of constituent effects, particularly the social composition of districts.

Economic issues generated quite different equations. On both the Pipeline and the Commerce scales, party displayed only modest correspondence to the patterning of voting scores, falling below the correlations rendered by constituent and personal factors. On the Commerce scale (which concerned bank examiners, a board of labor arbitration, antitrust proposals, and railroad regulation) both constituent and personal ethnicity correlated with the voting at similar levels, but neither factor appeared to exercise a decisive influence on the way Republicans or Democrats viewed these questions. On the Pipeline scale, however, personal social origins clearly had some connection with the division among the Democrats; personal ethnicity, in fact, accounted for 31 percent of the variation in their voting scores. Two further observations strengthen this point: first, constituency factors, either ethnic or urban, had no effect on the voting, and second, the addition of the age and the generational status of lawmakers as variables in the multiple correlation model increased the "explained" variance by 9 percent, a fairly substantial increment. Republican responses to economic issues, by contrast, demonstrated no significant independent tie to either personal or constituent factors.

The ethnic connection with Democratic voting positions on the pipeline bill was curious and unexpected, and thus it invites closer inspection. The pipeline controversy originated in competition between two water companies. Each was owned principally by Chicago businessmen, each held rights to springs in Waukesha, a village west of Milwaukee, and each intended to pipe water to other locations. One of the firms, the Wisconsin Water Company, sought authorization to lay its pipes on land occupied by the industrial school for boys in Waukesha, ostensibly to aid the construction of a water line to Milwaukee but actually, opponents charged, to sell water at the World's Fair in Chicago. The other firm, the Hygeia Water Company, lobbied to block the application. An additional complication developed in that the terms of the easement allowed the Wisconsin Water Company to lay pipe across Waukesha streets en route to the industrial school.

Supporters of the Wisconsin Water Company's request argued that the legislation was a routine application for right-of-way authorization, that the state should accommodate, not obstruct, the development of entrepreneurial interests, and that the company planned a public service by providing water to Milwaukee. Opponents saw the controversy in less sanguine terms. They argued that the state had no business extending the use of public land to a commercial venture, that such authorization would make the state the arbitrator of private economic conflicts, that the legislation threatened the jurisdictional prerogatives of local government, and that continued development of Waukesha's springs would exhaust its water resources and ruin it as a summer resort.[4]

Thirty-five Democrats favored the application and eighteen opposed it. At the core of the opposition was a bloc of twelve German Catholics and German Lutherans. All twelve were above the Assembly median age and eleven of them were immigrants. Joining them were two Irish Catholics, one German Evangelical, one Norwegian Presbyterian, one man whose ethnic background is unknown, and a lone Yankee, a 69-year-old resident of Waukesha. Among the thirty-five Democrats who approved the measure were all the other party members of Yankee and British backgrounds, as well as seven of the eight Continental Protestants and nine of the eleven voting Irish Catholics. Nearly all of the men in the last two groups were American-born sons of immigrants and were below the Assembly median age. Completing the list of Democrats who favored the petition were three German Catholics and three German Lutherans, who were distinguished from their ethnic brethren by age and generation: all but one were American-born, and five of the six were below the Assembly median age and three of them were in their thirties.[5]

These profiles suggest that personal cultural background affected the way some Democrats responded to the easement proposal. Such a conclusion does not mean that personal ethnicity alone shaped Democratic attitudes. It would be more pertinent to ask why ethnicity had any saliency at all in the pipeline issue. Part of the explanation must lie in the substance of the legislation. The pipeline bill empowered the state to favor one entrepreneurial venture over that of a rival, and in this respect it was similar to legislation that mandated standards of personal moral behavior. In both cases the state acted as an arbitrator over disputes that some lawmakers viewed as private matters beyond the legitimate reach of government. Democratic resistance both to the pipeline application and to legislation on mores, it would appear, stemmed from a common reservoir of antistatist sentiments.

If this conjecture is valid, the question about the reason for the ethnic connection with the pipeline vote remains. The biographical histories of the twelve German Catholics and German Lutherans appear to hold the key to the answer. Ten of these men had settled in Wisconsin before the Civil War, an eleventh had come during the war years, and the twelfth had arrived in the state in 1873. Nine had emigrated as children, usually accompanying their parents. Eight of the twelve had been in Wisconsin when the Know Nothing cultural intolerance had erupted during the mid-1850s, and all had made the state their home when the highly restrictive Graham liquor law had gone into the statute books in 1873. The twelve had remained rooted in or near the communities of their original settlement, the German enclaves of high Catholic and Lutheran density in eastern Wisconsin, and apparently had retained strong attachments to their ethnic subcultures.

A plausible inference to be drawn from these data is that similar sociopolitical experiences molded similar political outlooks. The twelve German Catholics and German Lutherans were members of ethnic groups whose norms had been frequently challenged by the core culture. Their foreign birth suggests that they may have felt less acclimatized to the American environment than their second- and third-generation Democratic colleagues. And, to the extent that political attitudes become more deeply internalized, and perhaps more doctrinaire, as individuals age, then the twelve Germans' long residence in Wisconsin provided the time to nurture strong allegiances to the principles of "personal liberty," local autonomy, and limited government. The roll call voting of the twelve men in 1893 followed a course that is consistent with such a political mind set, although voting behavior itself does not disclose the determinants of any particular pattern of political socialization. The twelve Germans provided a higher rate of support for the Democratic position on party-conflict votes generally in the session and on community mores in particular than any other ethnic faction of their party, including the six German Catholics and German Lutherans who favored the pipeline bill. Finally, it bears restating that whatever the validity of this interpretation, the existence of ethnic influence in the voting against the pipeline bill does not preclude the presence of other, and possibly even more immediate, stimuli in the decision-making.

The other six Democrats who opposed the pipeline bill underscore this caveat, for they possessed different ethnic origins. Yet their political outlooks may have been influenced in much the same way as those of the twelve Germans had been. With the exception of one Irishman who had been born in Wisconsin in 1863, the six pipeline dissenters had been in the state when the anti-Catholic, anti-immigrant virulence had crested in the mid-1850s. Like the twelve Catholic and Lutheran Germans, they had displayed higher rates of party loyalty and greater opposition to prohibition than had their ethnic counterparts in the party. Benjamin Goss, for example, the one Yankee among the pipeline opponents, had voted wet on all liquor votes in 1893, a stand quite unlike the ambivalent position of the other Democrats of core backgrounds.

The pattern of responses to the pipeline question is, nevertheless, an anomaly. Despite the religious, national, and ethnic heterogeneity of the 1893 Wisconsin Assembly, sharp voting conflicts occurred infrequently along ethnic lines. On none of the forty-eight roll calls on contested issues were Catholics unified against Protestants or immigrants arrayed against legislators of old American roots (computed at the 60 percent level of disagreement). Methodists and Catholics rarely disagreed sharply over policy, and Yankees rarely coalesced against men of Teutonic origin. Nor did ethnic influences introduce pronounced voting cleavages within either party. Democrats, more heterogeneous religiously than Republicans, took part in seven roll calls in which the majority of Catholics voted differently from the majority of Protestants, but none of these splits reached the 60 percent disagreement threshold. Independent ethnic effects on voting behavior, if present at all, were usually subtle, not massive, and they usually found their outlet through party voting. On Community Mores, the most culturally charged policy sphere in the late nineteenth century, for example, the major ethnic components within each party usually agreed.[6]

This nexus between party and culture helps to explain why the sharpest intraparty ethnic cleavage in the 1893 Assembly did not occur over substantive legislation but over the nomination of a U.S. senator, in the Democratic caucus. Three candidates entered this race: John Mitchell, a wealthy U.S. congressman from Milwaukee; Edward Bragg, a former congressman and old-time Democratic party activist from Fond du Lac; and John Knight, a resident of northern Wisconsin and a friend, business partner, and political protégé of William F. Vilas, whom the Democrats had elected to the U.S. Senate in 1891. Beginning with an informal canvas and continuing through thirty official ballots, the caucus remained deadlocked among the three aspirants. Since Knight trailed the other candidates, Vilas apparently asked him to withdraw and urged his followers to support Mitchell, who won the nomination on the thirty-first ballot.

Politicking was the name of this game, but in this case factional loyalties followed ethnic lines. Ten of the twelve Irish Catholics and six of the seven German Catholics (an eighth had not yet been seated) voted for Mitchell, while eight of the nine German Lutherans (a tenth won election at a later date) supported Bragg on the final ballot. Less unanimity marked the other Assembly Democrats, but the Continental Protestants and Yankees favored Bragg by a two-to-one margin. When this cultural division is cast in religious terms, the senatorial nomination provoked the sharpest single voting cleavage between Catholics and Protestants in the 1893 session. This alignment, moreover, remained stable through the sequence of ballots; when defections occurred, the result actually accentuated the ethnic-bloc contrast.

The Catholic-German Lutheran split was too wide to be a matter of chance. Since the historical accounts do not reveal any overriding cultural issue in the senatorial race, the explanation for the pattern must be contained in the broader sociopolitical fabric. Catholics and German Lutherans lived in an unstable political coalition in Wisconsin in the early 1890s. The Bennett law had attracted many German Lutherans into Democratic ranks, but it did not remove their underlying suspicion of Catholics. Bragg represented a troublesome ingredient in this tenuous accord. Not only was he an outsider to the Vilas clique, but also his volatile and outspoken personality ruffled ethnic sensitivities; he had won national fame at the 1884 Democratic national convention by defending Grover Cleveland from attacks by Tammany Hall leaders, who were mostly Irish. Writing to Ellis B. Usher, manager of his senatorial campaign and political confidant (and a Lutheran) during the speakership race, Bragg had also labeled Edward Keogh, who went on to become the presiding officer, "a pretentious Irish fraud."[7]

If the Catholics' negative reaction to Bragg's "uncomfortable personality" had been colored by ethnic overtones, the Marquette statue controversy had given them an opportunity to see his rival, Mitchell, in a positive light. In 1887 the Wisconsin legislators had received a congressional invitation to place the statue of an eminent citizen in the national Capitol. They chose Father Marquette, the French Jesuit explorer of the Mississippi River, for the honor. The Superintendent of the Capitol, however, ruled the priest to be ineligible because he had not been a citizen of Wisconsin. Special congressional authorization was needed, therefore, and Mitchell, then a congressman, offered such a resolution in the House of Representatives in 1892. The Catholic press of Wisconsin, which followed the matter closely, commended Mitchell for his initiative and scolded Wisconsin's senators, one of whom was William Vilas, for dragging their feet on the issue. And both the *Milwaukee Catholic Citizen* and the *Catholic Sentinel* supported Mitchell's elevation to the Senate. Without conclusive evidence, the link between the Marquette statue affair and the Democrats' choices for senator in 1893 remains a conjecture, but it certainly was the kind of controversy that could have aroused ethnic allegiances. Mitchell's role in the matter surely enhanced his stature among Catholics, though it did not help to diminish German Lutheran criticism of the Democrats as the "Catholic" party or endear Mitchell to them.[8]

Ethnic background is only one of a variety of possible factors influencing legislative decision-making. A realistic model of legislative behavior must incorporate several types of factors that are potential determinants of voting patterns: constituent as well as personal, economic as well as cultural, and of course the fact of party. Nor should any single factor be expected to dominate the pattern of voting cleavages present in a session, although such an outcome is possible. Numerous studies of legislative voting, as well as evidence already reported here, indicate that the saliency of particular determinants fluctuates with the content of the proposals under review. A model of legislative behavior must allow for all these topical variations.

Aage Clausen's exposition of policy dimension theory is helpful to the inquiry at this point. In brief, the theory posits "that legislators reduce the time and energy requirements of policy decision-making by (1) sorting specific policy proposals into a limited number of general policy content categories and by (2) establishing a policy position for each general category of policy content, one that can be used to make decisions on each of the specific proposals assigned to that category." The theory rests on the proposition that legislators select their decision-making rule "*after* the policy content has been determined," and that "legislators will concur in the classification of specific policy questions according to a relatively small number of *policy concepts*." Legislators do not fit all issues into these generalized schemes, but like the general public, they tend to reduce diversity to conceptual simplicity.[9]

Clausen adapted policy theory to the study of congressional voting in the mid-twentieth century, but his ideas are also applicable to the historical analysis of legislative behavior. The theory provides a reasonable basis for anticipating that different voting alignments will emerge for different classes of subjects. It follows that determinants of voting behavior will vary in accordance with the way legislators perceive particular policy concepts. The theory does not specify the conditions under which particular determinants become dominant, but Clausen does see policy theory as grounded in the assumption that lawmakers tend to evaluate policy in much the same way as informed members of the general public do. From this it can be inferred that the activities of interest groups are useful indicators of community attitudes concerning policy. In communicating their demands to lawmakers, such groups help to identify the key substantive dimensions of particular issues, and the locations of these groups in the social structure suggest the sources of cues that influence legislative decisions. The patterning of these pressure activities, moreover, can corroborate and illuminate the policy classifications that lawmakers appear to perceive. For example, Community Mores primarily attracted social or ethnic groups to the legislative lobby, and lawmakers responded to many of these issues as manifestations of a generalized policy construct. Economic issues drew a different configuration of community spokesman to the statehouse, and generated different voting alignments. To assert that, in essence, different types of policy have different constituencies is hardly novel or complex, but it is fundamental.

These reflections build a foundation on which to expand the earlier hypotheses. A plausible inference to be drawn from policy dimension theory and other evidence is that cultural factors should leave their most visible mark on voting on social legislation while economic factors should have their greatest impact on economic legislation. A corollary to this is that issues of greatest concern to constituents should generate the most pronounced patterns of voting along constituent lines. The methodological difficulties of reconstructing past public opinion inhibit a comprehensive prediction of the specific topics most likely to produce such cleavages. But the available evidence suggests that cultural issues ranked high in public attention and that attitudes toward many of these subjects reflected constituent cultural affiliations. Constituent cultural differences, therefore, can be expected to show their strongest connection with voting patterns on Community Mores.

Persistent partisan cleavage on Mores has already been established, but this evidence does not contradict the assumption about the effect of constituency. Parties are, to some extent at least, constituent organizations; their personnel, issue orientation, and electoral activities link them closely to their constituent clients. Hence, it is consistent with this relationship that party voting occurs over issues on which legislators perceive a functional relationship between constituent interests and the political fortunes of their party. Many cultural issues of the late nineteenth century fitted this condition. On these and perhaps other questions, the party served as the channel through which constituent expectations achieved legislative expression.

On economic issues, however, culture and party can be expected to be less important than other factors. As a rough generalization, party voting did not break sharply along economic lines, nor did party rhetoric or platforms consistently portray a distinctive partisan position on these issues. But on the issues of Government it is reasonable to expect that party did serve as a primary decision-making referent because policy concerning election procedure, governmental structures, and public employees and officeholders had a direct impact on the maintenance of party organization.

These predictions establish a baseline against which to review voting tendencies in the midwestern houses. The voting alignments manifested in five sessions of the three state legislatures constitute a reasonable sample of these patterns. Two of these sessions (Illinois 1893 and Wisconsin 1893) represent years of Democratic upsurgence and of relatively close party alignment in each house; two other sessions (Iowa 1894 and Wisconsin 1895) met when the national economic climate had worsened and midwestern Republicans had recaptured large house majorities; and the fifth session (Iowa 1888) was typical of political and economic conditions prior to the 1890s. The results of the analysis are expressed as the percentage of variance in voting responses on roll call scales attributable (statistically) to party, district ethnicity, legislator ethnicity, occupation, district economic characteristics, and an urban factor. The scores ("explained variance") are averaged by policy sphere for the sessions in which a scale on each topical domain emerged (see table 7.2). In addition to the five policy spheres described in chapter 4, a sixth scale category (Mixed Economic) congregates legislation that is essentially economic from several other subject categories. Correlation analysis, it should be noted, does not automatically disclose the motivations that governed individual decision-making. Hence, the scores in table 7.2 should not be interpreted as literal representations of the magnitude of voting determinants but rather as expressions of the relative importance of each factor.

Voting in the midwestern legislatures conformed roughly to the patterns anticipated; yet the basis of decision-making was more complex than the hypotheses had allowed. Party and ethnicity stood out as clear correlates with Community Mores. Constituent and legislators' ethnic affiliations manifested their closest connection with these issues. The relationship held true both for the fully assembled house and for each party separately, with the exception that, for Democrats, personal ethnicity correlated more closely with commercial than with social issues. But this exception may be peculiar to the 1893 Wisconsin Assembly, the only session for which personal ethnic information was available for Democratic voting on a Commerce scale. Still, the general movement of cultural indicators is consistent with expectations: the magnitude of the cultural correlates declines when attention shifts to noncultural issues. Differences in constituent ethnicity, for example, account on the average for nearly twice as much of the variation on social as on economic legislation.

Correlations rendered by the district economic factors, on the other hand, were only slightly higher for economic than for noneconomic legislation. The difference between the variance explained by cultural and economic factors narrowed, however, on economic subjects, though the

Table 7.2. Average percentage of variation explained in roll call scales by selected variables, three states, five sessions.[a]

Legislative party and variables	Community Mores	Commerce	Fiscal Policy	Mixed Economic	Government	Public Services
All legislators						
Party	68	13	19	77	87	12
Ethnic District	33	16	20	22	20	14
Ethnicity	38	21	18	26	27	9
Occupation	7	10	9	9	3	12
Economic	7	8	8	5	5	7
Urban	12	6	9	5	4	12
Republicans						
Ethnic District	34	15	17	10	21	14
Ethnicity	34	19	18	9	11	14
Occupation	14	17	11	24	10	14
Economic	14	13	12	9	8	19
Urban	15	7	6	3	16	13
Democrats						
Ethnic District	28	11	—	5	15	20
Ethnicity	17	27	—	19	6	9
Occupation	9	18	—	7	2	21
Economic	7	11	—	11	6	15
Urban	3	7	—	11	1	16
Scales (Roll calls) (N)	5 (72)	5 (35)	4 (24)	3 (26)	3 (35)	5 (24)

a. Sessions: Illinois 1893; Iowa 1888 and 1894; Wisconsin 1893 and 1895. Democrats were excluded for Iowa 1894 and Wisconsin 1895 because of the small size of their delegation. Mixed Economic scales are defined in the appendix.

change was due merely to the weaker connection of ethnicity with these topics. Generally speaking, economic variables, measured as constituent differences and lawmakers' occupations, aid little in describing the patterns of voting alignment recorded in any scaled collection of roll calls. Separate examination of each party delegation modifies these observations only slightly. In a few instances (Republicans on the Mixed Economic and Public Services scales, and Democrats on Public Services) economic indicators explain a larger portion of the variance in intraparty voting than do cultural factors. Yet these percentages are so small as to call their signifi-

cance into question. Midwestern lawmakers' responses to economic legislation differed from their responses to Community Mores, but their voting
decisions on economic policy appear to have owed little to economic determinants. The same was true for party affiliation, although the Mixed Economic scales are a noteworthy exception. Party affiliation accounted for
three-quarters of the voting differences registered on these scales.

Party affiliation bore a more consistent relationship to decisions on
the issues of Government. Party cohesion was the overriding alignment on
these questions; other factors provide little additional information. In the
legislatures of the late-nineteenth-century Midwest party voting was
clearly linked to policy content. On Mores, Government, and Mixed Economic topics, party was the dominant correlate; on legislation concerning
Commerce, Fiscal Policy, and Public Services, party seldom had a pronounced impact. Where party did have salience as a voting reference, it
generally overwhelmed all the other factors incorporated in the quantitative analysis.

Consistency of a different sort marked the effect of urban and rural
contrasts on voting behavior. The variable Urban scored poorly on all
scaled issues, and it ranked below both cultural and economic indicators
in magnitude. This does not mean, however, that urban-rural differences
had no connection with the patterning of yeas and nays; the scores in table
7.2 are averages, in which highs and lows are not shown. In some instances population density, as well as other locational indices, did manifest a tie to particular votes. But in terms of the broad features of the policymaking landscape, voting conflict displayed only a modest relationship
to constituencies composed of country folk, small town residents, or big
city urbanites.

The simple (bivariate) correlations on which the data in table 7.2
were based are useful for surveying the comparative relationships between
particular variables and voting behavior. But legislators' responses to a set
of scaled roll calls may be the product of several determinants. Individuals
who act similarly do not necessarily all do so for the same reason. Their
collective response perhaps is best explained by the cumulative (or additive) impact of a combination of influences. Simple correlations, moreover, do not indicate the independent importance of specific variables
when other indicators are controlled, and thus they may distort the actual
significance of some factors. Multiple correlation and regression analysis
provide a method of exploring these more intricate relationships.

The five sessions reported in table 7.2 along with the 1887 Illinois
session supply the data for this investigation. Attention is centered on two
distinct subject areas: community mores and economic policy. Paired with
the Mores index in each session is a scale constructed of economic issues

that produced a low correlation with party affiliation, the usual voting outcome on economic matters. A consistent set of factors was used in each regression calculation. First, party was introduced into the equation, and then measures of urbanization, economic conditions (various agricultural variables and Occupation), and ethnocultural patterns (Ethnic District and Ethnicity) were added sequentially in steps. Thus, the model contains cultural and economic as well as district- and individual-level factors. The ethnic variables come in for the severest test in the multiple correlation analysis. Entered last into each equation, their job is to explain the variance that remains unexplained by the factors first introduced into the model. Table 7.3 reports the cumulative proportion of variance explained by each factor, entered by steps into the equation, and also beta values (weights), which provide an estimate of the independent connection (correlation coefficient) of each variable with the scaled voting scores.[10]

The results of the analysis emphasized the contrasting character of the voting alignments on social and economic legislation. Party accounted for the lion's share of the variance on Mores scales. The independent estimates of these partisan effects (beta) are not materially different from their simple bivariate coefficients, which do not remove the possible inflation caused by other variables. Party had no close rival in explanatory power on Mores among the other variables in the model. Nonpartisan factors added little to the accounting, except in Wisconsin in 1895, where party discord over cultural questions had diminished greatly from the levels present in prior Assemblies. Cohesive party voting over Mores was accentuated in Illinois and Wisconsin in 1893 and in Iowa in 1888, years when Democrats launched their most successful attack on Republican control of the midwestern legislatures during the late nineteenth century. The fluctuation in party voting between sessions suggests that close margins between seats controlled by the majority and the minority parties stimulated increased party unity over cultural legislation.

Divisions over economic policy, by contrast, rested on considerations quite different from those that structured responses to mores. The combined effect of all factors, including party, explained no more than a third of the variation on any scale, and when this level was achieved (Wisconsin 1895), party carried one-half of the load. Sharp partisan division did occur on some economic issues (for example, in the Mixed Economic scales, not shown in table 7.3), and some economic matters occasionally displayed connections with urban and occupational characteristics. Yet the issues embodied in the scales on economic legislation featured in table 7.3 represent a fair sample of contested economic policy at the statehouse in the late-nineteenth-century Midwest. The Illinois scales contain legislation that mandated the regular payment of wages (1887) and that required street railroads to elevate their tracks in Chicago and increase their finan-

Table 7.3. Cumulative percentage of variance explained and beta values for scales on Community Mores and economic policy, three states, six sessions.

	Community Mores						Economic policy					
	Illinois		Iowa		Wisconsin		Illinois		Iowa		Wisconsin	
Variables	1887	1893	1888	1894	1893	1895	1887	1893	1888	1894	1893	1895
Party	58	93	83	67	70	27	10	0	0	0	16	4
Urban	60	93	83	68	75	38	15	15	8	5	19	12
Economic	67	93	83	73	76	38	19	23	16	28	25	12
Ethnic	71	94	84	76	80	56	24	27	27	29	33	22
Beta values												
Party	0.59	0.95	0.83	0.70	0.64	0.32	0.51	0.04	0.28	0.18	0.21	0.07
Urban	0.02	0.05	0	0.03	0.17	0.27	0.39	0.66	0.14	0.13	0.06	0.15
Highest Economic	0.24	0.03	0.06	0.12	0.03	0.01	0.32	0.58	0.11	0.35	0.20	0
Highest Ethnic	0.25	0.08	0.08	0.20	0.10	0.24	0.56	0.17	0.33	0.10	0.18	0.21
Party (Pearson r)	0.76[a]	0.96	0.91	0.82	0.83	0.51	0.11[a]	0.05	0.07	0.01	0.40	0.21
Roll calls (N)	10	11	24	14	11	12	3	4	5	5	7	8

a. The Pearson correlation coefficient (r) differs from its reciprocal square ("variance explained") because of the three-party circumstance in Illinois 1887; two dummy party variables were used in the multiple correlation.

cial liability for causing wrongful deaths (1893). In Iowa, legislation regulated the liability of fire insurance companies (1888) and established the biennial tax levy (1894). A variety of regulatory measures made up the Wisconsin scales: in 1893, the creation of the offices of bank examiner and board of labor arbitration and the prohibition of trusts and free railroad passes, and, in 1895, proposals affecting railroad rates, station requirements, free passes, and taxes. Particularly striking in view of the diversity of these issues is the failure of party, urbanization, or economic or ethnic factors, separately or in concert, to describe the basic fault lines over economic policy in any state. Whatever the precise mixture of influences on these voting decisions, two quite different sets of perspectives underlay legislative disagreement over economic and social policy.

The comparative impact of ethnic and the other nonpartisan factors further illustrates the contrasting sources of conflict over the two policy domains. Ethnic factors had a small independent effect on the voting indexed by five of the six scales on Mores in table 7.3; these variables provided little additional information about voting decisions that could not be attributed to partisan, urban, and economic factors. On the sixth Mores scale (Wisconsin 1895), however, the ethnic variables boosted the explained variance by eighteen points (from 38 to 56 percent). Though not massive, the increase is sufficiently large to suggest that when partisan cleavages over cultural issues diminished, at least in Wisconsin, cultural factors picked up some of the explanatory slack. Urban-rural differences also correlated significantly with the voting on mores in the 1895 Assembly (the scale consisted entirely of votes on liquor), a fact that complicates the analysis. Tests for the independent effects of urbanization, constituent ethnicity, and lawmakers' personal cultural backgrounds on this scale indicate that each of the three factors had approximately equal influence on the voting, and that they mutually interacted. In Illinois and Iowa, on the other hand, constituent differences along urban and rural lines showed little tie to voting on Mores.

Urban, economic, and ethnic indicators all had somewhat greater explanatory power when the voting analysis shifted from social to economic issues. Rather than following a single pattern, the saliency of specific factors varied among sessions and issues. Urbanization manifested a close tie to the division over the Chicago street railway bills of 1893. Occupation accounted for over a fifth of the fluctuation in voting scores on the Iowa fiscal legislation of 1894. The two ethnic variables displayed some correspondence to voting in Wisconsin (1893, 1895) and in Iowa (1888); they registered a greater independent tie to the voting on these economic issues than on Mores, a finding that went against initial expectations.

The contrast in the ethnic connection with voting on social and on economic subjects is largely due to political party. Unlike the voting on economic legislation, Mores tended to divide lawmakers into two partisan blocs. As a result, party unity could obscure ethnocultural influences that may have affected responses to cultural policy. Such influences may be more visible, at least in a quantitative sense, in the alignments within each partisan delegation. Intraparty voting analysis (not shown tabularly) confirms the speculation. Ethnic indicators correlated more closely with the voting scores of each partisan delegation than with the responses of the full membership of each house, although the extent of these effects remained modest. Cultural attributes explained no more than two-fifths of the variation in any party's voting on any of the social policy scales constructed from the six sessions referenced in table 7.3. Republican responses to prohibition in the 1886 Iowa house represented the only scale (not shown tabularly) constructed for the fifteen sessions in which cultural factors accounted for more than one-half of the intraparty variance. The ethnicity of constituents and of lawmakers and urban-rural differences jointly explained 53 percent of the variation in Republican voting on Mores in the 1893 Wisconsin Assembly. But the interwoven connections among these three indicators in Wisconsin makes it difficult to isolate their separate contributions in the voting.[11]

Ethnicity, in short, played some role in legislative decision-making; yet the broad implication of the multivariate analysis is that party loyalty incorporated but transcended the potentially disruptive effects of constituency and personal background in intraparty responses to Mores. These issues were, after all, a key substantive test of legislative party policy differences in the late nineteenth century, a condition that helped to cause unity as well as division. The total contribution of urban, economic, and ethnic factors accounted for one-half of the differences in Republican scores on only two of the six Mores scales reported in table 7.3 (data not shown); and the same group of indicators failed to reach even this explanatory level on any of the Democratic alignments.

Ethnicity, nonetheless, displayed a closer statistical tie to intraparty voting on social than on economic issues, a finding that partly redeems earlier expectations. Conversely, urban-rural differences and economic characteristics provided for a larger share of the explained variance within each party on economic issues than on Mores. In view of this comparative relationship, the tie between the Democratic responses to the pipeline bill and their personal ethnic background was unusual, although analogous correlations of lesser magnitude occurred in conjunction with Republican voting on railroad legislation in other sessions. As a rule, however, Republican voting showed a greater sensitivity to cultural attributes on Mores than on economic issues. Although they were more culturally heterogeneous than Republicans, the Democrats put up a greater show of unity on cultural legislation. But on economic questions ethnic factors accounted for more division among Democrats than among Republicans. This comparison is based on the relative, not the absolute, value of correlations, however, for the analysis was more successful in locating the sources of Republican than of Democratic disagreement, both for cultural and for economic policy.

The lines of legislative cleavage were therefore neither uniform nor always clear. What can be said with some assurance is that lawmakers relied on different policy cues when they faced different policy domains, and that the combination of factors underlying Republican voting was not a replica of the calculus of Democratic decision-making. This intricate nature of legislative behavior is made clearer by focusing attention on two specific factors, urbanization and farmers.

Urbanization has often been identified as a source of political conflict in the decades after the Civil War. According to this line of argument, disagreements between residents of the city and the country arose because of divergent policy goals and mutual political jealousies. Whatever the perspectives of individual politicos and their constituents might have been, legislative behavior in the midwestern statehouses evidences little support for the urban-rural conflict thesis. The index of urban-rural differences between constituencies seldom explained more than one-fifth of the variation in the voting scores from any set of scaled legislation, and usually far less. This proportion, moreover, nearly always declined substantially when ethnic factors were controlled. Controlling for urbanization, on the other hand, frequently left the relation between ethnicity and voting virtually undisturbed. In some instances the magnitude of the ethnic correlations was higher among rural lawmakers than among the fully assembled house. In other words, the ethnic connection with legislative voting owed little to differences between urban and rural location. The reverse, however, was not true: the urban connection with legislative behavior was frequently induced by the geography of ethnicity.

Despite this poor comparative showing, urbanization did have some bearing on legislators' policy performance. Voting differences between urban and rural lawmakers were most evident in Illinois, where ethnicity had less impact on voting than in Iowa and Wisconsin, and where Chicago ranked as a bona fide metropolitan center. Although Prairie State legislators seldom divided into unified urban and rural camps, the reclassification of the Urban variable for Illinois into a Chicago and downstate dichotomy (downstate meaning all other legislators) yielded some substantial correlations, mainly for Commerce and Service issues, during the Four sessions held between 1887 and 1893 (see table 7.4). Legislation directly affecting the Windy City, such as the regulation of the stockyards, construction of the sanitation canal, funding of the World's Fair, and the im-

Table 7.4. Association (average gamma coefficients) between roll call scales and locational factors by policy sphere, Illinois, 1887 to 1893.[a]

Party and locational factors	Policy Sphere					
	Mores	Commerce	Fiscal Policy	Mixed Economic	Govern-ment	Public Services
All legislators						
Urban	0.19	0.28	0.23	0.06	0.12	0.38
Chicago-						
Downstate	0.34	0.54	0.39	0.20	0.15	0.69
North-South	0.13	0.30	0.35	0.25	0.30	0.35
Republicans						
Urban	0.24	0.29	0.22	0.24	0.16	0.43
North-South	0.31	0.32	0.32	0.24	0.30	0.28
Democrats						
Urban	0.24	0.41	0.40	0.26	0.36	0.35
North-South	0.29	0.44	0.52	0.29	0.39	0.49
Scales (Roll calls) (N)	4 (43)	6 (31)	4 (45)	4 (50)	2 (24)	4 (16)

a. The gamma coefficients were averaged for the scales in each policy sphere for the sessions of 1887, 1889, 1891, and 1893. Intraparty data for Chicago-Downstate are not shown; the Chicago Republican and Democratic delegations contained relatively few members, and this produced some misleading coefficients.

position of safety requirements for railroad tracks laid at grade level in Chicago's streets could draw the big city lawmakers into common cause. Later, in 1895, Chicago solons unified in favor of establishing standards for the horseshoe trade, granting powers to cities to regulate department stores and public utilities, and bestowing street railroad franchises on Chicago entrepreneurs. Downstate representatives seldom acted with equivalent cohesiveness. Their usual disarray is understated in the coefficients reported in table 7.4, as unity among the relatively small Chicago delegation sometimes greatly inflated gamma scores.[12]

Legislation with urban implications also spawned the sharpest urban-rural divisions in Iowa and Wisconsin. The school textbook bill in the 1888 Iowa house, amended to apply only to cities, produced the highest Urban correlation among the scales reviewed in that state; and in Wisconsin a proposal to locate the state agricultural fair in Milwaukee county evoked the sharpest urban-rural split. In some instances urban-rural disagreement marked the response of one party but not the other. Appropriations earmarked for Chicago, as well as other issues of interest to urban constituents, such as the regulation of pawn shops and milk dealers, stirred Chicago Democrats to deviate from the voting position of downstate colleagues. Chicago Republicans followed suit occasionally on urban matters, but they were more likely than Chicago Democrats to part company with downstate colleagues over Community Mores. Milwaukee Republicans also broke with their party over Mores in some sessions. But even in the battle over liquor in 1893, when Milwaukee Republicans deviated substantially from the views of rural colleagues, ethnic factors appear to have been responsible for a sizable proportion of the urban-rural cleavage.

Generally speaking, urban-rural differences made an unimpressive contribution to voting conflict in the statehouses. Demography provides part of the explanation, for city dwellers constituted a minority of the population in all three midwestern states. Illinois and Wisconsin allotted only one-quarter of their house seats to urban constituencies, while in Iowa the ratio was only one in nine. Unless urban delegates found allies in other blocs, they could not unilaterally carry a roll call vote. Lawmakers from semi-urban districts, such as those that included a small city, could be a source of coalition support, but such alliances were extremely rare. City representatives therefore had little to gain by regularly challenging the general legislative will, especially if such action provoked rural opposition. Cooperation and accommodation, not confrontation, was the wisest strategy for urban lawmakers.

A second factor further diffused potential urban-rural conflict in Wisconsin and presumably in other states as well. By custom, the Milwaukee delegation constituted an unofficial standing committee of the Wisconsin Assembly, to which pending legislation concerning the city and county was assigned. The Milwaukee city council channeled its special requests through the city's statehouse delegation; interest groups lobbied with its members and provided spokesmen to appear at its hearings. Acting like a permanent committee, the Milwaukee delegation reported to the full Assembly, which generally agreed with its recommendations. Some legislation concerning Milwaukee did, of course, provoke controversy among the general membership. Yet the infrequency of sharp Milwaukee-rural voting divisions appears partially attributable to the special consideration extended to Milwaukee's local affairs.[13]

The minority status of the urban delegations and the patterns of deference to city legislation do not exhaust the explanations for the muted urban-rural dissonance in the midwestern legislatures. The nature of the contested issues and the kinds of perspectives that legislators brought to bear on them are also explanatory factors. Some legislation that conceivably could have driven policy wedges between representatives of the city and the country, such as direct economic assistance for urban working-men, seldom provoked dispute in the three midwestern houses. And questions that did occasion controversy and might have evoked urban-rural voting disagreement, such as Community Mores and Government, usually divided lawmakers in other ways. Party, not population density, was the principle fulcrum on which bloc alignments broke on these matters. Illinois illustrates the point. More urbanized than Iowa or Wisconsin, Illinois recorded a greater rate of urban-rural legislative division than did the other two states, and yet party had its greatest impact in Illinois. Partisan conflict over social issues, moreover, was rooted more in divergent cultural outlooks and competition between ethnic subcultures than in factors innate to urban and rural environments. Perhaps in the twentieth century as social welfare and redistributive policy commanded higher priority, as urbanization proceeded, as urban malapportionment followed, and as the nexus between party and ethnicity weakened, the preconditions for urban-rural policy dispute increased. Available evidence indicates, nevertheless, that urban-rural disagreement never has been the principal fault line of legislative conflict in any state of the upper Mississippi Valley.[14]

Some accounts of the late nineteenth century draw particular attention to the dissatisfaction of farmers. Squeezed by periodically declining prices and escalating costs, beholden to middlemen, railroads, creditors, and large landowners, and, on occasion, victimized by natural calamity, many farmers experienced economic hardship in the decades after the Civil War. The rapid growth of a variety of agricultural organizations in the 1880s and 1890s reflected these frustrations. Some farmers saw these associations as vehicles for radical politics, but probably the majority supported more conventional pressure-group activities, such as petition to their state legislature. Roy V. Scott has provided a careful case study of the political demands of farmer organizations in Illinois during the last decades of the 1800s. The Farmers' Mutual Benefit Association (FMBA), for example, whose stronghold lay in southeastern Illinois, sought the assessment of property at true cash value, a state income tax, and the abolition of the state board of tax equalization, which the FMBA contended was controlled by business. The Association also urged the regulation of trusts and stockyards, a reduction of loan and railroad rates, and the popular election of Illinois railroad commissioners. According to Scott, the goals of other agricultural groups in Illinois differed only in detail from the FMBA's position.[15]

The Farmers' Mutual Benefit Association also managed to elect three of its candidates to the Illinois house in 1890. Independent third party activity by farmers, however, seldom achieved electoral victories in the upper Midwest. Farmer politics appears to have had greater effect on the major parties; at least, in 1890 approximately fifty successful candidates for the Illinois house reportedly pledged to work in the interest of farmers. Farmers in the house went on to organize a Farmers' Club, which by charter excluded nonfarmers and which met irregularly during the session to discuss farm-related legislation. Such caucuses were not new in 1891: similar gatherings had taken place earlier in the Illinois Assembly, as well as in the Iowa and Wisconsin legislatures. But in the light of the agricultural agitation in Illinois in 1890 and the slender Democratic majority in the newly elected house, the Farmers' Club received special press notice.[16]

The farmer-legislators of the 1891 Illinois house may have shared general frustrations about prevailing economic and political conditions, but they did not translate these grievances into concerted voting unity on specific legislation. Men who listed their occupation as farmer (no roster of members of the 1891 Farmers' Club was located) voted with 80 percent unity (60 percent Rice cohesion) on only two contested-issue roll calls. At the 60 percent disagreement threshold just four of the sixty-nine contested votes in the session found the farmers opposed to the Chicago delegation; three of these cleavages occurred over the funding of the Illinois exhibition at the World's Fair, a matter in which Chicago had considerable interest. The three representatives who were members of the FMBA had entered the house amid great fanfare due to a pending senatorial election and the fact that no party held a majority of the seats in the combined membership of the upper and lower houses. But they did not have a noticeable impact on policy deliberations. Their votes provided the margin of difference between the winning and losing sides of voting divisions during the session on only five contested roll calls, none of which found the major parties cohesively opposed or farmers drawn into a tight voting phalanx. And without these conditions the FMBA could not have held "the balance of power" over policy outcomes.

In Iowa, heightened political interest in the agricultural regions of the state reportedly brought a large group of reform-minded farmers to the legislature in 1888.[17] Yet the farmer members of this house displayed little more group unity and little more disagreement with urban legislators than was the case in Illinois. Only in the 1889 Wisconsin Assembly (among the seven sessions in which occupation was used as a variable in the voting analysis) did farmers regularly reach a modest level of voting cohesion: 60 percent unity on nineteen of the fifty-two roll calls. And only in that session did disagreement between farmers and metropolitan delegates occur more frequently than between Republicans and Democrats. The 1889 session, however, was notable for its extremely low rate of party conflict. And, even this modest amount of farmer cohesion was not replicated in the three Wisconsin Assemblies that followed. In both the 1889 and 1895

Assemblies, Republicans held large majorities and party disagreement was infrequent. Despite the fact that farmers occupied more seats in 1895 (thirty-one) than they did in 1889 (seventeen) and that the economic climate had deteriorated by the middle 1890s, the policy posture of farmers in 1895 was virtually indistinguishable from that of nonfarmers.

While neither close unity among farmers nor sharp farmer-urban conflict was common in the midwestern legislatures, farmer-legislators stood relatively apart from some or most of their colleagues on some issues. Farmers in the 1893 Illinois house, for example, were opposed to making Saturday a half-day bank holiday, to extending the term of office of Chicago mayors, and to allocating road tax monies to county treasurers. On the small Service scale that indexed this voting, farmers scored 89 percent in contrast to 34 percent for lawyers and 27 percent for service workers. In Wisconsin, lawmakers who claimed to be farmers took a timid lead in supporting antitrust legislation in 1891, and in favoring a state board of labor arbitration and the regulation of trusts and railroad switching rates in 1893. In Iowa, farmers were among the most supportive of occupational groups in the 1888 house on the question of imposing stricter regulations on fire insurance companies.

Yet only in Iowa, in the 1894 house, did farmers behave as a distinctive group on more than a handful of votes. In that year the division of legislators into farmers and nonfarmers produced a gamma coefficient of 0.5 or higher on four of the session's eight scales. One farmer watchword was fiscal constraint. Farmers provided less support than most other occupational groups for a variety of fiscal authorizations for state institutions and local government functions, legislation that included the proposed rate of state taxation and funds to construct homes for widows of Union veterans. Legislation to restrain "trespassers" from hunting on farm lands also produced a distinctive farmer vote, but an appropriation to relieve the indebtedness of the State Agricultural Society and a bill to regulate insurance companies did not.

On strictly empirical grounds, it is clear that in 1894 Iowa farmers, especially the Republicans, exhibited a modest amount of policy agreement. The reason for this unity is less apparent. Quantitative analysis cannot completely resolve the question of whether the farmers' behavior was prompted by attitudes derived from agricultural experiences, or whether the occupational correlations merely coincided with other sources of policy conflict. Occupation was only one of several characteristics shared by these farmers. Three-quarters of them were Republicans, and they were substantially older than their nonfarmer party colleagues. Sixty percent of the Republican farmers had sat in the previous session ("incumbents"), as against only 23 percent of the nonfarmer Republicans. And, like most of their constituents, the G.O.P. farmers were primarily of core cultural backgrounds. These personal and constituent attributes provide clues that may explain the performance of the Republican farmers, who returned to Des Moines in 1894 apparently as ready to advance temperance as any other policy goal.

By the slenderest of margins, Iowa Republicans had resolved at their state convention in 1893 to retreat from their rigid prohibitionist stance in the hope of recapturing electoral supremacy. In the subsequent meeting of the General Assembly, revisionist Republicans carried through the party's new policy of moderation on liquor by passing a thinly disguised local option law, popularly known as the mulct bill. This was the premier event of the session, and the closeness of the numerous roll calls on the measure attest to the depth of controversy that persisted over the liquor question.[18]

In view of the earlier battle lines over the saloon issue, the joint opposition of Democrats and prohibitionist Republicans that emerged over the mulct bill created an unusual alliance. Democrats displayed their distaste for the "hypocritical" provisions of the new policy by abstaining on most preliminary roll calls and by uniting against the bill on third reading. On this motion they joined Republican farmer-legislators, the bloc of the G.O.P. that was the least willing to abandon cultural ideology for the sake of partisan expediency. The most determined of these Republican opponents to the mulct principle were incumbents who represented constituencies that "always" or "usually" elected Republicans to the state legislature (see table 7.5), localities where antisaloon sentiment flourished and rural and small town Protestants predominated. This cadre of seventeen Republicans scored 75 percent on the Mulct scale, in contrast to 13 percent for the

Table 7.5. Republican voting scores (percent) on the Mulct scale by Party Competitiveness, Occupation, and Term, Iowa, 1894.[a]

Party Competitiveness	Farmers		Nonfarmers		Category mean
	Freshmen	Incumbents[b]	Freshmen	Incumbents[b]	
Always Republican	71 (3)	74 (6)	34 (7)	60 (8)	57 (24)
Usually Republican	44 (5)	75 (11)	35 (13)	— (0)	52 (29)
Swing or Democratic	100 (4)	79 (1)	13 (17)	52 (3)	22 (25)
Category mean	45 (12)	75 (18)	25 (37)	58 (11)	44 (78)

a. Lower scores indicate greater support for the mulct bill (local option principle); higher scores signify greater support for rigid prohibition. Figures in parentheses indicate number of legislators in each category.

b. Incumbents denote legislators who had served in the 1892 Iowa house.

seventeen nonfarmer freshmen elected in competitive ("swing or Democratic") districts. The profile of these polar blocs suggests that constituent
and political considerations were as influential as were policy outlooks
associated with occupational roles in explaining Republican disagreement
over moderation of the party's traditional liquor policy. Further analysis
of the alignment on the Mulct scale shows that both incumbent status and
district competition (which was related to constituent ethnicity) had some
independent connection with Republican responses.

Whatever their motivations, the Republican farmers in the 1894
Iowa house also took the lead in defending their party's stand on other
community mores. Although party was responsible for the basic cleavage
among all legislators on these roll calls, the incumbent Republican farmers
from normally Republican districts registered a score of 13 percent on the
Mores scale, in comparison with the 37 percent score of the newly elected
nonfarmer Republicans from the most competitive House districts in the
state. The Fiscal scale of this session manifested similar policy distance
between these two banner blocs, which averaged scores of 48 and 12 percent respectively.

The contribution of occupation as an explanatory factor in the 1894
session, however, should not be exaggerated. Occupation accounted for a
healthy yet still fractional share (23 percent) of the variation in Republican
responses indexed by the Mulct scale. The factor explained a smaller proportion (15 percent) of the party's voting differences on Mores and made
its greatest impact (28 percent) on the Fiscal scale, which consisted of legislation on economic questions. Generally speaking, the 1894 Iowa farmers
had a small part in producing the cleavages over other legislation, with
some exceptions. Hence, the question whether personal ties to farm life
among members of the 1894 Iowa house produced a policy outlook that
clashed with the views of men from other occupational pursuits remains
unanswered and conjectural. But the role of occupation in the midwestern
legislatures in general can be summarized more conclusively: it seldom
was a significant determinant of policy decisions.

The lack of cooperation among midwestern farmer-lawmakers
should not be interpreted as prima facie evidence that some of them turned
their backs on their agricultural constituents. Such a verdict assumes that
rural residents expected their lawmakers to approach policy from the perspective of a farmer, and that some of the legislators, though cognizant of
these expectations, chose to defy them. Only if candidates emphasized
their farm ties in campaigns and promised to channel their energies toward
farm interests, and only if constituents evaluated legislative nominees and
officeholders on the basis of a coherent agriculturist standard, would it be
legitimate to assess the behavior of farmer-lawmakers on these terms. De-

spite instances of farmer dissatisfaction in the late nineteenth century, there is little evidence that midwestern farmers, as a class of constituents, developed a unique and self-conscious political ideology predicated primarily on agricultural interests. They certainly did not sustain a broadly based political organization of their own to nurture such goals. Policy fragmentation, rather than a coherent politics of agriculture, characterized midwestern farmers in the late nineteenth century. They certainly were not a homogeneous economic bloc. Commodity specialization, differentials in wealth and property ownership, and local conditions produced a heterogeneous agricultural structure in the Midwest.

What conclusions can be drawn, then, about farmer-legislators in terms of the larger theme of this chapter, the dimensions of legislative behavior at the statehouse? Although some farmer-lawmakers may have viewed some issues from the perspective of the economics and politics of farm life, the model of policy resolution on which this study rests cautions against the presumption that such one-dimensional attitudes predominated. Rather, the model assumes that a logical basis exists to anticipate that voting alignments vary with policy content, and that differential voting alignments imply shifting influences on voting decisions. But these changes in the calculus of decision-making do not necessarily mean that legislators substituted one single determinant for another. Unless evidence indicates otherwise, a realistic model of legislative behavior posits that a cluster of influences molded the sequence of responses to any related set of policy problems.

The farmer-legislators illustrate this variegated basis of policymaking. These lawmakers shared not only a nominal occupational background but also, to varying degrees, partisan, ethnic, regional, and friendship affiliations. The voting analysis implies that each characteristic at times supplied a reference for policy decisions. But even relative voting cohesion among farmers does not automatically signify that their behavior flowed from a common agriculturist outlook. Whatever the determinants of such similar voting behavior might be, the diversity within farming itself suggests the likelihood that farmer-legislators (and their constituents too) would hold a variety of opinions on policy questions pertinent to agricultural and rural interests. Given these diverse and potentially competing policy cues, farmers in the midwestern houses performed consistently with a multidimensional view of legislative behavior.

Voting behavior in the midwestern houses was complex. When attention shifts away from the issues of high partisan discord and away from social policy, no simple generalization about the sources of legislative conflict suffices. Yet this diversity itself deserves emphasis, for it contradicts commonly held notions about past American legislatures. Oversimplification of the legislative process distorts the history of lawmaking.

8

ECONOMIC POLICY

Community Mores caused impassioned battles in the midwestern legislatures, but lawmakers spent more time reviewing economic policy. Legislation on Commerce and Fiscal Policy, along with measures on Public Services, many of which had a distinctly economic character, constituted more than one-half of the contested bills and contested-issue roll calls in the fifteen sessions examined. That these subjects claimed such a sizable share of the legislative docket attests to the impact state action could have on the acquisition and allocation of society's scarce resources. The content of these proposals was quite different from the goals contained in legislation on Community Mores, yet in both instances the state made authoritative decisions that endorsed certain interests and philosophies and rejected others. Such consequences, inherent in the exercise of governmental power, insure policy disagreement over numerous subjects in a representative political system. The particular sources and structure of these controversies, however, are related to the objectives of these actions. Such conceptual distinctions help in understanding the nature of legislative conflict over economic policy in the late nineteenth century.

Policy theory holds that the content of legislation affects voting behavior, and it predicts that the saliency of specific decision-making referents will differ from one set of policy issues to another. This supposition rests in part on the contention that different policy objectives affect different interests. To the extent that particular lobbies were concerned with some subjects but not with others, potential influences on legislative behavior shifted. This fact is illustrated by the kinds of advocacy groups that raised their voices over economic policy. Whereas cultural issues drew an assortment of social and religious groups to the legislature, economic questions primarily attracted lobbyists from entrepreneurial and occupational groups. And whereas the pattern of pressure on Community Mores often involved broadly based organizations that focused their attention on a few highly visible policy questions, lobbying activities of an economic nature tended to lure advocates from a wide variety of specialized backgrounds who concentrated on specific and often parochial issues. The lineup of supplicants favoring one aspect of economic policy usually bore no relation to those who were pushing for action on other economic subjects.

Emissaries from railroad companies headed the list of lobbyists found most often in the legislative halls when commercial policy was before lawmakers. The sheer scale of railroad operations and the potential harm state action could do to them explains this presence. Because contested legislation on railroads generally threatened corporate autonomy, the railroad lobbyists usually assumed a defensive posture.[1] They were most concerned about measures affecting their own business practices, but they also gave attention to some tangential questions. The railroad lobby in Illinois, for example, attempted to scuttle the Chicago Drainage Canal bill, and it closely monitored the progress of the tax reform bill in 1889. Generally, it was the issue at stake that drew the line between the railroad's allies and its opponents. Railroad shop workers, conductors, locomotive engineers, and firemen allied with the managers in Iowa in protesting the reduction of passenger fares, which workers argued would lower their wages. By contrast, legislation to place greater liability on railroads for injuries to their employees brought representatives of railroad workers into conflict with the companies. And various merchants, shippers, manufacturers, and farmers, all groups that used railroad carrying services, joined in urging lawmakers in Iowa and Wisconsin to regulate railroad freight rates.[2]

Lobbying activities on railroad bills illustrate the general pattern of pressure brought to bear on commercial matters. The groups whose voices and petitions were most likely to be heard at the statehouse usually included the members of the industry, occupation, or locality whose economic interest was at stake. Most business and occupational groups did not maintain permanent lobbyists in the state capital, although some of the larger enterprises apparently did employ such individuals to keep watch over legislative proceedings on a more or less regular basis. Trade and civic associations appointed committees on legislation, to which they delegated advocacy assignments. But as a rule, entrepreneurial, occupational, and other groups turned their attention to the state legislatures on an ad hoc basis, when legislation pertinent to their interests arose.[3]

Whatever the merits of their case, lobbyists, the members of the so-called "third house," must be recognized as potential influences on policymaking during the late nineteenth century. The Milwaukee Manufacturers

Association, for example, informed Wisconsin Assemblymen of its reservations about state antitrust legislation. Officials of insurance companies appeared at the statehouse when their industry came under review. Chicago real estate dealers actively worked for the passage of the Torrens system of filing land titles. Craft and trade workers associations communicated with legislators on matters directly affecting their occupational specialties. Trainmen urged broader railroad liability for employee injuries and safer working conditions; coal miners sought reform of the methods of weighing coal; stonecutters lobbied against the use of prisoners in their trade. In other instances, coalitions of workers urged policy innovations. Representatives of joint labor committees from Chicago pressured their state legislature for an eight-hour day, a board of labor arbitration, and a minimum wage rate on publicly financed work at the Chicago World's Fair. The Knights of Labor opposed the private employment of convict labor.[4]

An equally diverse array of supplicants sought state appropriations. The Iowa Stock Breeders Association resolved to petition the state for passage of a bill that paid bounties on wolves' scalps, while beet sugar producers in the Hawkeye State told lawmakers that their industry deserved subsidy. The Illinois Bee Keepers Association was one of innumerable agricultural and trade organizations that claimed a share of the state treasury. Such applications usually did not provoke significant legislative conflict; few Illinois representatives, for example, begrudged the award of five hundred dollars in 1891 "to promote the growth and develop the apiarian interest." Veterans' organizations claimed that they were entitled to state funds for a variety of projects. The state militia told lawmakers of their need for new armories and training installations. Reuben Gold Thwaites, long associated with the State Historical Society of Wisconsin, joined with the president of the University of Wisconsin in soliciting fiscal support for the construction of "a grand building upon the lower campus of the Univ.," which would house the Society and function as a joint library for the two institutions.[5]

Competition between rival claimants of state favoritism was especially pronounced on Fiscal Policy. Legislation on taxation, which affected wide segments of the society, drew lobbyists from diverse backgrounds who presented different recommendations. No policy area demonstrated the competition more clearly than proposals to construct new state institutions. Decisions about where to locate insane asylums, orphans' and veterans' homes, normal schools, militia camps, and similar public facilities lured contestants on a regional basis, as constituents sought to win these prizes for their own localities. From the cities came policy recommendations from public officials, men of commerce and labor, civic action groups, and newspaper editors, who spoke to the special needs and interests of urban life and their particular municipality. Not all such petitions carried an economic message, but many did. The Chicago Real Estate Board, for example, initiated legislation that enabled Chicago to levy additional taxes in order to improve the physical appearance of the city in anticipation of the World's Fair. Spokesmen from the Windy City traveled to Madison to urge Wisconsin legislators to allot a generous subsidy for their World's Fair exhibit. The *Chicago Tribune* regularly exhorted its city delegation to attend to innumerable matters, a practice replicated by urban dailies throughout the Midwest. Legislative battles fought at the statehouse often raged simultaneously in the press, as rejoinders from downstate newspapers to Chicago papers attest.[6]

Entrepreneurial groups carried their competitive struggles into the legislative process. Competition between establishments in the same industry, as witnessed in the controversy over the Wisconsin water pipeline bill, illustrates one dimension of these contests. The other dimension, conflict between groups from functionally different sectors of the economy, was evidenced in Illinois when packers, shippers, livestock dealers, and producers entered the fray over the regulation of stockyards. The demands of rival economic groups presented legislators with the difficult problem of deciding whose application best coincided with the public interest. In view of such tough choices, legislators no doubt welcomed compromises that competing groups themselves arranged.[7]

This sampling does not exhaust the list of commercial and local groups that aired legislative preferences. But the lobbyists identified in this discussion typify the pattern of pressure over economic policy. These groups tended to represent narrowly defined interests. And when the objectives of economic legislation changed, so did the roster of lobbyists.

Pressure groups had become a fixture in the legislative process by the late nineteenth century. Since the lack of modern survey research data for this period makes it difficult to weigh their impact on legislators' decisions, the reaction of lawmakers to lobbyists must be deduced largely from roll call voting. Hence, the parallel between the sequence of specialized advocates who lobbied on specific economic legislation and the pattern of shifting legislative voting blocs on these issues is suggestive. The coincidence proves nothing in itself, but it is consistent with the likelihood that voting alignments on economic legislation owed some debt to the structure and character of pressure activities.

Legislative voting on economic topics manifested neither regular nor uniform lines of division. Decision-making on these subjects fitted no single attitudinal or ideological mold. Aside from some partisan splits, the voting in a session on one set of economic legislation seldom bore a close relationship to the configuration of responses on the other economic issues. In the 1893 Wisconsin Assembly, for example, the Pipeline and Commerce scales, both essentially nonpartisan alignments (see table 7.1), did not generate similar arrangements of legislators. And in the 1887 Illinois house the voting pattern on labor legislation did not resemble the alignment on the revision of the tax code. In Iowa in 1888, representatives rearranged their bloc voting relationships to give one alignment on roads, another on railroads, and still another on insurance. The same pattern appeared in all sessions subjected to scale analysis.[8]

Party was an irregular frame of reference on economic policy. The scales on Commerce, Fiscal Policy, and Public Services (see table 8.1), in which the majority of scaled roll calls on economic issues were located, generally failed to divide lawmakers sharply along partisan lines. The scales on Mixed Economic policy were an exception. These voting indices bridged several policy spheres and were constructed mainly of economic issues that did not correlate closely with the voting alignments on the

Table 8.1. Association (average gamma coefficients) between economic policy scales and selected variables, three states, twelve sessions.

Policy scale and state	Scales (N)	Roll calls (N)	Variables				
			Party	Ethnic District	Economic	Urban	Farmer
Mixed Economic							
Illinois	4	50	0.99	0.15	0.30	0.06	—
Iowa	3	20	0.97	0.62	0.33	0.33	0.40
Wisconsin	1	8	0.99	0.45	0.32	0.41	0.30
Commerce							
Illinois	6	31	0.53	0.32	0.34	0.28	—
Iowa	5	21	0.36	0.30	0.29	0.19	0.20
Wisconsin	8	48	0.45	0.28	0.27	0.27	0.26
Fiscal Policy							
Illinois	4	45	0.69	0.24	0.30	0.23	0.11
Iowa	5	22	0.45	0.25	0.27	0.24	0.43
Wisconsin	4	19	0.54	0.21	0.17	0.20	0.18
Public Services							
Illinois	4	16	0.22	0.36	0.32	0.38	—
Iowa	4	24	0.48	0.36	0.33	0.24	0.31
Wisconsin	3	13	0.26	0.19	0.29	0.31	0.18

other economic policy scales. The Mixed Economic scales joined legislation from a variety of topics: assorted appropriations and licensing authorities of state officials (Illinois), veterans' benefits and the political composition of the railroad commission (Iowa), and railroad liability and a memorial to Congress requesting the repeal of the Sherman Silver Purchase Act (Wisconsin). Also included in the Mixed Economic scales for Illinois were such diverse issues as regulation of medical practitioners, tax reform and antitrust proposals in 1889, several measures concerning the procedures of local government, and conservation. The coefficients summarized in table 8.1 indicate that the Economic policy scales aligned legislators primarily along a partisan dimension.[9]

This pattern was more the exception than the rule. Neither party nor any other indicator dominated response patterns on economic legislation. Neither ethnic nor economic differences among constituencies consistently described the basic fault lines over these issues, although traces of their influence were visible. The joint impact of economic variables (Manufacturing Workers and selected agricultural indicators) rarely accounted for more than 15 percent of the variation in voting scores, either among the fully assembled house membership or within each party delegation. And when party and ethnicity were first entered into multiple correlation equations, the contribution of economic indicators in explaining the residual variance generally shrank to insignificance.

The classification of constituencies along an urban-rural continuum similarly failed to disclose a regular basis of cleavage on economic legislation. The same was true for the division of lawmakers into groups of farmers and nonfarmers. In Iowa, farmers assumed some distinctive voting positions on legislation contained in the Mixed Economic and Fiscal scales, but across the broader policy landscape occupation was not a major determinant of legislative behavior. Lawmakers' economic class standings were not examined systematically; yet it is doubtful whether such differences would go far to explain the sources of disagreement over economic matters. If class had any impact, it probably functioned more as an element of consensus than of conflict. Most representatives, broadly speaking, were middle-class.

Since the underlying criterion in scale construction is high intercorrelation among roll calls, the logistics of locating scalable clusters of votes insures that the major voting alignments in a legislative session are incorporated within the resulting indices. Votes that do not, by definition, "fit" into these sets reflect idiosyncratic voting alignments. Yet it is possible that such nonscaled responses corresponded to economic circumstances more closely than did the scaled legislation. To test this possibility, the roll calls from three Illinois (1887, 1889, 1893) and two Iowa (1888, 1894) sessions were correlated with agricultural and other variables.[10] The results of these calculations showed little indication that differences in legislators' voting on any issue at all in these five sessions were related to differences among constituencies in terms of rates of farm tenancy, size, or indebtedness, the value of farms or of their commodity output, or comparative emphasis on wheat, corn-hog, or livestock production. Some legislators on some occasions may have followed cues derived from these constituent tendencies, but the majority did not. None of the 427 roll calls in these five sessions showed a (Pearson) correlation of 0.5 or higher with an agricultural factor. And separate intraregional analysis of southern and northern Illinois turned up only three votes that reached this threshold.[11]

Economic policy, in short, generated a diversity of voting alignments. None of the quantitative indicators used in this study, including party affiliation, consistently described the underlying basis of these disagreements. Most of the indicators rose to prominence on some divisions, but none carried significant explanatory weight across the aggregate of economic legislation. The shifting alignments and the fluctuating salience of voting determinants indicates that midwestern representatives tended to view each economic proposal as a relatively separate and distinct question rather than as an extension of a larger, more generalized policy framework, as was often the case when social and cultural issues were under consideration.[12]

The structure of constituent interest accounts in part for this contrast in policy orientation. Highly symbolic in character and intent, Community Mores probed the emotionally sensitive and normatively oriented matters of life-style and social identity. In a sociopsychological sense, these issues affected nearly everybody, and they were easily understood in lay terms. That point did not escape party activists, who exploited the cultural facts of life in election campaigns. And their legislative arms voted in sufficient conformance with general party outlooks on social issues to retain credibility with the voters.

Economic issues had a different relationship to the community. Whereas the political aroma of the debate on liquor carried into the country crossroads, the small towns, and the heterogeneous neighborhoods of the big city, the questions of fencing livestock, granting small stipends to dairy and firefighters' associations, licensing department stores, and other matters of similar specialized character and scope affected only small segments of society. Lacking the emotional bite of the saloon and school issues, the majority of economic bills concerned mundane matters and did not evoke a passionate response or even any particular attention from most people. Some issues, of course, such as the regulation of railroads and "trusts," struck responsive cords among midwesterners. But consensus as well as cleavage could prevail among constituents on these questions. And when economic policy did cause disagreements, political parties eschewed an electioneering strategy to exploit these divisions. Neither party cultivated a distinctive class base in its election support or significantly challenged the public norm that allotted a limited rather than an expansionist role to government in economic management.

Thus the policymaking imperatives that proved instrumental in regard to Mores were largely absent from economic policy. Since they lacked a generalized policy standard that linked numerous economic topics to a single decision-making rule, lawmakers followed a comparatively unstructured path in their responses to economic policy. Both personal philosophy and interest group activity became increasingly important as frames of reference on such questions, although elements of party, culture, and constituency had a place too in these decisions, depending on the issue at stake. The diversified bases of these responses are illustrated by the legislative histories of six specific subject areas, which were selected as samples of economic policy. Railroads and trusts, two component subjects of the policy topic on Business, and Private Finance and Labor were drawn from legislation on Commerce. Expenditure was the topic related to Fiscal Policy that was selected for closer analysis, and legislation on Roads is indicative of some questions concerning Public Services that contained an economic dimension.[13]

Railroads

As the nation's largest business, the railroads inevitably were drawn into the web of politics. In keeping with the pattern of American enterprise, the railroads were privately owned and operated, but few businesses acted with total immunity from public interference during the late nineteenth century. Because of the nature of their service, the railroads in particular were viewed as performing a quasi-public function, and thus their activities were viewed as a legitimate object of state policy. Some state action took the form of assistance, such as approval of licenses, right-of-way applications, and preferential tax treatment. But railroad practices and charges also occupied public attention. In the early 1870s Illinois, Iowa, and Wisconsin had all regulated freight rates and established railroad commissions invested with several oversight functions. Soon afterward, however, Iowa and Wisconsin repealed these so-called Granger laws and despite the passage of the federal Interstate Commerce Act in 1887, grievances against the railroads mounted in the Midwest.

Excessive rates, their discrimination between destinations, undertaxation, lax safety precautions, and inadequate liability responsibility were the most commonly heard complaints. Added to these charges were allegations that the railroads possessed exorbitant political influence, a motif that some historians magnified into assertions that the lines dominated state politics and lawmaking.[14] Although these contentions overstated political reality, many leading politicians did maintain close relations with railroad company personnel. Wisconsin's Ellis Usher, for example, privately reviewed his recommendations for certain legislative leadership posts with railroad officials. Both Henry C. Payne and Edward C. Wall, chairmen of the Republican and Democratic parties in Wisconsin during the early 1890s, had personal economic ties with railroad companies and were associated with Milwaukee streetcar franchises. In Iowa, too, railroad officials reputedly exercised considerable influence in high Republican councils.[15]

Cognizant of the potential threat state action posed to their enterprise, railroaders actively defended their interests through public and private activities. A mainstay in their public relations campaign was the provision of free transportation to state lawmakers. The visiting committees of the Iowa house, for example, traveled to state institutions at the courtesy of the railroads and sometimes in the company of their officials. Wisconsin Assemblymen journeyed to the World's Fair in Chicago at the expense of the railroads. The pass system, attacked by some as indirect bribery, was highly popular with lawmakers, whose low legislative salaries precluded extensive travel and whose constituents clamored for transportation favors. Wisconsin railroad reformer Albert R. Hall was labeled an eccentric by the statehouse reporter of the *Milwaukee Journal* when he refused to accept free railroad transportation to the Fair in 1893. The railroads sometimes issued passes selectively, which exacerbated the ill feelings some critics harbored against the system. Wisconsin Assemblymen Charles Moore sent his wife several free tickets with the admonition: "Don't say anything to anyone about having passes. It makes people jealous you know."[16]

Until after 1895, efforts to eliminate the pass system made no headway in the three midwestern states. The Wisconsin Assembly did approve antipass measures in 1891 and 1893, largely due to cohesive Republican support, but the senate killed both initiatives. Two years later, when the G.O.P. returned to majority status in the Assembly, the party took less interest in the reform. Bills to regulate other railroad practices also fared badly. No *contested* issue on these subjects became law. But several contested measures favorable to the companies, such as delaying the time of implementing automatic brakes and couplers in Iowa and authorizing street railway franchises in Chicago did advance through the house. Railroad legislation that found its way onto the statute books usually won approval without sharp voting division. None of the nineteen railroad laws enacted in Wisconsin between 1887 and 1891 qualified as contested issues by the standard used in this study.[17]

The absence of roll call contests over railroad legislation is best illustrated by the 1888 Iowa house, which wrestled with the most concerted railroad reform campaign mounted during the fifteen legislative sessions studied. Despite conflicting positions of railroaders, shippers, and farmers, despite disagreement over whether or not the legislature should write a schedule of maximum freight rates, and despite some lawmakers' torrid denunciations of railroads, the major regulatory bill of the session failed to generate substantial voting dissent in the house. The measure glided through engrossment and passage without a negative vote and encountered no opposition when the house approved the house-senate conference report. Amendments to the bill provoked only scattered protest. Details of the new railroad law were hammered out prior to its consideration on the house floor, where legislators displayed a willingness to compromise on unresolved differences. In the end, Iowa outlawed rebates, long haul-short haul discrimination, and pooling arrangements. The state railroad commission was empowered to revise freight rate schedules, which courts were to regard as reasonable maximum charges. A companion statute changed the railroad commission from an appointed to an elective body and required the state, not the railroads (as was current practice), to pay the salaries of commissioners. Voting conflict did not arise over the principle of elected commissioners but over election procedures, and especially over Democratic attempts to insure minority party representation on the board.[18]

With the exception of the employee liability bills in Wisconsin, votes on railroad legislation were nonpartisan. Across the three states, Republicans and Democrats divided over the issue in nearly equal proportions. Still, the balance of proregulation sentiment in all three states lay with the Republicans, especially those who represented Scandinavian and Yankee constituencies and who were of core cultural backgrounds. Scandinavian and British Republicans, for example, provided strong support for the several regulatory measures in the 1895 Wisconsin Assembly, in sharp contrast to the attitudes of their German colleagues. Yankee Republicans in the Assembly took an intermediate position. Farmers and the delegates from rural constituencies registered more positive sentiments toward state control of railroads than did urban representatives and nonfarmers, but these differences largely flowed from the ethnic contrasts in the voting. Still, the predominance of support for railroad regulation among delegates from western Wisconsin, where field crops were relatively more important than in eastrn sections, suggests that agricultural conditions also entered into voting calculations. In Illinois, on the other hand, Yankees of both parties tended to oppose the regulation of street railway fares (applicable primarily to Chicago), while southerners and Germans, especially among the Republicans, leaned toward approval of these proposals. Overall, ethnicity displayed a connection to voting on railroad regulation, but the patterning of these group outlooks contrasted on intercity and urban railways.

Trusts

Few members of the late-nineteenth-century polity liked "trusts," and the midwestern legislators were no exception. To their most hostile legislative critics, these symbols of monopoly were "hydraheaded monsters that prey on the people and drink their heart's blood." Most lawmakers' sentiments ran in similar directions, although they spoke with greater moderation when they addressed the subject. But consensus in the abstract over the evils of monopoly did not translate automatically into agreement over concrete antitrust legislation. Part of the explanation for this lies in the phrasing of the bills. Their concise but broad language exposed them to the criticism that they were too vague and that they threatened the activities of labor unions and small business. Other delegates expressed the apprehension, heard frequently in debate over commercial policy, that strict control of business would drive capital from their state. The realities of federalism worked to the advantage of such spokesmen, who warned that restriction of trade would impel entrepreneurs to seek more hospitable political climates; if any statutory remedy was required, these critics argued, it should come from the national government.[19]

Such reservations, nonetheless, did not deter most midwestern state representatives, especially after Congress blazed the trail in 1890 with the enactment of the Sherman Antitrust Act. The Illinois house passed antimonopoly bills in three successive sessions beginning in 1889. The Wisconsin Assembly defeated an equivalent proposal in 1889 but approved similar measures in the next two sessions. The senates, not the popular houses, proved the more intractable bodies in outlawing monopoly. In the midwestern lower houses a slight majority of the members of each party voted for the antitrust legislation.

As with most business regulation measures, voting on the antitrust bills did not split clearly or consistently along any behavioral axis. None of the ten roll calls on legislation that outlawed monopoly, for example, generated partisan conflict. Yet although they were not sharply etched, certain tendencies were perceptible. Antitrust legislation received its greatest support in the rural and Protestant districts and among delegates of core and farming backgrounds. Opponents tended to possess opposite characteristics. The pattern of responses to the antimonopoly bill in the 1893 Wisconsin Assembly illustrates the composition of these polar blocs. The British and Yankee Assemblymen who represented the most rural Protestant constituencies in the state voted 20 to 0 in favor of the measure whereas delegates from Milwaukee and the highly German counties that surrounded it accounted for most of the seventeen dissenting votes. Wisconsin farmers took the lead both in this session and in 1891 (though they had not in 1889) in calling for legal restraints on the economic giants. Personal outlooks unrelated to conventional socioeconomic categories appear to have been the leading determinants of decisions on business regulation. Yet the Wisconsin data in particular suggest that antimonopoly and anti-railroad sentiments, on the part of both lawmakers and constituents, were especially prevalent among agricultural and Yankee Protestant populations.

Private Finance

Insurance companies and financial services represent another segment of the Midwest's private money economy for which lawmakers groped to find the proper measure of state interference. Economic ideologies may have governed the way legislators responded to questions regarding the regulation of private financial institutions, but if so, these dispositions did not correspond consistently to any single variable dimension. Rather, a complex and diversified structure of voting materialized on these bills.

Division along cultural, economic, and locational lines, for example, were visible in Iowa over legislation that compelled insurance companies to pay the full amount specified in policies when property owners suffered a total loss. Delegates from Iowa's most Yankee districts were the legislative bloc most supportive of the proposal, scoring 87 percent on the Insurance scale. Farmer-lawmakers registered an 80 percent mark, and legislators from rural constituencies, regardless of occupation, averaged 74 percent. By contrast, a slight majority of the lawmakers with commercial backgrounds and a larger proportion of lawyers objected to the legislation. But the largest clusters of nay-sayers were found among representatives of the German and Catholic districts (scale score of 38 percent), urban locations (28 percent), and the Mississippi River counties (26 percent), whose socioeconomic features differed considerably from those of the southern regions of the state, the geographic locus of support for the bill. Whether the responses to the insurance bill reflected broad philosophic attitudes conditioned by distinctive socioeconomic cultures or whether specific insurance practices and needs, which varied with location, governed the voting is not answered by the available evidence. Some opponents contended that the proposed statute would encourage overinsurance and incendiarism, and thus higher insurance rates. Conceivably, delegates from the Mississippi River counties, the region of the greatest population density and highest property valuation in the state, had greater reason to fear increased insurance costs than did lawmakers from interior farming communities.[20]

The regulation of savings institutions in Illinois raised a different set of issues and a different configuration of votes. Party and section underlay these conflicts. In 1889 northern delegates and Democrats threw their support behind bills designed to protect depositors by specifying standards for the organization of savings institutions. When supporters acclaimed these proposals as legislation for the "working men," rural and southern lawmakers countered that they would create a "monopoly" among savings institutions, work a hardship on small country banks, and increase the fiscal burden on farmers by exempting savings deposits from taxation. In a session of extraordinary bipartisan dissonance between northern and southern representatives, the savings bank bills provoked the sharpest sectional voting of any contested issue, including bills to regulate the charges of stockyards, which northerners opposed, and to construct the Chicago sanitary canal, which northerners favored.[21]

Contrariwise, a measure proposing stiff standards for the incorporation of building and loan associations triggered pronounced partisan, not sectional, discord. On this measure Democrats voted in sympathy with allegations that the bill would penalize working men and foreign-speaking proprietors of such institutions, and would mandate unwarranted and costly inspections. As with other legislation that threatened to bring public inspectors into homes and offices, Democrats displayed a cohesive aversion to the intrusion of officials into domains regarded as beyond the legitimate reach of government. Two years earlier Illinois Democrats had been even more unified in opposition to the regulation of pawn shops, including their interest rates, a legislative step that the bill's Republican sponsor justified as one needed to make the business "respectable." Party voting also marked the division over Wisconsin's memorial to Congress protesting the repeal of the Sherman Silver Purchase Act and over Iowa's attempt to make silver full legal tender. By the early 1890s party animosity over the silver issue extended from the halls of Congress to the floors of the state legislatures.[22]

Yet financial policy did not consistently pit Democrat against Republican, as the question of interest rates in Iowa makes plain. Legislation to define usury in the 1886 and 1888 houses provoked the largest set of roll calls on private finance in the fifteen sessions examined, but without aligning lawmakers along any discernible behavioral axis. The rhetoric was as impassioned as it was lengthy. To proponents, the state had an obligation to "protect the honest yeomanry" and "the creators of wealth" from financial "sharks" by reducing the legal rate of interest and protecting the "innocent" and the "weak" from extortion. Citing Scripture for moral justification, these men appealed to colleagues to drive the usurers from the money temples of Iowa. But what was moral rectitude and economic fairness to some minds was contrary to "the law of nature" and simply bad business practice to others. Legislating the price of money, dissenters claimed, was economic folly, for "money like water would seek its own level." The debate incorporated the classic arguments over the inherent principles of capitalism, the competition between states in attracting investors and stimulating enterprise, and the preservation of economic equity among citizens. In the end, most Iowa lawmakers decided these questions without apparent reliance on constituent or other recognizable bloc references. And the terms of financial contracts continued to be a troublesome subject in the Hawkeye State, as representatives rediscovered in 1892 in considering a bill to protect signatories from assuming debts under circumstances of fraud. A long series of roll calls revived the debate over the question of when the state should restrain private financial transactions and replicated its nondescript voting alignments. Unlike their behavior on community mores, lawmakers honored no consistent ideological modalities when they defined the relationship between the state on the one hand and entrepreneurs and consumers on the other.[23]

Labor

Despite unrest among many nonagricultural workers in the last decades of the nineteenth century, midwestern legislators fought relatively few battles over labor policy. The infrequency of such disputes is particularly conspicuous in Illinois, given the state's rapidly expanding industrial base. The large body of labor legislation in that state, as well as in Iowa and Wisconsin, met either a bipartisan death or broad legislative approval. The presence of the new but slender Democratic majority in the 1891 Illinois house, for example, did not produce cleavage roll calls over the compulsory weekly payment of money wages, the prohibition of truck stores, the expansion of the powers of mine inspectors, an eight-hour day and minimum wage for construction workers at the World's Fair, or the state's first child labor law, all of which were enacted during the session. Iowa representatives spent days fighting over liquor policy, textbook purchase procedures, and a variety of financial and fiscal measures in 1888, but they did not contest the passage of three statutes concerning procedures for the weighing and screening of coal or of a law that prohibited truck stores, proposals intended to benefit coal miners. Although labor law was often insipid in character and poorly enforced, consensus usually guided these measures through the midwestern houses.

A fear of social disorder weighed as heavily on the minds of lawmakers as did a commitment to promote the welfare of workers. Illinois' swift reaction in 1887 to the Haymarket Square riot is instructive on this count. The Merritt Conspiracy Law, the harshest of several antilabor responses, held "formenters and inciters" of riots accountable for the damages to person and property committed by others. The object of the bill, explained sponsor Thomas Merritt, house leader of the downstate Democrats, was "to strike at those men whose names could not be spelled in English that came here to incite honest workingmen to believe that our government was a sham and a curse." Nearly all Republicans consented to the tenor of the bill, if not to Merritt's brief, and the majority of Democrats followed suit, although a large number sought refuge in abstention or absence. The only partisan resistance came from Chicago's United Labor men. When the Illinois legislature reconsidered its action in a less impassioned atmosphere in 1891, the house repealed the law with as much ease as it had passed it.[24]

Apprehension of renewed conflict between labor and capital lingered on, however, and on occasion served as justification for public supervision of industrial disputes. A Wisconsin lawmaker, for example, reminded colleagues who moved to sidetrack a bill to create a board of labor arbitration in 1893: "With the crack of the Winchester at Homestead still ringing in your ears, with the memory of the Haymarket riots at Chicago and the May riots in Milwaukee yet fresh in the minds of the assembly, I cannot see, gentlemen, why you should vote for indefinite postponement." The measure survived until the vote on passage, but it did not win enactment until the next session.[25]

In contrast to the voting on the regulation of railroads, trusts, and financial institutions, party formed the most common bloc division on labor legislation, especially in Iowa and Wisconsin. One-third of the roll calls on Labor (including the railroad liability bills on Wisconsin) qualified as party votes by the 60 percent disagreement criterion, and six out of every ten of these votes found the majority of Democrats opposed to the majority of Republicans. Partisan discord materialized primarily because Democrats unified on a labor issue; their party achieved high cohesiveness on the topic twice as often as Republicans.

On such divisions Democrats customarily stood with the interests of working men, although exceptions existed, especially when labor legislation ran afoul of Democratic antistatist sentiments. In Wisconsin, for example, Democrats opposed a board of labor arbitration and an eight-hour day for municipal employees. The party's effort to end the practice of leasing prison labor to private employers constituted a proworker stance but nevertheless one consistent with hostility to state interference with private contracts between labor and employers. A similar thematic cord was touched in Iowa when Democrats gave virtually unanimous support to legislation that restrained employers from compelling workers to forfeit union membership as a condition of employment. The bill delegated enforcement responsibility to county attorneys and provided for no significant increase in state authority. In general, labor legislation confronted Democrats with a perplexing policy dilemma. Which master should the party honor: the demands of laboring men, the philosophic distaste for expanding state administrative power, or the sanctity of contractual freedom among private groups? When the political merits of the first consideration outweighed the ideological loyalties to the other two, Democrats joined together in a prolabor and anti-Republican posture.

The history of the railroad liability bills in Wisconsin suggests that pressure from labor could have influenced this decision. Although it is not clear if the railroad brotherhoods lobbied disproportionately among Democrats, spokesmen for the employees did appear at committee hearings to urge removal of the "fellow servant" doctrine from the arsenal of railroad defenses against compensation claims of workers killed or injured on the job. The Republicans, who in effect sided with employers on the issue, argued that railroad work was no more dangerous than other occupations, and that state action on behalf of trainmen therefore favored a single "class" of labor. Such observations attested more to the hazards of many industrial jobs than to the absence of risk in railroad work. The railroad employee fatality rate in Wisconsin exceeded sixty deaths in some years during the 1880s; injuries were ten times as numerous, and their incidence was increasing. In the years before automatic couplers, few railroad brakemen worked for long without losing one or more fingers. As rail traffic increased, such mishaps mounted.[26]

The historical record does not disclose how such evidence played on legislators' policy decisions, but whatever their motives Democrats sided with the workers on this issue. Although Democratic voting unity varied on the ten roll calls examined on the liability issue between 1887 and 1893, a majority of Democrats always favored stricter railroad responsibility for injuries whereas most Republicans, with the exception of one roll call, voted against these proposals. When the issue reached a showdown in 1893, Democrats discussed various proposals in caucus and went on to rally all but a few mavericks behind key floor amendments to the bill, including a provision that made evidence of a defect in a railway car presumptive evidence of railroad company knowledge thereof. The Democrats turned back Republican substitute bills with a unanimous vote from their entire seated delegation, a combination of unanimity and perfect attendance rarely seen in the midwestern houses.

Illinois Democrats displayed no equivalent purposefulness. Whereas both the Iowa and the Wisconsin party supported the frequent payment of money wages, Illinois Democrats split evenly on this question in 1887, along with the Republicans. Clayton Crafts, later Democratic speaker of the house, scoffed at the bill as "buncombe," the product of labor "demogogues." The constituency factor played only a slightly greater role in relation to the Illinois wage bill. Many representatives from metropolitan, foreign-born, Catholic, and mining constituencies were among the supporters of the proposal, but no single constituent factor clearly described the structure of the division. Republicans from smaller and middle-sized city districts, as distinct from entirely rural constituencies, opposed the bill. Delegates from these semi-urban districts often took a probusiness and antilabor position.[27]

Party, moreover, did not underlie the division over urban safety legislation in the Prairie State. The bill to elevate the tracks of steam railroads operating on city streets (amended to apply only to Chicago) and the bill to remove the monetary limit on liability for deaths caused by the negligence of railroads did not affect workers alone. But these measures had special relevance to urban working class populations, who used streets as social and recreational space. Voting responses to these issues varied along a number of lines. Cook county men gave the measures wholehearted support, but delegates who represented small and middle-sized cities withheld their approval, a posture especially pronounced among the lawmakers who resided in these smaller urban localities. Rural delegates divided too, with Republican opposition greater in the affluent than in the poorer agricultural counties. Although responses varied regionally within each party delegation, neither party split along a north-south axis. Regardless of party affiliation, lawmakers of Irish and European backgrounds tended to favor the legislation whereas Yankees, Britishers, and Scandinavians opposed it. Despite these several tendencies, the quantitative summary of the joint relationship of personal and constituent factors accounts for less than a third of the variation in the voting scores on the street safety legislation.[28]

When party failed to direct the course of voting on labor legislation, constituency took up very little of the slack. Legislation of interest to mine workers in Illinois, for example, received strong support from representatives who resided in mining counties in 1887, but not in 1895. Iowa Republicans who won election in mining counties sided with owners over the question of strengthening the laws that prohibited truck stores and that governed the screens used in shifting coal. Some legislators apparently acted in concert with personal and constituent feelings concerning the welfare of workers; the Chicago delegation frequently displayed unity on these matters. Yet these tendencies did not grow into sharp voting cleavages along an urban labor-rural farmer axis.[29]

Expenditure

The obligation to fund the agencies that administered state policy produced a regular flow of appropriation legislation each session. Most of these measures did not provoke significant discord; a compromise was ordinarily reached over disputed details prior to floor consideration. Such settlements were based on the pervasive sentiment of "economy" in government, which conditioned most deliberations over public finance during these years. Beset by criticism about the inequities in the revenue system, yet constrained by public fears of new taxes and unnecessary expenditures, lawmakers endeavored to confine spending to the meager resources raised by traditional means. General reluctance to expand the administrative role of the state reinforced these predispositions. Hence, bills that tapped new sources of revenue at the state level and awarded generous stipends for new social services rarely won legislative acceptance.

Controversy over money bills was not unusual. Although the lines of voting divisions can be reconstructed, the reasons for them are not always clear. Philosophic parsimony stimulated some dissent, but fiscal conservativism alone does not explain all the conflict over appropriation legislation; hostility to the purposes to be served by the funding proposals played as large a role. The reduction or the refusal of financial support for an administrative function could be tantamount to injuring severely or wounding mortally the policy objective itself. The evidence provides no certain verdict about the relative importance of these several sources of disagreement. Not only are the motives underlying legislative behavior the most elusive of historical phenomena, but the legislative record implies that voting decisions across the body of fiscal legislation depended upon a variety of considerations.

The actions of the 1891 Illinois General Assembly, which entertained the largest collection of contested appropriations among the sessions examined, illustrate these dimensions of conflict. Legislation that provided for the state's ordinary administrative expenses, the creation of a boy's reform school, financial support for the national guard, an appropriation for the Pasteur Institute (the bill included monies for the treatment of alcoholics at the Keeley Institute, located in northern Illinois), the construction of the Chicago World's Fair, and the discontinuance of the collection of agricultural statistics produced thirty-seven contested votes in this house. Each bill drew on the state treasury, although amendments to some proposals concerned nonfinancial issues.

Party dominated the voting on most of these measures, with Republicans proposing higher funding and most Democrats favoring lower grants. Partisanship rather than fiscal liberalism appears to have been instrumental in motivating Republican behavior. Cast into an unfamiliar minority status, house Republicans seemed bent on forcing the majority to compromise its pledge of "absolute economy" in government, a motif reiterated in Democratic platforms between 1886 and 1894. And the G.O.P. had the votes to implement such a strategy. They achieved 80 percent cohesion (on the Rice index) on twenty-seven out of the thirty-seven appropriation-bill roll calls, while Democrats did so on but nine. Republicans kept all but one or two members in line twenty-three times, a level of unity matched by Democrats on only six occasions. Comparative fiscal liberalism probably contributed to Republican cohesion, but the purposefulness with which they resisted the spending reductions that Democrats sponsored conveys a decidedly partisan intent. The Republicans, for example, not only unanimously opposed a $52,000 reduction in the initial national guard allotment of $132,000, but they also achieved near unanimity in rejecting a proposed cut of $2,500. Further, by more than two-to-one margins, they opposed cuts of 50, 40, and 25 percent in the original million dollar World's Fair bill, although some downstate Republicans deserted their colleagues on the votes over the smaller reductions.[30]

Caught between their avowed commitment to "frugal government" on the one hand and sharp regional dispute over the merits of several bills on the other, Democrats were unable to match the Republicans' cohesiveness. Proposals that earmarked money for northern Illinois largely accounted for the disarray. Chicago was to host the World's Fair and was also the home of the Pasteur Institute. The proposed sites of the new reformatory and an additional rifle range contained in the national guard bill similarly channeled money (and thus jobs and patronage) northward. Southern Democrats took a dim view of all four measures. Although sectional political jealousy fed this uncharitable gesture, southern Illinois' relatively poor economy had no doubt disposed the party's southern wing to embrace Democratic pledges of frugality. Northern Democrats tended to support the full amount of these proposed awards; Chicago Democrats voted to a man with Republicans on each one. Speaker Crafts' attempt to reduce the Fair appropriation to three-quarters of a million dollars, for example, found no takers among his Chicago colleagues. The rift between the southern and metropolitan wings of the Illinois Democracy over appropriations was unusually sharp in 1891. Although regional splits of this magnitude were not the rule in the Prairie State, combined historic, economic, and sociocultural contrasts between the metropolis and downstate fed an undercurrent of policy antagonism throughout the late 1800s.[31]

Democrats did pull together on some appropriations. They voted, for example, to reduce the salary of John Rauch, the executive secretary of the state board of health, as they had done in earlier sessions. Rauch's quarantine and vaccination policies had irritated Democrats throughout the 1880s. The secretary's stipend was contained in the general appropriation bill, which cleared the house on a unanimous vote once the parties ceased to quibble over other minor items of expenditure. Most Democrats also moved to stop the collection and publication of agricultural data, and they took a cohesive stand on a variety of amendments to appropriation legislation that dealt with political concerns. For example, Democrats proposed and Republicans opposed the annual rotation of chaplains for the boy's reformatory.

The conflict over the budget for Iowa's state university presents an instructive contrast in appropriation politics. In 1886, 1888, and 1890 a coalition of Republicans from Iowa's Yankee and Scandinavian districts mounted an attack on university funding measures. The remainder of the G.O.P. joined Democrats to block the proposed cuts. The issue was unique in the Hawkeye State, both because it was the only controversy over a specific item of expenditure that reappeared in several successive houses and because of the anti-elitist views articulated by the university's critics. Advocates of the reductions denounced the appropriations as extravagant and wasteful, contending that the university favored a privileged minority whose professional careers were being sponsored by the taxes of most other Iowans. Democrats said little in rebuttal, but one party leader hailed the institution as Iowa's "crowning glory."[32]

The Republicans' anti-elitist objections to the university funding measures sound hollow in view of their usual policy posture and their sources of popular support. But some may have had other thoughts in mind. The state university was situated in Johnson county, which was very Catholic and very "wet." Charges and rumors circulated about student drunkenness and the antiprohibition views of faculty and trustees. Anti-university Republicans tended to win election in prohibitionist counties; unified opposition to prohibition was a characteristic Democratic response to restrictions on Community Mores. While the suspicion that ethnocultural considerations lurked behind the attack on the university rests on circumstantial evidence, the pieces of the puzzle interlock suggestively.[33]

The behavior of Iowa lawmakers on the university issue and the actions of Illinois legislators in 1891 do not exhaust the voting divisions manifest on fiscal policy. Although party affiliation corresponded with these alignments more closely than did other variables, a variety of shifting coalitions best describes the voting configurations on appropriation legislation. The diversity of these measures accounts for the pattern, or, more aptly, for the lack of one. While categorically similar in their ties to the treasury, these proposals in fact funded a myriad of functions and beneficiaries. Legislators did not approach financial legislation as a unified policy sphere; their voting shows no regular division into blocs of fiscal liberals and conservatives. Rather, within a general framework of fiscal caution, midwestern lawmakers decided the merits of each appropriation proposal in terms of its particular purpose and claimants.

Hence, fiscal policy in general and legislation containing appropriations in particular spawned a wide spectrum of voting configurations. Republicans and Democrats from Chicago, for example, faced bipartisan opposition in the attempt to grant cities additional tax powers. Despite the supporters' assertion that the bill would enable Chicago to improve its streets and public facilities in anticipation of the World's Fair, many opponents apparently agreed that such an alteration of municipal charters would open a Pandora's box of further tax authorizations. Local and regional loyalties were pronounced in responses to legislation that created new normal colleges in various corners of each state, and in fights over the location of permanent homes for state fairs and for other public institutions, such as insane asylums. State subsidies to agricultural and trade associations usually incurred little voting dissonance, although on occasion a handful of lawmakers questioned the propriety of these awards. Only when legislation to assist quasi-public agencies touched more conventional sources of controversy did discord flare up. One such instance occurred when Wisconsin Democrats thought that the Catholic Industrial School for Girls deserved state support equal to the allotment voted to a similar, though public, institution under Protestant administration. Lawmaker's ethnic background seldom distinguished these divisions, yet exceptions existed, as was the case over an assortment of legislation in the 1895 Wisconsin Assembly. Here, Democrats and German Republicans supported fiscal austerity, contrary to the attitudes of Scandinavian and British Republicans. Oddly, these blocs reversed positions on the measure providing for the construction of a building for the State Historical Society of Wisconsin, which the bill title indicated would house the "relics of the late Civil War." Claims on the public treasury rode on a merry-go-round of legislative politics.[34]

Roads

Road policy was formally classified as a topic in Public Services. But legislation on the subject can also be discussed with economic policy because the maintenance of rural roads and city streets involved taxation and the flow of commerce. In addition, road policy concerned intergovernmental relations. Historically, state governments had delegated the planning, financing, construction, and maintenance of roads, bridges, viaducts, and sidewalks to political subunits—rural towns, counties, and incorporated villages and cities. The essence of the system was local option, the administrative arrangement common to the late-nineteenth-century polity. Towns and counties had the authority to lay out roads. Residents of each town could decide whether to pay their road taxes in money or to "work out" their obligations, and the second option was the more popular by far. Cities had similar control over their streets and assessed abutters for their construction and improvement. Beginning in the mid-1880s advocates of "good roads" urged revision of country road policy, but old ways were hard to change. Most of the contested road legislation through 1895 concerned minor adjustments to prevailing practices.

Legislative voting patterns on road policy varied widely, reflecting both the diversity and the limited scope of such bills. Seldom did these patterns bear any resemblance to the bloc alignments evident on other topics of economic legislation. In Iowa and Wisconsin, in fact, the closest behavioral analogue lay with the divisions over liquor and other legislation on Community Mores. In Illinois, road legislation usually generated its own unique voting dimensions. Nor did road policy divide midwestern lawmakers sharply along partisan or urban-rural lines. On only four of the thirty-eight roll calls on roads did the parties disagree at the 60 percent threshold, and no urban-rural division reached this level of conflict. But partisan and urban-rural factors did show some modest connections with voting. A simple majority of the two parties were opposed on over one-half of those motions, and urban delegates disagreed with country representatives (though not necessarily with legislators from semi-urban districts) on one-third of them.

Some of these apparent urban-rural disparities were actually the product of partisan voting differences. In 1890 and 1892, for example, Democrats, who occupied nearly all the house seats of Iowa's urban districts, opposed legislation that ordered local residents to destroy Canadian and bull thistles along roadsides (with penalties for noncompliance) and to trim the Osage orange hedges bordering rural roads. A bare majority of Assemblymen from Wisconsin's urban constituencies differed with an equally slender margin of the nonurban delegates over a request to bar commercial traffic from Grand Avenue in Milwaukee, but this voting pattern was largely the product of sharp party disagreement over the proposal. Regional tendencies were more pronounced than either party or urbanization in the voting on some road bills. Local variations in wealth, the availability of gravel and other surfacing materials, terrain, and customs concerning town governance and road work underlay these interregional contrasts. Illinois legislation, for example, which allowed counties under township organization (a pattern common in the north) to employ a road superintendent from "outside their own body" but required that overseers reside in the district in which they supervised road work, received majority support from southern Democrats but not from the party's northern wing. Republicans from southwestern and western Iowa joined Democrats in opposing an amendment to the statute concerning the issuance of bonds for drainage ditches, whereby the taxes to amortize the loan were explicitly confined to the district that benefited from the improvement. Farmers in Iowa took no cohesive stand on this or on most road legislation, but more innovative proposals did produce recognizable voting differences between legislator occupational groupings.

The structure of voting on road policy assumed a clearer profile in 1893 over legislation in Wisconsin that promised some substantive changes in traditional road management. This bill created a three-member commission with jurisdiction over county roads, levied road taxes in money, and provided that county road work be supervised by a "competent civil engineer." The measure also would have established a state board of highway commissioners, a feature that some interpreted as an omen of increased state involvement in local road construction. The county road proposal originated with the Madison Businessmen's Club and its road committee, chaired by John L. Olin, a lawyer and former gubernatorial candidate of the Prohibition party. Olin solicited Senator Adam Apple, a Democrat and farmer from Racine (in southeastern Wisconsin) to sponsor the measure, and he also lobbied with farmers' organizations and appeared before appropriate Senate and Assembly committees. Additional pressure came from the Wisconsin League of American Wheelmen (headquartered in Milwaukee), a cyclist's organization that had been among the leaders in advocating "good roads."[35]

Engaging the support of Senator Apple was sound strategy on the part of the reformers, but it was insufficient to overcome the weight of tradition. Although the county bill passed the Senate, it failed in the Assembly at the hands of the senator's own party, region, and occupational colleagues. Irish and German Democrats, whose districts lay mainly in the east-central and lake portions of the state, and ten of the eleven self-styled farmers in the Assembly, presented a solid phalanx of opposition. Only Democrats of core cultural backgrounds, men who tended to win election in Yankee districts, broke with their party. As for the Assembly Republicans, 70 percent supported the bill. Culture had little direct connection with their voting, but occupation and region did. The Republican opponents clustered among delegates from the southwest and among farmers, manufacturers, and contractors. Merchants, bankers, real estate dealers, lumbermen, and teachers, on the other hand, cast most of their votes in favor of the bill, as did representatives of small city constituencies.[36]

The division over Senator Apple's county road bill reflected the crosscurrents of opinion that greeted reform of road management. Several considerations underlay the Democrats' opposition. Preference for local autonomy was one apparent reason for their objection. The behavior of Democrats who were of Irish and German backgrounds and came from constituencies of peripheral nationalities suggests that cultural factors fed this disposition. Although fiscal conservatism may have affected some ethnic groups (Germans in particular), at the same time the county road bill, like prohibition legislation, probably symbolized a threat to the sociopolitical independence of the peripheral cultural groups. To the extent that the non-core-culture groups identified Yankees and their ethnic kin with efforts to shift administrative functions from local to wider jurisdictional arenas, these groups may have perceived political centralization largely in

terms of negative cultural implications. But Democratic opposition probably rested on another ground as well. Most Assembly Democrats represented the oldest and wealthiest region of the state, areas where gravel was
abundant and a substantial portion of the roads had already been improved. Many constituents in this region probably feared the inauguration
of a policy that could eventually require them to contribute financially to
road construction in other regions of the state.

Geography bore a different relationship to Republican votes on the
county road bill. Members of the G.O.P. from southwestern Wisconsin,
where hilly terrain raised the cost of road construction, cast the majority
of their votes against the bill, whereas thirteen of the fourteen Republicans
from southeastern Wisconsin favored the measure. Yet the general pattern
of Republican responses, which also varied between occupations and to a
lesser degree between small town and open country constituencies, suggests that geography was not the only element in the G.O.P. outlook.
Whereas farmers and residents of the countryside may have seen a county
road network mainly in terms of a higher tax burden, the small town merchants, bankers, and school teachers had associational and economic ties
that could have enabled them to visualize the broader implications of better roads. As members of the ethnic core establishment, moreover, Republicans had less cause than Democrats to see cultural threats in political centralization.[37]

The Wisconsin legislature, however, did advance the cause of good
roads in 1893. By voice vote, the Assembly joined the Senate in the enactment of a bill requiring towns to pay their road taxes in money unless they
voted otherwise and placing road work under a town-appointed superintendent, who held office for three years. An effort to repeal the statute in
the next Assembly, now under Republican control, failed; Yankees were
the law's staunchest defenders. Iowa inched forward on reform in 1894 by
requiring that a portion of the local road tax be transferred to the county,
for expenditure at the discretion of the board of supervisors. Once the bill
was amended to specify explicitly that local jurisdictions retained primary
control over road taxes and their mode of payment, all major legislative
blocs supported the bill. But in Illinois a more advanced measure, which
provided for boards of town highway commissioners to construct gravel
or macadam roads, fell before bipartisan and rural opposition in the 1895
house.

The perspectives on economic policy displayed by midwestern legislators tie in well with a variety of commonly held notions about the late
nineteenth century. Consensus reigned over the fundamentals of the economic system. The legitimacy of private enterprise and the sanctity of private property existed as a priori assumptions, scarcely challenged. Domi-

nant opinion asserted that natural laws governed economic activity, and that government interference should be selective and limited. The state also had an obligation to promote enterprise, and not just to restrain abusive business practices and to protect consumers. Corporate arrogance was occasionally denounced, but successful businessmen were viewed as witnesses to the opportunities provided by the system.[38]

Yet economic realities changed rapidly during the latter decades of the nineteenth century, and with the revised order innumerable demands arose that government should respond accordingly. In fact, the states collectively enacted thousands of statutes that brought government into a closer relationship with the commercial system during these years. Many more proposals were debated and discarded. The social service-managerial state still lay in the future, but the oversimplified stereotype of a laissez-faire policy is an equally inappropriate characterization of the performance of government during the last quarter of the 1800s.[39]

A duality had evolved between traditional economic premises and a realization that conditions imposed new tasks on government. Legislative behavior in the Midwest reflected the ambiguities and uncertainties spawned by this changing economic order. Lawmakers proposed no overarching schema for revising the relationship between government and economic interests, but they offered timid reforms in numerous areas. Voting on economic issues did not polarize legislators into rigid or consistent ideological blocs, yet some faint partisan tendencies are perceptible. The balance of sentiment for the regulation of commerce and the centralization of public administration lay with Republicans, while Democrats supplied the largest measure of support for urban consumers, workers, and financial equity. But the exceptions to this blurred pattern tell the larger story. As with the complex medley of entrepreneurial, property, and local interests competing for economic advantage, a diversity of referents guided policymakers on commercial and fiscal legislation.

9

THE ISSUES
OF GOVERNMENT
AND THE ROOTS
OF PARTISANSHIP

State legislators were not deaf to the demands of their communities, but neither were they marionettes that moved automatically with the tug of public opinion. Lawmakers acted in an institutional environment that nurtured its own dynamics, built around rules of procedure, custom and tradition, and personal and political loyalties. It is in this context that political parties assumed such importance in the midwestern legislatures of the late nineteenth century. Parties bridged the related but separate worlds of community and statehouse. That midwestern legislators voted more often in partisan than in other bloc arrangements is consistent with this strategic stationing. Regardless of the wisdom of their stances or the motivations that drove them, parties affected policymaking in the late nineteenth century.

It is easier to identify the occurrence of a party vote than to explain its basis. As with most empirical measures of behavior, the incidence of party voting is not self-explanatory. A variety of considerations may underlie such dissidence, and these factors can vary over time, space, and subject. Although policy content and ethnicity affected rates of party voting, other determinants were also involved.

Several axioms of political life in the United States shaped the context of legislative conflict over the issues of Government. With its town, village, city, county, and state governments, the Midwest epitomized the nation's diversified and overlapping structure of governance. These diverse centers of public authority attest to the strength of political localism in America, a tradition that thrived on nineteenth-century suspicions of centralized governmental power. Americans, moreover, displayed a tenacious loyalty to the basic structure of their political arrangements; yet at the same time they were inveterate tinkerers with these institutions. State legislators occupied a key position in this process, for they determined the conditions under which all nonfederal officeholders served. Since this prerogative included the power to advance personal and partisan ends, its exercise was bound to find critics.

Midwestern legislators devoted considerable attention to the details of governmental structure and procedure. Eighteen percent of the contested roll calls and 25 percent of the contested bills dealt with Government. The measures contained in this policy sphere ranged in scope from important alterations of institutionalized power to minor adjustments in the routines of officeholding. Some questions embraced "reforms" that enjoyed broad popularity; other proposals were virtually ignored by the larger society. Interest and objectives, in short, varied greatly across this topical landscape. In terms of these criteria, the issues of Government fell into three general but overlapping categories: "reform" measures, many of which were advocated by various civic associations; changes in governmental procedure, mostly of a minor nature, which aroused little general interest; and proposals that provoked party disagreement.

Few of the policy proposals that circulate in the political arena at any moment attract broad public notice. Some that do, however, generate a momentum of their own; metaphorically speaking, their time has come, and resistance to "reform" melts away. Such consensus had developed over the secret ballot and the direct election of U.S. senators. The Iowa and Wisconsin houses easily passed resolutions that petitioned Congress for the popular election of senators. Secret ballot bills won virtually unanimous final approval in all three midwestern houses, although amendments on details, such as ballot format, occasioned sharp and sometimes partisan dispute. The establishment of boards of labor arbitration in Illinois and Wisconsin and the popular election of railroad commissioners in Iowa had similar legislative histories in the 1890s. Wisconsin's constitutional amendment substituting uniform for special laws for cities never aroused more than a handful of opponents during the five Assemblies that voted on it between 1887 and 1895. Legislative performance paralleled public consensus and apathy: voters approved the constitutional change in 1892, but the referendum attracted the smallest turnout of any proposed amendment in late-nineteenth-century Wisconsin.[1]

Sentiment for political "reform" contributed to the passage of Illinois' municipal civil service act of 1895. This law provided for civil service examinations and a probationary period for new appointees, and it forbade employees to solicit or pay political assessments or engage in partisan activities. Initiated by the Civic Federation and the Civil Service Reform League ("good government" organizations based in Chicago), the bill had the support of the Chicago Republican committee and of Democratic Gov-

ernor John Altgeld. Other proponents, including the mayor of Chicago
and various civic groups, joined the civil service lobby in Springfield.
Pressure for the bill had Republican overtones, a pattern manifested in
preliminary roll call skirmishes. A Democratic motion to exempt policemen from the terms of the act, for example, was tabled on a strict party
vote. Despite some partisan fears that the measure threatened Democrats
on city police forces, passage carried easily, 110 to 23. Public sentiment
was an apparent factor in persuading the majority of Democrats, including half of their Chicago delegation, to vote yea. Chicago residents voted
to implement the law shortly after its legislative enactment.[2]

But most legislation on government failed to arouse general community interest. Where lobbying was evident, a narrower range of supplicants pushed specific policies. Bar associations sought changes in administrative procedures, especially for the judiciary and county attorneys. City
and town officials monitored proposals that affected their localities and
their offices. "Taxpayers" protested increases in public salaries. Prohibition lurked beneath the surface of several proposed administrative adjustments; in the Iowa bill that provided for grand jury clerks, for example,
opponents saw more rigorous enforcement of liquor laws as the real objective.[3]

Politicians had a direct interest in the details of government. They
sensed what later research has confirmed, that the rules of the political
game affected political fortunes, which in the context of the late nineteenth
century often meant party welfare. When opportunity knocked, party
activists outside as well as inside the legislature pooled their resources on
behalf of their organization. Cooperation peaked on apportionment legislation because alterations of existing statutes could translate into gains or
losses in state legislative or congressional seats. Activists in the majority
party drafted these bills and shepherded them through the legislature, usually in the face of cohesive opposition from the minority. High party unity
was the rule on this issue, but isolated defections occurred, especially
among members whose districts were to be erased. Party leadership focused attention on these mavericks, and the scale of pressure applied was
related to the partisan balance in legislative seats. The efforts of Democrats in the 1893 Illinois legislature, where the party needed the support of
every party member to carry a congressional reapportionment scheme,
dramatically illustrate this tendency. With the outcome of the bill hanging
on the vote of one laggard, the house Democratic steering committee,
Governor Altgeld, and the party committee from the member's district
variously coaxed and threatened the wayward colleague, but to no avail.
Such tactics provided grist for the mills of antiparty critics. But in a day
when popular politics was party politics, such stratagems had their own
logic.[4]

The partisanism of apportionment and the relative unanimity accorded some political reforms represent polar responses to the issues of Government. As with other spheres of policy, voting alignments varied with governmental subjects. Party was the most pronounced characteristic in these alignments, but rates fluctuated, as the percentages of party votes on the following issues show:

Issues	60% disagreement threshold	Party majorities opposed
Apportionment	67%	83%
Elections	48	67
Constitutional conventions (Illinois)	43	71
Fee system	22	55
Salaries	19	43
Urban incorporation (Wisconsin)	0	0

In contrast to the predictable substantive direction of their response to most Community Mores, the parties displayed considerably less policy consistency on governmental affairs. Proposals to call a constitutional convention in Illinois between 1889 and 1895 illustrate this meandering. Republicans supported and Democrats opposed this proposal in 1889, but four years later the parties reversed themselves. At the intervening session (1891) both had divided equally on the measure. Finally, in 1895, mild partisan disagreement greeted a motion to temporarily postpone consideration, only to be followed by bipartisan opposition on third reading. Illinois voters, who had no trouble recognizing where the two parties stood on the liquor issue, must have been justifiably confused about partisan intentions on the convention issue.

Party responses to Mores and Government differed in another essential way. Whereas cultural dissimilarity contributed to party disagreement over Mores, ethnicity had little direct connection with party divisions over Government. Social factors also were linked with breakdowns in party unity on Mores, but this pattern was not replicated in the intraparty variations on the Government scales. When party was a reference on these issues, it frequently dominated the voting, leaving little more to explain. When party did not enter fundamentally into the decision-making, no other factor consistently suggested the bases of disagreement.[5] Mores and Government were the two most partisan collections of legislation in the midwestern houses, but the roots of these disagreements sprang from different political soils.

Partisan conflict in the midwestern legislatures over government and other issues raises the question: what determined party voting? Students of legislative behavior have offered a variety of explanations for variations in partisanship in the states. Broadly speaking, these studies have examined two dimensions of the problem: circumstances that account for variations in the levels of party voting between states and over time, and for variations in the levels of support that individuals give to their own party in the same session.[6] Both approaches rest on sound rationale, although neither has produced universally applicable theory. Equally pertinent, generalizations derived from mid-twentieth-century voting may be inadequate explanations for activities in the nineteenth century.

Consideration of this question focuses on the lawmakers themselves. Which legislators provided their party with the greatest support? What factors distinguished party regulars from party mavericks? Data drawn from five sessions were used to examine these questions, although closest attention was given to the 1893 Illinois and Wisconsin houses and to the 1888 Iowa house, meetings for which the largest array of information on variables was collected. In each meeting lawmakers were assigned a "party support" score, which is the percentage of times a representative voted with his party on party votes during the session. A party vote, again, is a roll call on which the parties disagreed at the 60 percent threshold (40 percent on the index of likeness).[7]

Since political calculations bear on legislative behavior, it would be reasonable to assume that legislators' comparative political status affected their rate of party support. Men in leadership positions (measured in terms of the occupants of committee and speaker chairs), for example, may have possessed attitudes toward party that differed from those of nonleaders. Similarly, experience in prior legislatures may have affected party loyalty. Partisan voting behavior may also have been linked to electoral circumstances, such as the competitiveness of legislative districts. Given the varied research findings on these questions, the direction of the relationships between measures of political status and party support are not predicted. Rather, the analysis is confined to an exploratory concern: did political variables account for a substantial proportion of the variations in party support? The same question is posed in relation to lawmakers' socioeconomic attributes and those of their constituents.[8]

Use of an array of variables permits a comparative examination of several types of possible influence on party support. On the one hand, the indicators permit estimates of the relative salience of political, social, and economic effects on party support. On the other hand, they allow determination of whether lawmakers' personal characteristics carried more weight than constituent features. In addition to the summary index of party support, the index is subdivided according to the content of its legislation into Mores and non-Mores. Table 9.1 provides an overview of the relative importance (percentage of variance explained) of selected variables as correlates with overall rates of party support in three sessions. A review of these correlations and of the support scores on which they are

Table 9.1. Percentage of variance in party support index scores explained by selected variables, three states, three sessions.[a]

Variables	Republicans			Democrats		
	Ill.	Iowa	Wis.	Ill.	Iowa	Wis.
Political						
Chairmen	—	4	—	3	—	2
Term	4	1	1	0	0	6
Vote Margin	2	20	9	8	6	9
Party Competitiveness	3	5	—	3	18	—
Personal						
Ethnicity	13	—	16	11	—	12
Occupation	8	1	24	6	0	6
Age	—	5	1	—	2	8
District						
Ethnic	22	15	18	5	22	7
German	6	14	26	0	3	1
Urban	5	4	28	0	1	8
Economic	7	3	17	6	6	8
Party mean score	93	85	83	95	93	88
Standard deviation	7	17	13	6	9	13

a. Session years: Illinois, 1893; Iowa, 1888; Wisconsin, 1893.

based disclose several suggestive relationships, but the most persuasive message is that no single factor consistently explains the variations in party support.

Political influences seemed particularly unimpressive. Neither legislative experience (Term) nor leadership status (Chairmen) showed substantial association with the scores. Republican freshmen did display slightly less loyalty than incumbents, but Democrats did not follow suit. Chairmen of important committees averaged lower support scores than other chairmen and nonleaders, but the differences were too small to say with confidence that these officials behaved more independently than others on party votes.[9] The voting performance of the important chairmen, moreover, differed from that of speakers. The majority leaders scored substantially above the average party mark in all five sampled houses. Only one speaker failed to deliver a perfect record on Community Mores, and this modest defection occurred in Iowa (1888), where cultural policy generated more than a score of party disagreements. So, while neither leadership status nor experience was especially pertinent to rates of partisanism, speakers did take a lead in the voting conflicts with the opposition party.

Measures of electoral competitiveness (see Vote Margin and Party Competitiveness in table 9.1) were more successful correlates, but they reached suggestive size only in Iowa. Cultural issues predominated among the party votes in this state, however, which implies that the empirical ties between competitiveness and support owed something to the ethnic factor in the Hawkeye political system. Constituent ethnicity, for example, correlated as closely with support scores on Mores as did indices of competitiveness.

Illinois' multi-member house districts provide a special opportunity to analyze the connection between political competition and party support. The state's scheme of plural balloting permits a ranking of the three victorious candidates by the number of votes each received in the general canvas. This system of minority representation induced local party organizations to offer a two-man (and rarely, a three-man) field in districts where electoral prospects were good, and to restrict their slate to a single nominee in places where they anticipated minority status. Since a legislator's rank in the ballot returns was partially a function of the size of party slates, the ranking index has been adjusted for this circumstance. In combination, these two features should capture some of the conditions of nomination and election to the Illinois house. Republicans or Democrats whose party placed two men in the field against just one partisan opponent and who ranked first in the final canvas, for example, probably felt more comfortable about their standing with the party hierarchy and the electorate than did representatives who ranked third in a field of four major party candidates. Without denying the likelihood that numerous conditions determine competitiveness, one can inquire whether Illinois' special electoral arrangement affected party voting support.

If the index has validity and if the 1893 session is representative of other Illinois houses, then the competitive gradation indigenous to minority representation had only minimal impact on individual variations in party support. Overall, the index (not shown tabularly) explained 1 percent of the fluctuation in Republican scores and 15 percent in Democratic scores. The lone Democrat who occupied the weakest category of districts in his party's competitive scale (third rank in the voting in a district where Democrats ran only one nominee) voted with his colleagues only 64 percent of the time, compared with the party average of 95 percent. This extreme deviance, however, was not matched by his single Republican counterpart, who stood with his colleagues on every party vote.

On average, Illinois lawmakers who ranked second or third in the canvas returned slightly lower support scores than did the top vote-getter

in each district. But a larger voting differential corresponded to the comparative size of party slates. Both Democrats and Republicans who were
their party's only nominee in their district deviated from the party fold
more often than did men from districts where the party claimed two legislators. This margin was trivial among Republicans but of suggestive proportions among Democrats. In all three states, in fact, representatives
whose electoral footing was relatively uncertain, as indexed by both the
frequency with which the rival party had captured the district in prior elections (Illinois and Iowa) and the closeness of lawmakers' electoral victory
(Wisconsin and Illinois), registered lower support than did party colleagues whose districts lay safely in Republican or Democratic hands. It is
not the magnitude of the contrast that is of particular note, for the spread
is small, but rather the direction of the relationship, which is similar in the
three states. It is less clear, however, how much the factor of competitiveness actually entered into the individual dynamics of decision-making.

Varied competitive situations may have bred influences that affected
party loyalty and defection, but it is doubtful whether lawmakers' hopes
of reelection ranked high among these considerations. Not only were single terms the customary length of service at the time, but freshmen and
prior incumbents registered similar support scores. Other factors, moreover, correlated more closely with support than did the indices of individual political status.

In Illinois and Wisconsin, personal ethnic background offered more
productive clues to party loyalty. Predictably, the ethnic tie showed up
more strongly on Mores than on non-Mores. Irish and German Republicans and Yankee and British Democrats displayed the greatest reluctance
to toe the party line on cultural questions, a pattern that withstood controls for competitiveness. An analogous association, especially among the
G.O.P., existed with constituent ethnicity. The Grand Old Party found its
most reliable representatives in districts where core subcultures predominated, and it could count least on colleagues whose districts contained
numerous voters of peripheral ethnic background. High cohesion, particularly on Mores, largely explains why the Democrats failed to duplicate this
pattern.

Given Illinois' diverse urban-rural landscape, Democratic unity in
the Prairie State warrants particular notice. Illinois Democrats did not suf-
fer consistent defections from either urban or rural quarters when they
opposed Republicans. In the sessions of 1887, 1889, and 1893 neither
party's Cook county delegation assumed a decidedly different posture
from downstate colleagues on party votes. The large size and the multi-
member feature of Illinois house districts, however, may obscure some
urban effects on partisan behavior. To check this possibility, an alternate
urban-rural indicator was devised, whereby the population size of each

representative's home area (see the variable Post Office) was used as a measure of local environment. Conceivably, the density of population of his residential area might have affected his response to party policy and partisan cooperation. For 1893 at least, tests do not confirm this speculation. Whether Prairie State lawmakers made Chicago, a smaller city, a little town, or the open countryside their home had no observable connection with their record of party support. Only in Wisconsin, among the three states, did constituent urban-rural differences manifest some empirical tie to party voting. But even there, the relationship held only for Republicans and was inflated by other factors. As with nonpartisan voting, urbanization had a limited impact in conditioning the modes of partisanship.

The riddle of partisan voting behavior resists simple solution. Indicators of socioeconomic and political conditions point to no single determinant of fluctuations in party voting among each delegation. The possibility remains that party cooperation and defection were the cumulative products of numerous stimulants. To pursue this idea, selected political, personal, and district variables were entered into separate multiple correlation models and tested on two sessions, the Illinois and Wisconsin houses of 1893. Mores were examined separately from non-mores. In addition, a comprehensive model pulled together leading variables from each topical cluster and was applied to the overall index of party support.[10]

This more robust quantitative investigation yielded some additional information, but not much. The best the comprehensive model could do with any partisan group was to account for 43 percent of the fluctuation in the support scores—for the 1893 Wisconsin Republicans, as shown in table 9.2. Calculations for Democrats failed to explain even one-quarter of the differences in their scores. Evidently the larger story lies with the unknown ingredients of party loyalty.

Still, these quantitative profiles provide some light. In the first place, political factors do poorly in comparison with personal and district attributes, regardless of legislative content. And second, the last two indicators are considerably more successful in describing voting alignments over mores than over non-mores. The second observation underscores a theme reiterated throughout this study: issue content strongly affected legislative decision-making.

To the extent that clues to the basis of individual voting performances can be estimated with available indicators, the inference to be drawn is that legislators' constituent environment, in combination with their personal social backgrounds, exercised some influence on decisions to agree or disagree with party on community mores. Political factors had at best a negligible bearing on this calculus. The quantitative controls used

Table 9.2.   Percentage of variance in party support index scores explained by multiple correlation models, Illinois and Wisconsin, 1893.

State and model	Republicans		Democrats	
	Mores	Non-Mores	Mores	Non-Mores
Illinois 1893				
Political	2	6	3	10
Personal	16	7	17	20
District	21	8	19	6
Comprehensive[a]	28		23	
Wisconsin 1893				
Political	8	4	3	4
Personal	40	17	13	14
District	39	15	17	8
Comprehensive[a]	43		22	

a. Used to analyze the overall index of party support, which combined both Mores and non-Mores.

with regression analysis (partial correlation and beta values) sharpen and refine this contrast. Legislators' ethnic background emerged as the most influential indicator in the personal model, and constituent cultural and urban-rural features headed the list of district indicators. Age, occupation, the size of lawmakers' home towns, agricultural conditions, and section had either less or no effect. The apparent constituent link to party voting on Mores, moreover, is suggested in the political model: in all four partisan groups examined, electoral competitiveness rendered a stronger independent tie with party support than did the other political factors.

Party voting on non-Mores depended on somewhat different factors. Legislator ethnicity and district cultural features declined as correlates with this category of votes, which contained numerous bills on Government. Moreover, on average, chairmanships, legislative experience, and membership on a house steering committee bore a stronger relationship to support scores on non-Mores than did indices of electoral competition, although none of these correlations reached impressive levels.

Numeric analysis, in other words, does not fully disclose the sources of variance in party support. But it does imply that the conditions that spawned deviancy on Mores differed markedly from those affecting party votes on other issues. A review of partisan behavior in all five of the sessions sampled reinforced the point. Intraparty correlation between the

Mores and non-Mores support indexes was uniformly low, averaging 0.3 (Pearson correlation). Moreover, constituent ethnic factors made a much better showing on Mores than on non-Mores, whereas district economic conditions had little apparent connection with responses on either type of issue.[11] Whatever impelled lawmakers to join or desert party, the cast of maverick lawmakers on Mores changed materially when other subjects were on stage.

The limited success of the correlation analysis in locating the sources of partisanship may owe as much to high cohesion on party votes as to conceptual faults in the explanatory models. Since the large majority of delegates voted with their faction on party votes, most support scores fell into a constricted range, an outcome that hampers numeric analysis. Only 2 of 302 Democrats and 11 of 343 Republicans whose voting qualified for study in the five sampled sessions failed to join their party at least half of the time. When the line between loyalty and disloyalty is raised to a support rate of 75 percent, 7 percent of the Democrats and 18 percent of the Republicans qualify as mavericks. Party voting conflict subdivided lawmakers into two general camps: one, the vast majority, whose voting record hovered around the party average; and a handful of party apostates. The party stand on Mores more than on other issues tended to drive a wedge between party loyalists and party renegades. A closer look at the apostates in three sessions (see table 9.1) further reveals the properties of partisanship.[12]

To take one illustration, Democrat James Wilson of Illinois cast more votes for the Republican position on compulsory education in 1893 than did any other party colleague. Wilson was a Yankee farmer from heavily Republican Winnebago and Ogle counties, a district in northern Illinois where Yankees, Britishers, and Swedes predominated. No stranger to legislative ways, the Ogle county Democrat had served his first term in Springfield in 1887. That year his constituents had also elected the only nominee of the Prohibition party to sit in all of the fifteen sessions studied. Wilson did not match the antiliquor regularity of his Prohibition colleague, but he cast more dry votes in 1887 than any other Democrat. The coincidence of these facts proves nothing in itself. But Wilson's attributes are typical of a renegade Democrat voting on the issues of "personal liberty." Speaker Clayton Crafts perhaps understood these cross-pressures when he asked Wilson to chair the revenue committee in 1893.

The two Democrats who ranked just behind Wilson in deviancy in 1893 had earned their maverick status, like Wilson, principally by challenging the party position on Community Mores. Both men represented competitive districts, where the Prohibition party was strong and where Republicans regularly captured the majority of the house delegation. Like

Democrats, most members of the G.O.P. stood firm on the school issue in 1893. The most notable exception was a German, whose constituents in rural Cook county numbered more Germans than Yankees. Two Chicago Republicans, an Irishman and a southerner, had slightly lower rates of defection, mostly over non-Mores.

In Iowa, in 1888, tight Democratic unity was still insufficient to bind all colleagues on Mores. William Theophilus, the party's leading renegade, was a young Welshman, a bank cashier, and the only Democrat that rural Howard county sent to Des Moines between 1882 and 1894. Republican Governor Larrabee had carried the district handily in 1887, and five years earlier its voters had favored prohibition in the 1882 referendum. Theophilus' middle course on the liquor issue suggests that he took account of these political realities. The other Democratic deviants in the session reflected similar, if not so extremely, competitive conditions.

Prohibition was the litmus test of Iowa Republicanism for much of the 1880s and the early 1890s. Therefore the four members of the 1888 house who customarily joined the Democratic opposition on this and other social issues must have had compelling reasons for their disloyalty. That three of these lawmakers represented constituents who had rejected prohibition in 1882 may have been one of them. Polk county, highly Yankee, dry, and Republican, seems an unlikely home for the fourth G.O.P. defector, Albert Cummins. A younger lawyer in 1888, Cummins went on to national political fame by continuing to buck the Republican establishment.

The six Democrats in the 1893 Wisconsin Assembly with the lowest support scores present some intriguing contrasts. Mores issues again were the chief catalyst of defection. Three of the men who voted against the Democratic majority fitted the conventional profile of party dissenters on social policy. All were Protestants of core ancestries, all represented relatively Yankee districts (for Wisconsin), and all failed to gain a popular majority in their elections. Their districts had gone Republican two years earlier, drifted into the Democratic camp with the Bennett law landslide of 1890, and returned to Republicanism in 1894. The election data suggest that the defection of a sufficient number of normally Republican voters to the Prohibition party in 1892 was instrumental to this trio's victory. Such cultural and political realities certainly could have entered the scales of decision-making when these three lawmakers weighed their constituent and personal predispositions against party cooperation.

The second triad of Democratic deviants came from a different sociopolitical milieu. Two were Irish Catholics and the third was a German Lutheran. All won their seats handily in 1892. Germans and Catholics predominated in their districts, and unlike their three Protestant counterparts, they had served in prior sessions. By the political accounting of the time, one would expect to find such men among the Catholic and German "anti-paternalism" bloc. The fact that they were not there is largely inexplicable. The two Irishmen were out-and-out prohibitionists, at least on the issues on the agenda in 1893. Possibly they had been affected by the sober spirit of the late-nineteenth-century Catholic temperance movement, which was led mainly by Irish priests. The persistence of a factional grudge may have contributed too: these men were the only Irish Catholic Assemblymen who did no support John Mitchell's senatorial election in 1893.[13] As for the German Lutheran maverick, he did not support Mitchell either. Mores proved less troublesome for him than did other party votes; at least he displayed independence on several different subjects.

Since mild strains of independence seem to be innate in many men, it may be reasonable to expect party deviancy to occur randomly among legislators, and thus to show no relation to particular variable categories. That hypothesis is not confirmed by Republicans in the 1893 Wisconsin Assembly. The leading Republican defectors did not constitute a representative sample of the party's personal, political, and district characteristics. Of the five G.O.P. lawmakers who voted more often with Democrats than with their own party on social legislation, four represented Milwaukee and two of these were German Lutherans. The fifth man, a non-Milwaukeean, had entered office by a hair's breadth in the balloting. Surveying the Republicans who had slightly lower rates of party defection, one finds lawmakers with attributes common to the least steadfast G.O.P. members in other sessions, especially on Mores: urban and non-Yankee constituencies; Germanic or non-Protestant personal backgrounds; narrow election victories; and, in 1893 at least, legislative inexperience.

Except for their recorded votes, nineteenth-century state lawmakers left little information about their stay in office. In the absence of more incisive data about their behavior, limited and circumstantial evidence must be used in drawing conclusions about the dynamics of decision-making. Two features of party deviancy stand out in the review of the available information. First, sociocultural issues were the most frequent catalyst of defection; and second, party mavericks tended to represent competitive districts and to have constituent and personal backgrounds atypical of the majority of their colleagues. Not all defectors fit this profile, of course, but the data suggest that the most likely sources of party deviancy were personal normative outlooks on cultural issues, conditioned largely by subcultural associations, and relationships with constituents in which legislators assumed an instructed-delegate role.

The large majority of each delegation withstood such cross-pressures and voted with the party. Some of the influences that forged this unity have already been suggested by means of correlation analysis, but the glue in party cohesion must have contained at least three other active ingredients: shared policy preferences; the institutionalized presence of party; and the activity of party leaders.

The likelihood that shared policy preferences played an instrumental role in producing party cohesion rests on an assumption about the relationship between party leaders and the structure of policy attitudes among the party rank and file. It is widely conceded that party leaders in American legislatures lacked the power to demand loyalty from party members. Beyond patronage and favors, party leaders could use little more than persuasion to entice cooperation from their colleagues. Hence, a crucial determinant of leadership effectiveness was the degree to which recruitment patterns placed in office rank-and-file members with shared predispositions on issues.[14]

If one grants that family tradition, electoral convenience, and patronage expectations do not exhaust the reasons why politicians associate with a particular party, then it is reasonable to assume that attitudinal compatibility with party principle could contribute to these alliances. And if complementary opinions were not a cause of party affiliation, they could at least be its byproduct. To the degree that such policy consensus existed, the parties tended to nominate their legislative candidates from pools of relatively like-minded men. A rough partisan ideology had formed in the late 1800s around a set of evocative symbols. Numerous lawmakers brought with them to the statehouse compatible opinions on "personal liberty," "economy in government," and "local control". To this list should be added the psychology of partisanship: to the extent that lawmakers possessed loyalty to their political organization—to its history, its personnel, and its goals—they shared the partisan ethos of interparty competition. The sentiment probably had its greatest manifestation in the questions on Government, since these issues often had a direct bearing on party mechanics.

It is easier to hypothesize about shared policy attitudes than to document them historically. The voting performance of the party steering committees in the 1893 Illinois house, however, does speak to the problem by allowing a rough comparison of the behavior of appointed party spokesmen with that of the rank and file. Since steering committees promoted the party position when so charged by the caucus or leaders, their activity can serve as a benchmark of organized partisanism. Members of the Republican and Democratic steering committees disagreed with one another on thirty-six votes, compared with thirty-one disagreements between the fully assembled delegations. But on nine occasions the rank and file did not follow the lead of the steering committees, and on four votes the steering committees did not disagree (at a 60 percent threshold) when the whole parties did. Party voting in this house was not simply a case of the rank and file dutifully mimicking the leadership.[15]

The analysis can be carried a step further. The double requirement that each steering committee had marshaled a quorum of its members on a roll call (which frequently they did not do) and that those voting had displayed total unity created an approximate standard with which to identify instances when party establishment sought cohesive action. Out of seventy-three contested roll calls the Republican party committee met this condition twenty-five times and the Democrats but sixteen. And on only ten of these roll calls did both the steering committees and the full delegations lock in partisan conflict. According to these criteria, organized party unity occurred over the following issues: compulsory education and an increase in business incorporation fees (three votes each); dissolution of the commission to propagate fish (two votes); and the publication of the reports of agricultural societies and the substitution of formal courts for urban justices of the peace (one vote each). But on twice as many party votes the actions of steering committee members provided less unified direction for a party voting position, if the leadership took one at all. As leadership voting cues diminished, shared policy preferences among the rank and file potentially increased as a factor in forging party cohesion.

The mere presence of the party was another likely inducement to cohesive voting. The signs of party were everywhere in the midwestern legislatures; hence it served as a ready and convenient policy reference. Partisan contacts, in fact, lined the path of legislative service. Party played an instrumental role in nominations and in the election campaign, in the early-session organizing activities, including the selection of the speaker, and in subsequent interpersonal contacts. The partisan dimension of housing and seating arrangements increased opportunities for intraparty exchanges, as did social and business activities throughout the term. Legislative manuals and newspapers invariably referenced state legislators by their partisan affiliations. The majority and the minority were basic facts of political life in these institutions, and both press editorials and party spokesmen asserted that these affiliations carried particular obligations.[16]

Legislative party caucuses brought the delegations together formally. The parties used the device in every session, although the frequency of meetings appears to have depended on circumstances, such as a close balance of house seats (as in Illinois and Wisconsin in 1891 and 1893, and in Iowa in 1890), or a pressing policy dilemma (the mulct liquor law in Iowa, 1894). Apportionment, appropriations, appointments, and adjournments were the most regularly discussed subjects, but agendas included other key contested issues.[17]

The scant surviving records of these caucus meetings indicate that they served as occasions for mutual discussion, not as command performances in which leaders dictated instructions to the rank and file. Unanimity was not universal, for walkouts, absenteeism, and complaints were recorded. The important point, however, is not how much leaders may have attempted to twist members' arms at these gatherings, but rather that caucus meetings actually occurred. They offered yet another way in which the institutionalized presence of party was manifested. Caucuses facilitated intraparty communication, reminded lawmakers of their partisan attachments, and further elevated the visibility of party as a set of symbols and a collectivity of specific people. In this regard, no comparable rival existed in these forums. Given its omnipresence, the wonder is not that party cued some voting responses but that its impact was not greater.[18]

The influence of legislative leaders is one of the thorniest problems for historians to decipher. Without the aid of contemporary interview techniques, they lack the kind of data best suited for evaluating leadership effectiveness. This methodological limitation raises doubts, therefore, about the wide powers that writers sometimes ascribe to politicians in the American past. Notwithstanding the growth of analytic sophistication in recent years, old myths about the "bosses" live on.

It is important to recognize that the identification of formal leadership positions, or even of apparent leaders, including a review of their activities, is no certain index of their degree of influence. Form must not be mistaken for substance. Theoretically, speakers held top rank in the majority party, and committee chairmen acted as lieutenants. Minority parties had formally designated spokesmen too, presumably elected in caucus. Steering committees existed, at least in some sessions, but it is unknown how much party leaders relied on them. At times leaders attempted to give direction to their party. Democratic Speaker Clayton Crafts and the party steering committee, for example, lobbied actively among the membership for support of the party's apportionment plan. C. W. Robinson, whom Democrats elected as caucus chairman in the 1894 Iowa house, recounted that he accepted the post on the condition that when circumstances prevented the calling of a caucus on questions "which smelled in the least of politics," members would follow his voting instructions ("a nod or shake of the head") signaled from the floor. Although Robinson had discretion about exercising his prerogatives, his authority originated in policies adopted by his caucus. The Democratic caucus, for example, had resolved to abstain on preliminary votes on the Republican mulct liquor bill, a tactic that Robinson helped to implement.[19]

Other parallels in leadership efforts to coordinate the party could be cited, but at the danger of exaggerating leaders' power. Their influence was limited, largely because of the nature of the legislative process. The high turnover of legislative personnel and the brief, biennial session worked against the development of an experienced and entrenched leadership cadre. Clayton Crafts, for example, was one of only two men reelected as speaker in the fifteen sessions studied. Since seniority had not emerged as a prerequisite of leadership authority, party chiefs derived their powers from personal alliances and popular support. Power was not equally distributed among party members, but neither was it totally concentrated in the hands of a few party "bosses."

Governors provided little assistance to legislative party leaders. Restraint, not active involvement, characterized their relations with the legislatures in the late-nineteenth-century Midwest. Governors outlined their views on policy needs as their constitutional duty dictated, but most concurred, at least in spirit, with Governor Horace Boise's remark that "such recommendations are advisory only." John Altgeld displayed the most energetic policy role among the midwestern chief executives who sat between 1886 and 1895. He appeared at the legislative party's caucus to urge various policy courses, summoned recalcitrant Democrats to his office, and used patronage as a lever of compliance. But illness during the early months of the 1893 session hampered his only opportunity to work with a Democratic majority in both the upper and lower chambers.[20]

The present-day leadership structure in Congress and the modern active Presidency have no analogue in nineteenth-century state government. Because strong party commands did not come from the statehouse, the influence of political leaders outside its confines was potentially greater than it is today. The list of these interested partisans included chairmen of the state party committees and their committeemen, the heads of local party organizations, city and federal officers, and the editors of the large partisan newspapers in each state. The names and activities of these participants in legislative party affairs varied with time and place. A portrait of one such individual suggests the dimensions of this leadership pattern.

Edward Clarence Wall, a native of Milwaukee, was forty-seven when he assumed the chairmanship of the Democratic state committee in Wisconsin in 1890. For the next four years he was intimately connected with the fate of his party in the Badger State. No stranger to politics, he had served in the Assembly in the 1870s and later had sat on the state party central committee. But his major triumph came in the fall of 1890 when Democrats swept into the statehouse. Victory earned the party new opportunities, including the election of Assembly speaker and the appointment of committee chairmen. Wall took an advisory role in the negotiations over these selections and personally convened the first Assembly caucus, where Democrats chose the presiding officer. The state party chairman's relations with the legislative party did not end with these preliminaries. Periodically during the sessions of 1891 and 1893 he worked with the Democratic delegations in Madison, sometimes from his "lookout" post on the Assembly floor.[21]

For his labors Wall won the epithet of "boss" from the opposition press. Assemblymen "were whipped into line by the Democratic chairman," snarled the *Milwaukee Sentinel*, Wisconsin's most powerful newspaper.[22] Was Wall really such a strong man? Did he dictate party policy in Madison during the winters of 1891 and 1893? To see Edward Wall as a commander who marshaled party troops with the authority of a general is to misjudge his rank. His commission was closer to that of party chaplain.

Despite their legislative majority, Wisconsin Democrats faced a leadership vacuum. No permanent party leadership structure existed in the Assembly, partly because of the brevity of legislative careers. Fifty-three of the sixty-six Assembly Democrats in 1891 were freshmen; only fourteen of these newcomers reclaimed their seats two years later, when another crop of thirty-six first-termers made up two-thirds of the Democratic majority in the Assembly. Wall filled an important void in this unstructured environment.

Wall acted as a conduit through which various party luminaries—especially U.S. Senator William Vilas, former state party chairman Ellis Usher, and *Milwaukee Journal* publisher Lute Nieman—fed policy recommendations and patronage preferences to the Democrats in the house. To their ideas Wall added his own. "Economy—that's what I am here for" was his persistent refrain. Persuasion was his customary weapon and a creditable Democratic "record" his battle cry. Wall outlined his tactics to Vilas in March 1893:

> I spent last week in Madison. On arriving there found that there was every prospect of enormous appropriations . . . I saw pretty much every Senator that was in favor of liberal appropriations . . . using the argument that the party could not succeed in 1894 unless this Legislature made a record. I showed them that the Bennett Law would no longer be an issue . . . On Thursday the sentiment seemed to change and I think now that I can see that we can get through and keep appropriations within bounds.

Through his network of contracts with party chiefs, his demonstrated skill as a campaign tactician, his attention to detail, and his devotion to party affairs, Wall was the grand lobbyist in Madison.[23]

But there he found party atomization, not a pliant delegation. The sources of this disunity, in Wall's view, were "personal ambitions," "demagogues undertaking . . . all sorts of so-called reforms," and a "regular scramble" to spend state money.[24] The chairman may have transformed some of this independency into party cooperation, yet Democrats voted with only moderate unity in 1891 and 1893, as table 9.3 documents. The rate of cohesion in those meetings showed no substantial deviation from adjacent sessions, when Democrats formed the Assembly minority. Five of the six unanimous Democratic responses in 1891 occurred over the repeal of the Bennett law, the state issue most responsible for the party's 1890 victory. Despite its partisan purpose in exaggerating Wall's power,

Table 9.3.   Democratic voting unity in five sessions of Wisconsin Assembly.

Cohesion levels (Rice index)	Percentage of contested roll calls				
	1887	1889	1891	1893	1895
100%	11	4	11	4	12
80%	27	23	28	23	28
60%	36	38	33	37	47

even the rival press conceded that his control over the delegation was limited.[25]

Wall had several inducements to seek a successful record in Madison. As public estimation of Democrats rose, so, thought Wall, did his political and financial future. He attempted without success to parlay his contributions to Grover Cleveland's presidential election in 1892 into a cabinet position. Like many public figures in the nineteenth century, moreover, the chairman combined business with politics. His main income apparently came from street railways in Milwaukee, including some lines controlled by Henry C. Payne, Wall's G.O.P. counterpart. This curious relationship was matched by Wall's lobby against a bill to tax street railways in 1893. At the time he was employed by the Edison Electric Illuminating Company, a transit franchise controlled by Henry Villard, the railroad financier and Democratic patron. The party's fall from power in the state elections of 1894 did not end the flexible relationship between Wall's private and public affairs. Still party chairman in 1895, Wall chose to lobby for brewers and oleomargarine manufacturers in Washington, D.C., instead of counseling the Democratic minority in Madison.[26]

Wall saw no conflict in this dual role. But neither did business opportunism appear to be his sole political motivation. Whatever his private ambitions, Wall was a partisan. His letters to party officials, while often patronizing, unveil the self-portrait of a dedicated and dignified loyalist laboring for the party, often with considerable self-sacrifice. His complaint in private about his vilification in the Republican press as a "spoilsman" and "pot-house politician" reveals his distress over the public distortion of this self-image. Since Wall enjoyed being in the public limelight and craved the reputation it might bring, these criticisms hurt all the more.[27] How much the desire to enhance his personal esteem drove Ed Wall to work for the Wisconsin Democrats must remain a historical conjecture. But the result of his partisanship embodied the ethos of party competition that was so characteristic of his age.

10

LEGISLATIVE DEMOCRACY IN THE LATE NINETEENTH CENTURY

For the greatest portion of their national history Americans entrusted most policymaking authority to the states and their legislatures. The decision reflected eighteenth- and nineteenth-century premises that government should be representative and decentralized. These attitudes and the comparative scale of state and national governmental activities made state assemblies the keystone of the federal arch throughout the nineteenth century. This historic relationship no longer exists. A series of developments, some evolutionary, others dramatically swift, some national in character, others tied more closely to local and institutional decisions, have deposed state legislatures from their former primacy over domestic policymaking. Many if not most Americans now regard these bodies as of secondary importance in a complex social service-managerial polity that is directed essentially by executives and the national government.

Reflection on the scope of public functions in our own time offers an instructive contrast with the character of governance in the 1880s and 1890s. The massive policy load that government now carries bears slight resemblance to the velocity of public activity in the nineteenth century. The proliferation of redistributive policies, highlighted by direct payments to individuals, revenue collections equal to a third of the gross national product, a matrix of intergovernmental monetary transfers and federal grants-in-aid, a veritable maze of both state and national administrative authorities that collectively manage the economy and supervise a plethora of services, an unprecedented "peacetime" defense establishment, and an active, "personalized" Presidency, which symbolizes government, form the cornerstone of a polity whose leading features matured in the middle of the present century. Strip away these tools of modern statecraft and one comes closer to the political world of nineteenth-century state legislators.

The questions before lawmakers of any era and the solutions they arrange are conditioned largely by the traditions of governance they inherit. The policy context of the late nineteenth century embodied the assumptions of the later 1800s and not those indigenous to post-New Deal America. The contested issues among the larger corpus of policy considerations illustrate the content of legislative deliberation during the last years of the nineteenth century and disclose its topical breadth. State lawmakers determined the legality of enjoying a glass of beer in the neighborhood tavern, of speaking German in the classroom, and of allowing women to participate in politics. They debated the responsibilities of commercial enterprise toward its employees and the conditions under which these ventures could do business. Representatives established priorities among public functions when they composed state budgets and when they specified how local government should manage its fiscal affairs. Control over the duties and structure of administrative bodies, state and local, lay within the legislative prerogative, as did the rules that governed election procedure, the management of rural roads and city streets, and the protection of public health. These and dozens of other distinct categories of contested policy filled legislative dockets in the late-nineteenth-century Midwest and elsewhere.

Critics past and present have dismissed the deliberations of many of these older state assemblies as devoid of constructive importance for society. Students of government, of course, must distinguish clearly between editorial complaint, whatever its era and merit, and the patterns of activity disclosed by systematic reconstruction of past behavior. Weighing the wisdom of policymakers' performances and analyzing their origins are separate intellectual functions. When attention is directed to the process of legislative deliberation, viewed from the perspective of its participants, one encounters a broad range of substantive disagreements that divided lawmakers. Some legislation concerned long-standing disputes in host communities; many matters were debated with passion and apparent conviction. By these criteria politics of the late nineteenth century, at least at the policymaking level, was neither issueless nor inconsequential.

Preoccupation with electoral politics, in which the specifics of public policy seldom play a major role, can obscure this substantive dimension of American governmental history. Most legislative proposals and decisions do not attract wide public notice at any time, but this fact does not lessen the presence of conflict over policy. The extent of issue orientation in the American political system varies with the roles of the participants in it. Officials in positions of policymaking authority, politicos stumping the campaign trail, interest groups intent on securing particularistic goals, the press and other commentators on public life, and the general public maintain different perspectives on the political process and bring different interests to it. The behavior of distinct groups of actors in the governmental system does not emanate from a common reservoir of political stimuli. Their functional relation to the polity affects their responses to it.

How, then, did midwestern state legislators respond to contested issues of public policy in the late nineteenth century? What factors shaped their disagreements? What should we conclude about the way representatives conducted the business of lawmaking? One paramount feature of these older state legislatures, at least the lower houses of the Midwest, is seldom emphasized in the recollections of them: they were eminently democratic. In many regards they were representative of the societies they served. In terms of their structure and composition, their modes of decision-making, and their accord with contemporary norms of governing, the midwestern state legislatures were open rather than closed corporations.

One reason for this representative character was the high degree of accessibility of legislative office. Freshmen lawmakers—amateurs without prior legislative experience—held most seats in these forums. Not only did new faces predominate in each session, but also fresh recruits were not hard to find. Despite its defects, the two-party system that flourished in the late-nineteenth-century Middle West was able to offer candidates in virtually every legislative race. Election outcomes, moreover, always placed a sizable bloc of the partisan minority in office, which provided the opposition with a forum for vocal if not always constructive dissent.

Lawmakers' backgrounds reflected the social fabric of the wider society. In an era when religious and ancestral traditions served as boundaries for much of everyday life and underwrote their own status hierarchy, most major ethnic groups won at least nominal representation. Catholics, Lutherans, and Methodists, and Yankees, Swedes, and Poles—to cite selectively from a long list—occupied the same legislative chamber and seldom allowed their individual cultural loyalties to seriously impede the flow of public business. Representatives similarly brought a diversity of occupational experiences to state capitals. Admittedly, the profile of these officeholders was predominantly middle-class and middle-aged, virtually all white, and exclusively male. However skewed their membership appears now, the midwestern legislatures contained as broad a sample of society as did most private institutions of the age.

The structure of representation to the lower house fostered accessibility to the machinery of policymaking in another way. The large number of lower house districts insured representation of a wide spectrum of constituency types. And their relatively small populations, with a single representative who lived in the district, facilitated legislator assessment of constituent interests. The larger spatial and population size of Illinois' legislative districts impeded this general relationship, but their multi-member feature probably offset some of this liability. Frequent contact with various sources of opinion, nonetheless, was a fact of legislative life. The short, biennial meetings of the state legislatures meant that lawmakers spent most of their time in their districts and thus among constituents. But the flow of information between representatives and the represented continued while lawmakers were at the capital. Besides their frequent trips home during breaks in the session, they received letters, petitions, and remonstrations from constituents and visitations from a panoply of interest organizations. A vigorous press and partisan networks fed more information into the policymaking arena. Power and influence are never equally distributed, and all groups did not have equal access to legislative attention. But state legislators were not political recluses. Many legislative minds may have remained closed, but, figuratively speaking, legislative doors remained opened.

Legislators' responses to policy options followed directions consistent with democratic premises. The point is not that lawmakers always mirrored constituent opinion or that their decisions always promoted the public good, for they did not. Nor did legislators march in lockstep to any single determinant or ideological command. Rather, their behavior was the product of a diversity of factors. Viewed in totality, their responses reveal a process of decision-making in which numerous references circulated and shaped voting outcomes.

The fluctuation of these voting alignments was tied closely to the subject matter under review. Representatives tended to condense the diversity of legislative specifics into fewer, more generalized policy constructs. Policy content thus guided legislators to their decision-making rules. Economic questions generated less stable voting arrangements than did other issues, but this lack of consistency does not lessen the impact of content on decision-making. Instead, it demonstrates that lawmakers failed to reduce economic subjects to any overriding policy classification. No overarching voting structure emerged that set economic liberal against economic conservative, those for capital against those for labor, prostatist against antistatist, or even rural agriculturist against urban commercialist. Elements of each scheme of conflict appeared in the late nineteenth century, but agendas of the era lacked broadly developed social welfare and economic management policies and hence the kind of substantive reference points that can condition fixed economic reflexes. In later years parties imposed greater voting order on these questions. In the late nineteenth century, however, state lawmakers, much like the general public, manifested an ambiguity toward the relation between state and estate.

Social policy had a different legislative history. A high degree of consistency in bloc arrangements, largely partisan in composition, marked responses to community mores. The pattern was woven from several distinct sociopolitical threads. Americans entered an era of sustained social upheaval in the late nineteenth century. The ethnic fabric of the population progressively altered, and the verities embedded in a pastoral, preindustrial existence clashed increasingly with the newer truths associated with urbanized and commercialized society. The tensions spawned by this changing cultural order were manifested in legislative agendas, as lawmakers battled over the legalization of competing social conventions. Unlike the more specialized impact of most economic measures, the general public easily personalized the meaning of revisions to their state's social code.

Political party activists recognized this reality and exploited its connection with the ethnocultural systems present in each state. The cultural strategies that were so important to party electoral success, however, obligated party legislative wings to redeem some campaign promises or, in their absence, to act more or less consistently with the unarticulated yet vital expectations of their electoral supporters. Political parties cannot survive indefinitely unless they are believed to stand for something. Partisan disagreement over cultural issues in the late nineteenth century provided such a policy distinction. The subjects of party battles in the midwestern legislatures were not mirrored in Congress, however, a contrast that is explained by the federal structure of decentralized elections and division of jurisdiction between the states and the national government. The prohibition of liquor in these local assemblies was the analogue, figuratively speaking, of the tariff to Republicans and Democrats in Washington.

State party leaders often endeavored to pull delegations together on community mores, as well as on certain other issues, but the power of legislative "bosses" was limited. Shared policy dispositions and internalized loyalties to party, reinforced at times by constituent influences, were the most active ingredients in the compound that molded party cohesion. The stability of decision-making alignments on cultural policy flowed largely from this relationship between cultural referents, constituency, and the complex sociopolitical dynamics of partisanism. Its product, in the Middle West at least, was a philosophic dualism that associated Democrats with cultural liberalism (though not on racial issues) and Republicans with Victorian moral rectitude.

Another factor promoted disputes over community mores. Social rule-making was relatively costless. The legalization of cultural values neither authorized large levies on state treasuries nor significantly disrupted private economic relations. Enforcement responsibilities promised no new state bureaucracy; local authorities were in place to do the job. Since government could write social rules without offense to other axioms of political life, community mores had ready access to legislative agendas. The same principle contributed to their role as a staple of state party discord. The social symbolism of legislative action occupied a higher priority among the functions of government in the nineteenth than in the twentieth century because the impact of economic policy remained underdeveloped in comparison with its present dimension.

The realignment of legislator voting positions between policy categories owed much to party, which imposed the dominant structure on responses to community mores and governed numerous divisions over the issues of governmental structure and operation. Fiscal policy, commerce, and public services, by comparison, elicited fewer conflicts between Republican and Democrat, although the pattern varied among specific policy topics and the states. Then too, the point at which partisanship is clearly manifested in a roll call vote and its motivational origins are open to discussion. Yet regardless of the measurement criteria, party had no comparable rival among policy determinants in the midwestern lower houses. Alternate sources of policy reference, whether indexed as constituent or lawmakers' personal attributes or as broad social, economic, and locational classifications, underwrote no generalized voting framework of their own. Voting cleavages along urban-rural, regional, and occupational lines occurred with sufficient frequency and magnitude of divisiveness to enable one to argue that they served as factors that affected policy outcomes, but they were not major independent channels of policy dissonance. Ethnicity correlated more closely than other nonpartisan factors with voting behavior, but its force was largely felt within the confines of party, often as a modulator of partisan support.

That party imposed order on legislative behavior in ways that other identifiable systems of influence did not is cause for rethinking its place in nineteenth-century governance. Partisan behavior affected policy outcomes and offered voters some standard of legislative accountability. The point is not that parties offered programmatic alternatives for the direction of public affairs, but that they provided an organizational touchstone that served the psychic loyalties and structural needs of both voters and officeholders. No other single component of the political system could claim so much. Admittedly the partisan collectivities of the late nineteenth century were extensions of the social and economic establishment, but unequal access to the councils of political influence is found in all political eras. Before dismissing these older parties as superfluous relics of a highly politicized age, one should recall their democratic features. Nor can one hold the venality of politicos solely responsible for failure of Republicans and Democrats to solve society's ills. The constraints on party grew out of the political soils that nurtured them.

Whether acting as partisans or in some other capacity, lawmakers operated within the normative boundaries of nineteenth-century governance. They eschewed radical solutions to societal problems, preferring the safety of consensus when it could be found. Competition over goals reduced the number of these safe havens, yet the conflicts over policy that did ensue seldom violated the principles on which the system rested. Incrementalism, not explosive policy reconstruction, characterized legislative performance. The occasional sharp break with policy precedent, moreover, did not disrupt democratic norms. The legitimacy of majority decisions was never challenged; no rump parliaments are on record in the upper Midwest. In the face of sometimes intense levels of disagreement, lawmakers normally conducted their deliberations civilly and in accordance with the rules of legislative procedure.

The eye of a wary public helped keep them on this narrow path. Popular surveillance was selective, of course, but a central motif of late-nineteenth-century political culture was the tradition of limited government. It is no coincidence that increasing state activism in the late 1800s and early 1900s unleashed older suspicions of political power, a fear that contributed to the imposition of new constitutional constraints on legislative authority, an escalation of judicial attacks on state action, and statutory assaults on political parties. Americans had long displayed a split political personality; they revered representative government but remained cynical about the intentions of elected officials. Hence, the same political ethos that nurtured the short session—a virtual obsession with some lawmakers—also supported state legislatures that collectively enacted thousands of authoritative decisions each decade in the late nineteenth century. It is instructive to recall that the mounting criticism of politics during the so-called progressive era ran parallel with an outpouring of reform measures enacted primarily by state legislatures.

The portrait sketched here contrasts with the conventional historical picture of the American state legislatures. Since the 1880s numerous articulate observers have criticized both the process and the product of state lawmaking. Although the complaints have followed several streams of thought, the classic image of these bodies owes more to allegations of individual wrongdoing than to any other bill of indictment. To many, the term state legislator has been synonymous with corruption.

Some commentators indicted whole legislatures, not just specific people, as purchasable and purchased. Both journalists and representatives raised some charges of bribery during the sessions reviewed here. Money allegedly was offered to influence the caucus nominations of U.S. senators in Illinois in 1887 and in Wisconsin in 1893. "Sandbagging," the practice whereby lawmakers feigned antibusiness legislation to extort payoffs from the affected enterprises, reportedly occurred in Illinois. Charges surfaced in the same state that corporations paid legislators to kill the anti-trust bill of 1889 and for similar favors in later sessions.[1] The midwestern classic in this genre is the story, told and retold, of Charles Yerkes, the Chicago street railway magnate, who sent his agents to Springfield "with bags of gold" to buy franchise legislation, and then surreptitiously offered Governor John Altgeld a "million dollar bribe" to ice the deal. Altgeld, the tale goes, discreetly resisted the temptation.[2]

It would be naive to assert that midwestern legislative politics of the 1880s and 1890s was untainted by corruption. Whatever the era, the opportunities for dishonest gain inherent in official station have tempted many individuals. Yet the contention that graft ran so rampant in the deliberative bodies of the late nineteenth century as to make a mockery of constitutional government is an exaggeration. Although the scale of illegality and its impact on policymaking is difficult to measure, circumstantial evidence rebuts the extreme exposition of the corruption thesis. Both midwestern legislators and the press, in fact, leveled few charges of bribery during the sessions that form the basis of this book. Illinois, Iowa, and Wisconsin, of course, do not themselves constitute the American political universe. Perhaps other legislatures are more deserving of the uncomplimentary reputation that commonly is assigned collectively to state lawmaking.[3] A fundamental characteristic of the federal system is the differences between the states, including, presumably, differences in the prevalence of corruption in their legislatures.

Accusations of malfeasance, wherever they point, must be balanced against the known dimensions of policymaking. Close inspection of the midwestern houses provides persuasive evidence that a variety of determinants directed the flow of lawmaking. That voting alignments varied between policy spheres and that this pattern assumed consistency on numerous topics over time and between states is particularly damaging to the case for the corruption thesis. Some kinds of policy customarily provoked partisan responses; other issues rarely did. Cultural, locational, and political factors each acted as influential references, depending upon legislative content and political circumstance.

Some voting patterns remain unexplained, it is true, but this says as much about the limitations of historical methodology as it does about the possible role of corruption. To doubt that the policy outcomes of the late-nineteenth-century state legislatures, of the lower houses particularly, rested primarily on the legitimate foundations of decision-making would deny that legislators acted in accordance with their values, policy dispositions, traditional loyalties, prejudices, and ignorance, and even with a sense of civic duty toward constituents and the welfare of their state.

Corruption has been the stereotypical complaint about the American state legislatures, but this charge does not locate the primary reason for their decline. Their fall from public grace stemmed more from their successful embodiment of older ways of governing. If anything, the deliberative forums of the nineteenth century suffered from an excess of democracy. The high turnover of personnel came at the expense of legislative experience and expertise. Legislative structure and electoral reality nurtured close ties between representatives and the represented, but they also encouraged an atomization of legislative purpose. Popular suspicion of governmental power and of the trustworthiness of officeholders perpetuated biennial sessions, low pay, and inadequate staffs. The system guaranteed short-term solutions to many long-term problems. Hence, the state legislatures entered the twentieth century laden with handicaps.

The timing was crucial, for two world wars and the Great Depression led to new levels of governmental coordination and national policy leadership. Washington used the new national income tax to meet these exigencies and to finance the subsequent expansion of the social service-managerial state, and in the process discouraged analogous fiscal reform in the states. Federalism entered a new era after 1945 and the state legislatures suffered in the competition. In contrast to their former ascendancy in domestic policymaking, these bodies increasingly lost control over the direction of public affairs in the twentieth century. Our own time has seen an effort to pump new breath into these ancient forums. Yet the logic of restoring vitality to state legislatures does not change the fact that we now live in an executive-centered and increasingly more nationalized political system.

APPENDIX
NOTES
INDEX

APPENDIX
ON SOURCES
AND METHODS

Many of the observations in this study rest on research strategies that need a more extended explanation than can be given in the notes. The emphasis in this appendix is on conceptual specification, generic sources, and the basic analytic principles followed in the research. The serious specialist knows how to take the story from there. Methodological details appearing in my other writings are paraphrased rather than repeated here in detail. Several techniques used in the dissertation from which this book grew, for example, have remained essentially unchanged in subsequent work.

The Legislators

Collection of information about the legislators began with the listings of names, districts, and party affiliations contained in house legislative journals and extant legislative manuals (*Iowa Official Register*, 1888-; *Wisconsin Bluebook*) for the sessions examined. Data for more comprehensive profiles were drawn from these manuals and from assorted biographical compilations extant for certain sessions.[1] The absence of an official legislative manual for the Illinois General Assembly during the late nineteenth century is the primary reason for gaps in some data series in regard to age, occupation, place of birth, and legislative experience.

The most difficult information to locate was among the most desired: lawmakers' ethnic background. Ideally, this index calls for information about an individual's national ancestry, religious affiliation or background, and generational history in the United States.[2] Since these three ingredients were not laid out neatly anywhere, I usually had to settle for less. Consequently, a comprehensive ethnic profile was compiled only for the 1893 Wisconsin Assembly. Biographical research on this session began with the *Wisconsin Bluebook*, which listed legislator's place of birth. From there I went to local histories and biographical albums, newspaper obituaries and other descriptions of life-cycle events, certificates of death, lodge and fraternal publications, and the federal manuscript censuses of 1870 and 1880. When these trails gave out, I contacted legislators' relatives and acquaintances, with surprisingly productive results.

Similar published sources were used to reconstruct ancestral or religious profiles for other sample sessions: Wisconsin, 1895; Illinois, 1883, 1891, 1893, and 1895; and Iowa, 1888 and 1894. The existence of the manuscript returns of the Iowa state censuses of 1895 and 1915 made it possible to construct a virtually complete religious profile of the 1894 Iowa representatives. Ethnic information was obtained for some members of all fifteen sessions studied, but comprehensiveness varies. Variables that are based on legislator's personal attributes are listed at the end of the appendix.

The Roll Calls and Contested Issues

A sample of 1,105 roll calls drawn from fifteen sessions constitutes the basic data on legislative voting. The sampling strategy was designed to complement the major purpose of the study, namely, to identify and analyze the contested legislative issues of general policy within the jurisdictions of Illinois, Iowa, and Wisconsin. The identification of these subjects began with the inspection of every roll call vote printed in the house journals of each of the fifteen regularly scheduled sessions studied. The subset of roll calls was extracted from this larger universe by a process of elimination, whereby votes that did not satisfy criteria for selection were discarded. This sifting procedure yielded 998 roll calls on contested issues (see table 4.1), to which were added 107 supplemental votes.

A contested issue was defined as a bill (and its accompanying roll calls) that passed three checkpoints. Briefly stated, these criteria encompassed standards of legislative content, parliamentary motion, and yea-nay division. Since the details of the procedure appear elsewhere, only a paraphrase is needed.[3]

The first checkpoint specified that only questions of general state policy qualified for selection. This eliminated private bills, legalizations of minor local ordinances, memorials to Congress regarding matters of national jurisdiction, and most details concerning the internal operation of each branch of state government, such as the confirmation of legislative staff.

The second checkpoint blocked noncrucial legislative motions from the sample. This ruling had no bearing on most bills, for only one or a few roll calls were taken on them. It is best to state the obvious: legislation that failed to generate a roll call vote could not qualify as a "contested issue." But some legislation generated a dozen or more votes. The standard used to pare down these large and sometimes repetitive sets of roll calls was to distinguish "minor" from "important" motions. The general rule employed was to regard as dispensable the motions that did not materially alter the content of a bill, or that carried nonfatal consequences for its legislative life. Thus a vote to postpone legislation indefinitely was usually retained, but reconsideration of that motion (if any) usually was not, unless a substantially different yea-nay division resulted, or if it was the final roll call on the bill. A comprehensive and hierarchically ordered checklist of legislative motions, keyed to parliamentary procedure in each state, was devised, and motions of marginal impact on each bill were discarded. As already implied, I remained sensitive to the contextual history of each bill. The more roll calls extant for any parent bill, the more stringently I applied the checklist criteria. The votes retained in the sample represent all stages of the parliamentary process: second reading, temporary and indefinite postponement, amendment, reference to committee, engrossment, response to conference reports, and so on.

The final checkpoint in the sampling process eliminated bills that failed to satisfy a quantitative test of divisiveness. Here, the proportion of the minority vote for every surviving roll call on each bill (which had qualified under the substantive test) was averaged. Votes with no quorum and with fewer than ten members in the minority were first discarded. The resulting quotient provided a "conflict" score for each bill. Next, a conflict threshold was established to weed out issues of lesser voting controversy in each session. A sliding scale was adopted for this purpose, whereby the conflict threshold was set equal to two-thirds of the percentage of all minority party members seated in each session. Conflict threshold levels ranged between 13 percent (Wisconsin, 1895) and 33 percent (three sessions), with a fifteen-session mean of 26 percent. The rationale for a sliding scale is twofold: it offered a fairly objective way to reduce thousands of votes to a manageable number, and at the same time it insured that party divisions in each session would be caught up in my sampling net. To these 998 roll calls I added 107 supplemental votes. These were bills that failed the contested-issues criteria because of content (for example, memorials to Congress on a subject of national jurisdiction) or because of low conflict scores.

Had this study focused on a single session or perhaps a few sessions, the "contested issue" sampling strategy would have had less justification than it does for a survey of fifteen sessions. Admittedly, an uncounted number of "important" bills, judged by substantive criteria, failed to survive my screening process. But the goal before this study was to survey the policy conflicts generally present in the late-nineteenth-century Midwest. Hence, what may have been lost in terms of some specific policy disputes in certain sessions was offset by a strategy that located the most divisive legislation across a field of view defined in both time and space. In other words, the sample is not comprehensive but it is representative.

A related matter, the identification of legislative content, bears an instrumental relation to the selection of issues, their topical classification (see chapter 4 and specifically note 6), and the interpretation of policy controversy. The identification of the substance of legislation is also one of the most difficult tasks faced by the student of nineteenth-century state legislatures. The process frequently requires that the researcher not only locate the complete text of a bill (or a paraphrase of it) but also the specific substantive provisions that triggered controversy. The latter issue often necessitates the reconstruction of the historical policy context from which legislation emerged. Because no single source, and too often, no two or three sources, provided adequate information about these questions, my description of content customarily drew upon numerous types of materials: the official journals of each legislature, session laws and statutes, newspapers (an absolutely mandatory source), secondary works, and the surviving copies of the original bills (as introduced, not as amended).[4] The printed bills are located in the State Library of Illinois (Springfield), the Iowa State Law Library (Des Moines), and the State Historical Society of Wisconsin (Madison). Given the diversity of materials that I used to reconstruct the content of hundreds of bills and their amendments, I have cited these sources very selectively; I generally do not reference materials drawn from official state publications.

Analysis of Legislative Voting

Two basic approaches were used to reconstruct voting patterns in the legislatures studied. One method examined every roll call separately; the second technique grouped roll calls together by a criterion factor, from which indices or "scales" were created. Each method has its own advantages and drawbacks. Processing roll calls separately allows uniform investigation of every vote, but their dichotomous yea-nay division limits analytic possibilities. The logistics of constructing multi-vote indices, on the other hand, usually forces the elimination of some roll call data, but the resulting continua of legislator scores provide a more finely graded measuring rod with which to analyze voting patterns. As with any methodology, the questions asked should dictate the techniques adopted. Since both an extensive survey of the voting of specified groups and an assessment of the comparative impact of various potential voting determinants were desired, a rationale existed for each method.

Percentages of the yea-nay division, and indices of cohesion and disagreement (the obversion of the index of likeness) were calculated for all 1,105 roll calls studied.[5] Party affiliation and the four variables Catholic, Immigrant, Section, and Urban, arranged dichotomously, were used in this survey for every session, while other similarly grouped indicators, such as Assessed Value, Farmer, Manufacturing Workers, and Term, were used for a lesser number of meetings. A more intensive analysis was performed on approximately fifty votes of special interest. One-way analysis of variance provided a convenient method of comparing the voting scores of legislators grouped into three or more nominal or ordinal categories (such as Occupation and Ethnicity), while cross-tabulations were a handy way of introducing control factors. Finally, for five sessions every roll call was transformed into a "dummy" variable (yea votes coded as 1, nays as 0), and each roll call was correlated with selected variables (see chapter 8, note 10). The resulting Pearson correlations produced coefficients similar in magnitude to the proportional scores (reported in the text as percentages) of the index of disagreement, but the advantage of the former technique was that it enabled the use of interval-level independent variables.

Votes were also clustered together to form incremental measures of voting behavior, a technique that offered greater analytic versatility than observations of individual roll calls. Two types of "scales" were constructed, each representing a different clustering criterion. The prohibition and party support indices were the simpler of the two. For these measures, votes in support of the prohibition position on liquor questions and in support of the Republican side on party votes were designated "positive" responses. Lawmakers were scored in accordance with the proportion of times they voted the positive option, based on their total number of responses to each set of legislation. Absences were ignored in the tally, but legislators with an absence-abstention rate of 50 percent or higher were removed from the index. Prohibition indices were calculated for nine sessions (see table 6.2) and party support scores for five sessions (Illinois, 1887, 1889, 1893; Iowa, 1888; Wisconsin, 1893).

The other scaling technique was relatively free-form, in that votes were combined into an index on the basis of patterns of legislator voting alignments. The basic logic here is equivalent to that of Guttman scalograms, although an alternate "scoring" device (the way each lawmaker was assigned a score on the index) was used. Following MacRae's recommendations, four-cell cross-tabulations and Q coefficients were calculated for all pairs of roll calls in a session, and within topical parameters, roll calls with an average Q relationship of 0.8 or higher with other intercorrelated votes (and with no single correlation below 0.7) were entered into the cluster.[6]

A useful feature of scale analysis is that it permits the researcher to note the connections among issues that legislators themselves disclosed through their voting behavior. Scaling, therefore, offers an alternative method of analyzing legislative content, allowing interpretive adjustments to a priori schemes of issue classification. I endeavored to restrict scaled clusters of votes to each policy sphere described in chapter 4, and especially to three very broad categories: Community Mores, Commerce and Fiscal Policy, and Government and Public Services. The effort was seldom totally successful, in part because legislators did not always group issues in the way I did and in part because of the sparse number of roll calls in some policy categories in some sessions. Since the fewest number of roll calls was drawn for Wisconsin, its scales have less substantive homogeneity than do those for Illinois and Iowa. The intercorrelation of the voting alignments between the scales constructed in each session provided further insight about how lawmakers differentiated among assorted policy considerations.

The naming convention used to reference scales combines the nature of my scaling procedure with the nomenclature adopted for the issue categories presented in chapter 4. Scales that bear the name of a policy sphere were constructed from votes predominantly or exclusively assigned to that issue classification. Mixed Economic denotes a scale that was formed essentially among votes from the policy spheres of Commerce, Fiscal Policy, and Public Services, but sometimes from Government as well. Finally, scales that were based upon one or several distinct bills in a particular session (for example, the Pipeline and RR/Silver scales in the 1893 Wisconsin Assembly) were identified by their particular component legislation. Like the other variable indices in this study, scale names have been capitalized.

Legislator responses to each set of clustered roll calls were indexed by an additive method, whereby "positive" votes (an arbitrarily designated tail of the distribution) were credited as 2, absences as 1, and "negative" pole votes as 0. The sum of these weights produced each legislator's scale scores. There is very little difference between the overall correspondence of this scoring convention and the ranking order produced by Guttman scaling. But the additive method is mechanistically easier.[7]

Because the summation scale scores rendered an ordinal level measure, contingency analysis (cross-tabulation) was the appropriate technique for identifying relationship in the voting. Scale scores were grouped into four or five ranked categories, depending upon the number of votes contained in each scale cluster and its correlative frequency distribution, and these group scores were cross-tabulated with independent variables. Four by four (sixteen-cell) contingency tables were the criterion format for this analysis, but categories varied in accordance with variable distributions. Examination of the voting of Republicans and Democrats separately (that is, intraparty analysis, which, roughly speaking, held party "con-

stant") generally rested on a more limited distribution of scores and usually forced the collapsing of table cells.

Besides the inspection of absolute cell frequencies, gamma (a statistic
of association for ranked categories of data) was calculated for each scale
cross-tabulation, including interscale associations.[8] Because gamma tends
to inflate when a variable is collapsed into fewer categories, the most important ordinal (independent) variables were handled in two ways: quar-
tile division and dichotomization. The latter form was used principally for
comparison with variables that came only (or usually) in dichotomous
form, such as party affiliation. Differences in gamma coefficients for cross-
tabulations with most constituency variables, such as Catholic, treated
both as quartiles and dichotomies, were minimal, but the reader should
know that I calculated them both ways, and that I have usually reported
the higher value.

The greater analytic possibilities present when both dependent and
independent variables are expressed as interval measures provided the rationale to transform scale scores into percentages for six sessions (see chapter 5, note 18). The scaled cluster of roll calls remained the same; only the
scoring expression changed. After experimentation with various methods
of handling absences and weighing response types, the scheme adopted
was the same as that used for the prohibition and party support indices.
Choice of an interval scoring convention mattered little, however, for all
variants were highly intercorrelated. With interval-level voting data in
hand, the analysis proceeded in conventional statistical fashion from measures of central tendency and dispersion, to one-way analysis of variance
(when variables were expressed as categoric measures), to simple and
multiple correlation. Scattergrams indicated when extreme values of independent variables disproportionately influenced correlation coefficients.

I find no persuasive methodological justification for repeating these
dual methods of scale scoring, should the objectives of this study be replicated. I began my thinking about "dimensional" analysis with the Guttman scalogram in mind. From there, I experimented with scoring techniques as new inquiries and data alternatives arose. If I had to do the work
again, I would use only interval-level scale data. For the broad patterning
of legislative voting under investigation in this study, the scoring technique selected has less bearing on the final analysis than the way roll calls
are clustered. And this step in turn is dependent upon the initial sample of
roll calls.

The Independent Variables

The listing of independent variables at the end of the appendix is
longer than is customary in most social scientific work. Index construction

did not proceed on the premise that the more variables generated, the better the final product. On the contrary, good theoretical grounds exist to confine measurements to the lowest number that can adequately satisfy the requirements of the questions posed. Only two basic variable dimensions have been used in this book. Schematically stated, the first type divided all observations into either constituent (legislative district) or lawmakers' personal attributes; that is, the unit of measurement defined a property of the variable. The second dimension classified phenomena by their substantive quality, namely, their social, economic, or political nature. When fused, these conceptual planes of measurement form six variable subclassifications. Legislators' ethnic background, for example, cuts across the two dimensions in that it is a social measurement of discrete individuals. Classification of legislative districts by political competitiveness simultaneously defines the variable by unit of observation and substantive character. And so on, for the remaining variable subgroups.

The translation of this conceptual scheme into applied measurements caused the variable list to grow. The brief discussion that follows belies the time and expense required by this phase of the research. Problems emanated from three sources, which can be summarized as district structure, data availability, and measurement validity.

Nine apportionment acts (four in Iowa, three in Wisconsin, and two in Illinois) governed the fifteen legislative sessions studied. Some of the changes they introduced were minor, but most statutes made substantial alterations in district lines. The impact of reapportionment on index construction depended in part on the geopolitical shape of each state's house districts and in part on the existence of census or similar systematic population surveys. The rule of thumb followed in constructing constituency variables was to use the data collected as near in time to each session as possible.

Iowa was the easiest of the three states to work with in this regard. All its legislative districts were formed of whole counties, and its censuses of 1885 and 1895 offered a mother lode of social and economic data with which to supplement the 1890 federal census. The information on "religious belief" in the 1895 Iowa census alone made this source invaluable, for the 1890 United States census provided only a survey of church "communicants" as stated by local clergy.[9]

Illinois and Wisconsin, on the other hand, each offered its own special degree of difficulty. Illinois' legislative districts conformed to county lines, with the crucial exception of those in Chicago. The act of 1883 (applicable to the meetings of 1885 through 1893) apportioned the city on the basis of the 1880 federal population counts and the 1882 ward lines. But ward lines had been redrawn by the time federal census enumerators returned to the Windy City in 1890. Since Illinois took no intradecennial census of its own, no alternative, systematic data existed by which to track census to legislative unit in Chicago and simultaneously to provide observations based on the same data source for "downstate." Interpolation techniques were therefore necessary.

Wisconsin Assembly districts represented a wholesale violation of the county-unit principle; two-thirds of its constituencies were formed within counties. Most constituency indicators for the Badger State, therefore, rest on my tabulation of town and ward data from the Wisconsin 1885 (in manuscript) and 1895 censuses, which, to my good fortune, the state had taken. Milwaukee's districts followed ward lines, so linking census with these legislative units was less problematical than for Chicago. But as with Chicago, interpolation and apportionment techniques were necessary to reconstruct some intrametropolitan indicators, such as the distribution of Catholics and manufacturing workers. The appendix to my dissertation describes the procedures and the supplemental data used for Chicago, Milwaukee, and Wisconsin's intracounty districts when census information did not correspond to the geography of legislative units.[10] Variables formed for these units at later stages of the project conformed to these principles; the details or modifications, if any, are reported in the notes to this book or have been published elsewhere.

The question of measurement validity contributed to the proliferation of variables. The research began with the goal of creating uniform indices, in terms of data series and quantitative expressions, across states and sessions. As my methodological thinking evolved, this objective began to seem as indefensible as it was mechanistically impossible. The heart of this issue can be expressed in the question: how well do quantitative indicators, based on extant historical information, measure the underlying phenomena of interest? Clearly, when research deals with dynamic concepts such as ethnicity, occupational and economic orientations, and partisan identity, their numeric representation by census or nominally classified data are approximations at best. In view of this generic handicap, continuing attempts to improve measurement validity justified, I believe, deviations from measurement consistency. To express the idea as a metaphor, the decision to chart the contours of a mountain top from only one location of the surveyor's transit, especially if the peak is enshrouded in mist, makes a methodological mistake. Readings of the same mountain from several sites make more sense.

Consistency was not wholly abandoned, however, for some variables are relatively uniform across sessions. The Catholicity of constituent populations, for example, was measured for all sessions. This and most other indices of population ecology (except the agricultural indices) were expressed as proportions of the total population of each district. But additional variables were created to meet particular requirements and as data and practicality permitted. Legislators' religion, membership on party steering committees, party success rates for a series of elections to the lower house, and agricultural features of constituencies are illustrations of variables used for a selected number of sessions. Intercorrelation of constituency variables helped to verify the validity of specific indicators, as well as to identify degrees of multicollinearity. Literary evidence also provided aids for evaluating the validity of variables, although I cannot claim to have systematically verified each variable.

Still, the utility of the measures reported in this study should not be discounted. One has only to recall the correlation performance of party affiliation with roll call voting to make this point. The potentially complex sociopsychological and political underpinnings that on occasion led legislators to vote with their party are not overtly measured by nominal indicators of party affiliation. But this simple classification carried a tremendous empirical punch.

The measures of agricultural patterns warrant a brief note. All are based on the 1890 federal census of agriculture, in which the county is the smallest unit reported.[11] For this reason I excluded Wisconsin from this variable series. Most measures were calculated per acre as well as the per farm expressions reported in the book. Urban districts were excluded from the series. Other agricultural indicators, such as the production of corn, swine, and cattle, and various ratios of farm debt, were generated, but they were discarded because of high correlation with the indices eventually used.

The list below defines the variables reported by name in the text, tables, and notes. Constituency measures, with a subdivision for the agricultural indices, are given first, and, where applicable, are stated in their basic mathematical definition. The indicators of lawmaker's personal attributes follow.

Constituency Variables

Assessed Value.   Assessed value of real property divided by district population.

Catholic.   Catholic communicants divided by district population. Religious "belief" used for Iowa 1892 and 1894.

Catholic and German Lutheran.   Catholic and German Lutheran communicants divided by district population; for Wisconsin only. See German Lutheran.

Chicago-Downstate.   Classification of Illinois districts into Chicago and all others.

Democratic Vote.   Percentage of vote received by Democratic legislative candidates in election to the house. Not available for Iowa.

Economic.   A generic reference to economic indicators. When Occupation is listed separately in tabular displays, Economic refers only to interval-level measures of district economic characteristics (see Assessed Value, Manufacturing Workers, and the agricultural variables). A variety of economic variables were used as the Economic cluster in multiple correlation analysis, while the highest single correlate of an economic indicator with voting was reported for bivariate associations.

Ethnic District.   A nominal classification of the relative ethnic tendency of each district.[12] Where interval data were appropriate, Ethnic District means a specific nationality or religious variable that produced the highest association with a voting alignment, or, in the instance of multiple correlation, a cluster of these indicators. See, for example, chapter 2, note 13, and chapter 7, note 9. In other instances, various interval-level indicators of constituent ethnicity were consolidated into a summary index. In Iowa, for example, the variable Demgroup (not referenced in text) combined German, Irish, and Southerner.

German.   Number of German-born residents divided by district population. Austrians, Bohemians, and Czechs were included when given in data sources.

German Lutheran.   Communicants of German Lutheran churches divided by district population.[13]

Immigrant.   Number of foreign-born residents divided by district population.

Manufacturing Workers.   Number of workers engaged in manufacturing and coal mining divided by district population.

Methodist.   Number of Methodists (communicants or religious "belief") divided by district population; for Iowa only.

North-South.   Dichotomization of Section in Illinois into northern and southern regions. See definition, chapter 2, note 17. Cook county (which contained Chicago) sometimes was added as a subcategory of North.

Party Competitiveness.   An ordinal classification of party success in prior elections to the lower house. For Illinois 1893, the index was based on the elections of 1884 through 1892. For Iowa 1888, the elections of 1881 through 1885 were used, and for Iowa 1894, the elections of 1883 through 1893. Not used for Wisconsin.

Scandinavian.   Number of residents born in Sweden, Norway, and Denmark divided by district population.

Section.   Classification of each state into geographic regions.

Urban.   Number of residents living in incorporated places of 2,500 or more people divided by district population. Fifty percent used as criterion to distinguish urban from nonurban units, where applicable.

Vote Margin.   Difference between the vote received by the house representative and the candidate who ranked second in the balloting for the office. Gubernatorial returns used as a surrogate for house election data in Iowa.

Yankee.   White population born in the United States of native-born parents divided by district population. Adjusted in Illinois and Iowa for white residents born in southern states. For Wisconsin, a nominal classification only.

Constituency Variables: Agriculture

Agincome.   Estimated value of farm products, 1889 divided by Farm Value. See Farm Value.

Debt Ratio.   Real estate mortgage debt on acres divided by valuation of land, fences, and buildings on farms.

Farm Owners.   Farms cultivated by owners divided by number of farms.

Farm Population.   Total population of district divided by number of farms.

Farm Size.   Total improved acres divided by number of farms.

Farm Value.   Valuation of land, fences, and buildings on farms divided by number of farms.

Value Agricultural Products.   Estimated value of farm products, 1889, divided by number of farms.

Wheat.   Number of acres in wheat divided by farm acreage, improved.

Legislators' Personal Attributes

Age.   Age of legislator at time of service.

Chairmen.   Committee chairmen. A subdivision of the index provided for chairmen of "important" committees, defined in chapter 3, note 25.

Ethnicity.   A nominal classification of lawmakers by their national ancestry, religious affiliation or background, and generational history in the United States. Except for the 1893 Wisconsin Assembly, Ethnicity is a generic term, for which Nationality or Religion is often used as a surrogate.

Farmer.   Classification of Occupation into farmers and nonfarmers.

Nationality.   National ancestry of legislators.

Occupation.   Occupation of lawmakers, usually as self-stated in official or privately printed biographical compilations.

Party.   Party affiliation of legislators.

Post Office.   Rank-ordered classification of 1893 Illinois representatives according to population size of the locality listed in their postal address.

Religion.   Religious preference or background of legislators.

Steer.   Members of the Republican and Democratic steering committees, 1893 Illinois house.

Term.   The number of prior sessions a lawmaker had served at time of service in each session. Incumbent designates legislator who had sat in the prior session. Freshman means first-term member.

NOTES

ABBREVIATIONS

APSR   *American Political Science Review*
IaDHA   Iowa State Department of History and Archives, Des Moines
IaHJ   *Journal of the House of Representatives . . . of Iowa* (Des Moines)
IJHP   *Iowa Journal of History and Politics* (later *Iowa Journal of History*)
IllHJ   *Journal of the House of Representatives of . . . Illinois* (Springfield)
IllSHS   State Historical Society of Illinois, Springfield
IOR   *Iowa Official Register*
JAH   *Journal of American History*
JIH   *Journal of Interdisciplinary History*
JISHS   *Journal of the Illinois State Historical Society*
MVHR   *Mississippi Valley Historical Review*
PSQ   *Political Science Quarterly*
WB   *Wisconsin Bluebook*
WisAJ   *Journal . . . of the Wisconsin Legislature. In Assembly* (Madison)
WMH   *Wisconsin Magazine of History*
WSHS   State Historical Society of Wisconsin, Madison

1. Introduction

1. Ballard Campbell, "The State Legislature in American History: A Review Essay," *Historical Methods Newsletter*, 9 (1976), 185-186, 193-194; Samuel P. Huntington, "Congressional Responses to the Twentieth Century," in David B. Truman, ed., *The Congress and America's Future* (Englewood Cliffs, N.J., 1965), 5-31; William J. Keefe, "The Functions and Powers of the State Legislatures," in Alexander Heard, ed., *State Legislatures in American Politics* (Englewood Cliffs, N.J., 1966), 47-64; Malcolm E. Jewell and Samuel C. Patterson, *The Legislative Process in the United States* (New York, 1966), v.

2. James Bryce, *The American Commonwealth* (New York, 1889), I, 411-

412. Unless indicated otherwise, quotations are cited first in each note. Everett C. Ladd, Jr., *American Political Parties: Social Change and Political Response* (New York, 1970), 133, 182-183; U.S. Bureau of the Census, *Historical Statistics of the United States: Colonial Times to 1957* (Washington, D.C., 1960), 711, 718-719, 726; U.S. Census Office, *Eleventh Census of the United States: 1890. Report on Wealth, Debt, and Taxation, pt. II, Valuation and Taxation* (Washington, D.C., 1895), 406. Also see Lance Davis and John Legler, "The Government in the American Economy, 1815-1902: A Quantitative Study," *Journal of Economic History*, 26 (1966), 514-552; Solomon Fabricant, assisted by Robert E. Lipsey, *The Trend of Government Activity in the United States since 1900* (New York, 1952), 188-197; and Charles Frank Holt, *The Role of State Government in the Nineteenth Century American Economy, 1820-1902: A Quantitative Study* (New York, 1977), 21-24. The broad outlines of fiscal federalism in the twentieth century are conveniently summarized in the U.S. Bureau of the Census, *Historical Statistics on Governmental Finances and Employment* (Washington, D.C., 1964), and subsequent quinquennial editions. An instructive supplement is the Advisory Commission on Intergovernmental Relations, *Significant Features of Fiscal Federalism, 1976-1977 Edition: 3. Expenditures* (Washington, D.C., 1977), esp. table 1. On the issues generally raised in the paragraph, see Harry N. Scheiber, *The Condition of American Federalism: An Historian's View*, a study submitted to the Senate Committee on Government Operations, 89th Cong., 2d sess. (Washington, D.C., Oct. 15, 1966).

3. Bryce, *American Commonwealth*, I, 515, 505-551, 653-661, II, 37-44. Writers of the early twentieth century included: Paul S. Reinsch, *American Legislatures and Legislative Methods* (New York, 1907), 126-128, 228-274; Charles E. Merriam, *A History of American Political Theories* (New York, 1928), 107, 113, 120, 454; Matthew Josephson, *The Politicos, 1865-1896* (New York, 1938), 344. More recent writings include: Richard Hofstadter, *The American Political Tradition* (New York, 1948; Vintage ed., 1954), 164, 169, 179; George E. Mowry, *The Era of Theodore Roosevelt, 1900-1912* (New York, 1958), 60, 68, 71; Robert H. Wiebe, *The Search for Order, 1877-1920* (New York, 1967), 28; Thomas C. Cochran, "The History of a Business Society," *JAH*, 54 (June 1967), 12-13; William J. Keefe and Morris S. Ogul, *The Legislative Process: Congress and the States*, 2d ed. (Englewood Cliffs, N.J., 1968), 35-36; Arthur A. Ekirch, Jr., *Progressivism in America* (New York, 1974), 104, 107-108. In recent decades historians have ignored state legislatures.

4. Ballard C. Campbell, Jr., "Political Parties, Cultural Groups and Contested Issues: Voting in the Illinois, Iowa and Wisconsin Houses of Representatives, 1886-1895" (Ph.D. diss., University of Wisconsin, Madison, 1970), 16-25. Also see Paul T. David, *Party Strength in the United States, 1872-1970* (Charlottesville, Va., 1972), 132-133, 140-141, 280-281.

5. *Eleventh Census of the United States: 1890. Population*, pt. II, cxxv. Unless otherwise cited, ecological characteristics subsequently discussed are based on the state and federal censuses listed in the appendix.

6. Allan G. Bogue, *From Prairie to Corn Belt: Farming on the Illinois and Iowa Prairies in the Nineteenth Century* (Chicago, 1963), 216-232; Roy V. Scott, *The Agrarian Movement in Illinois, 1880-1896* (Urbana, Ill., 1962), 6-14; Eric E. Lampard, *The Rise of the Dairy Industry in Wisconsin: A Study of Agricultural Change, 1820-1920* (Madison, Wis., 1963).

7. Robert C. Nesbit, *Wisconsin: A History* (Madison, Wis., 1973), 308.

8. The liturgical "outlook . . . stressed the positive values of institutionalized formalities and historic doctrines of the old orthodoxies" and the subordination of communicants to the moral teachings of the one true church. The pietistic response rejected ritualism, emphasized salvation through conversion experience, and had an evangelical character. Richard Jensen, *The Winning of the Midwest: Social and Political Conflict, 1888-1896* (Chicago, 1971), 64-65, 85-88.

9. My conception of ethnicity has been shaped by numerous authorities, but particularly by Milton M. Gordon, *Assimilation in American Life: The Role of Race, Religion, and National Origin* (New York, 1964), 19-59. Also see Arnold Dashefsjy, "And the Search Goes On: The Meaning of Religio-Ethnic Identity and Identification," *Sociological Analysis*, 33 (1972), 239-245; Wsevold W. Isajiw, "Definitions of Ethnicity," *Ethnicity*, 1 (1974), 111-124; Nathan Glazer and Daniel P. Moynihan, eds., *Ethnicity: Theory and Experience* (Cambridge, Mass., 1975). Culture is used in this study to mean ways of life, that is, patterns of attitudes and behavior characteristics of a society and its subgroupings.

2. Electing Representatives

1. *WB, 1897,* 327 (Madison, Wis., 1897), 327. Illinois switched from one- to two-year house terms in 1855; Iowa did so in 1858, and Wisconsin in 1883.

2. Ballard C. Campbell, Jr., "Political Parties, Cultural Groups and Contested Issues: Voting in the Illinois, Iowa and Wisconsin Houses of Representatives, 1886-1895," (Ph.D. diss., University of Wisconsin, 1970), 309, 317. A historical survey of apportionment in each of the American states appears in Robert B. McKay, *Reapportionment: The Law and Politics of Equal Representation* (New York: Twentieth Century Fund, 1965), 273-475 (Appendix: State Summaries).

3. Eighty-seven percent of the house districts in Iowa (1888-1890) and 91 percent of the Assembly districts in Wisconsin (1889-1891) fell within a range of plus or minus 50 percent of the median district population.

4. These conclusions were drawn from a reading of state party platforms in the *Chicago Daily News Almanac, WB,* and *IOR* for the appropriate years.

5. The nature of popular political life during the late nineteenth century, nationally and in the Midwest, is described in: James Bryce, *The American Commonwealth* (New York, 1889), I, 540-551; Walter Dean Burnham, "The Changing Shape of the American Political Universe," *APSR* 59 (November 1965), 7-28; Samuel P. Hays, "Political Parties and the Community-Society Continuum," in William N. Chambers and Walter D. Burnham, eds., *The American Party Systems: Stages of Political Development* (New York, 1967), 152-181; Richard Jensen, *The Winning of the Midwest: Social and Political Conflict, 1888-1896* (Chicago, 1971); Morton Keller, *Public Life in Late Nineteenth Century America* (Cambridge, Mass., 1977), esp. 522-564; Paul Kleppner, *The Cross of Culture: A Social Analysis of Midwestern Politics, 1850-1900* (New York, 1970); and Robert Marcus, *Grand Old Party: Political Structure in the Gilded Age, 1880-1896* (New York, 1971), esp. chap. 1.

6. Roll off for the two Illinois house elections averaged 1.4 percent; my calculation of voting returns is from the *Chicago Daily News Almanac* of 1889 and 1893. Drop off in statewide elections in Iowa averaged 15 percent between 1878

and 1898, according to Burnham, "American Political Universe," 10.

7. Estimates of ticket splitting in the three states, both before and after the introduction of the secret Australian ballot, show miniscule deviations from straight-party voting: Jerrold G. Rusk, "The Effect of the Australian Ballot Reform on Split-Ticket Voting, 1876-1908," *APSR*, 64 (December 1970), 1220-1238, esp. tables 3 and 5. Wisconsin adopted a statewide secret ballot in 1889, Illinois in 1891, and Iowa in 1892. Jensen, *Winning of the Midwest*, 42-43. Since Wisconsin's new ballot law was in operation by the election of 1890, the party-line voting suggested by the data in table 2.1 appears to have been little influenced by the old style of balloting. On straight-ticket voting in Illinois, see Ernest L. Bogart and Charles M. Thompson, *The Industrial State, 1870-1893*, Centennial History of Illinois, IV (Springfield, Ill., 1920), 142.

8. *Daily Illinois State Register*, Oct. 1, 1892. Also see Jensen, *Winning of the Midwest*, chap. 1; Joel A. Tarr, *A Study in Boss Politics: William Lorimer of Chicago* (Urbana, Ill., 1971), 61.

9. *Davenport Democrat*, Jan. 15, 1890; *Dubuque Herald*, Oct. 15, 1893; Diary of Willet S. Main, September and October 1888, box 2, WSHS; Journal of Archibald W. Hopkins, p. 203, microfilm, WSHS.

10. An urban district is defined as a constituency in which 51 percent or more of the population resided in incorporated places of 2,500 or more people. Also see appendix.

11. The variables are defined in the appendix. Variable names are capitalized in the text and tables in order to distinguish between discrete measurement constructs and the concepts underlying them. The variable Urban, for example, refers to quantitative indices of urban and rural populations (several measures created).

12. Gamma coefficients (a statistic of association for ranked categories of data) were calculated for cross-tabulations of legislators' party affiliation with constituency variables. Analogous to coefficients produced by simple Pearson correlations (r), gamma scores range between plus and minus one and zero; the closer the coefficient is to unity, the closer the relationship between the ranked pattern of two variable indices. Two-by-four tables (eight cells) were the criterion format for cross-tabulation analysis of the constituent characteristics of party legislative delegations.

Gamma coefficients for the association between legislator party affiliation (major parties only) and selected constituency variables in six Iowa sessions were as follows:

	1884	1886	1888	1890	1892	1894
Catholic	0.60	0.55	0.75	0.80	0.87	0.64
German	0.27	0.52	0.40	0.68	0.69	0.76
Yankee	−0.19	−0.36	−0.46	−0.48	−0.59	−0.64
Urban	0.34	0.37	0.41	0.36	0.48	0.43
Farm Owners	*	*	0.13	0.16	0.17	0.31
Farm Value	*	*	0.15	0.39	0.50	0.26

The asterisks indicate that values have not been calculated. The minus signs show that Republican victories tended to increase in districts with the highest proportion of Yankees.

Pearson correlations (r) between the party affiliation of representatives, expressed as a dummy (dichotomous) variable, and selected constituency variables for the 1888 house were as follows: Catholic, 0.43; Yankee, −0.34; Methodist, −0.39; German, 0.39; Wheat, 0.01; Farm Owners, 0.10; Value Agricultural Products, −0.02; Farm Value, 0.11; Farm Population, 0.30. On electoral politics in Iowa generally, see Ballard C. Campbell, "Did Democracy Work? Prohibition in Late Nineteenth-Century Iowa: A Test Case," *JIH*, 8 (Summer 1977), 87-116, and references cited therein.

13. For details, see Campbell, "Did Democracy Work?" esp. nn. 13 and 14. Yankee produced the highest beta weight (analogous to partial correlation) among five ethnic variables for the six elections, averaging 0.22. Beta for Farm Population averaged 0.06 and for Value Agricultural Products 0.10. Introducing each ethnic variable separately, rather than as a composite index, into the regression equation diluted the ethnic beta scores. For the 1888 and 1894 house sessions multiple correlations were calculated between party affiliation (dummy variables) and constituency factors. Five ethnic variables accounted for 34 and 45 percent of the variation in the two sessions respectively. Farm Population explained no additional variance while agricultural variables increased the explained variance 5 percent in 1888 and 9 percent in 1894.

14. Gamma coefficients for the association between legislator party affiliation (major parties only) and selected constituency variables in six Wisconsin sessions were as follows:

	1885	1887	1889	1891	1893	1895
Catholic	0.74	0.61	0.70	0.55	0.65	0.43
Immigrant	0.27	0.33	0.48	0.39	0.06	−0.13
Urban	0.33	0.44	0.50	0.32	0.25	0.16
Manufacturing Workers	*	*	0.30	0.12	0.21	−0.05

Asterisks indicate that values were not calculated. The minus sign indicates the tendency for higher ranges of Immigrant to associate with Republican victories. The following gamma associations were found between party affiliation and selected variables for 1893: German, 0.55; Scandinavian, −0.47; German Lutheran, 0.60; Assessed Value, 0.07; Section 0.74.

15. For a general analysis of popular voting in Wisconsin in the late nineteenth century, see Roger Edwards Wyman, "Voting Behavior in the Progressive Era: Wisconsin as a Case Study" (Ph.D. diss., University of Wisconsin, Madison, 1970). Main currents of Wisconsin politics can be followed in Robert C. Nesbit, *Wisconsin: A History* (Madison, Wis., 1973) and its bibliography.

16. The typology represents comparative ethnic tendencies among the several districts and not necessarily the ethnic majority in a constituency. See appendix for details. I defined a Yankee of the nineteenth century as an individual of

British descent whose ancestors had resided in the United States for several generations, who had been associated with northern rather than southern traditions, and
whose religious background or church affiliation was with an old-line American
Protestant denomination. Admittedly, this definition skirts several troublesome
issues, but finer distinctions are of marginal importance to this study. Extant data,
for example, allow only a rough approximation of the aggregate Yankee population in any one locality; usually my estimate is based on the number of native
whites born of American-born parents.

17. The demarcation between northern and southern Illinois (North-South)
for this study lay along the northern boundary of Adams, Schuyler, Mason, Lo-
gan, Dewitt, Champaign, and Vermillion counties. Southern Illinois embraced districts 29-51 under the apportionment act of 1882. I divided the state into nine regions for more refined geographic categories.

18. On settlement patterns see: Allan G. Bogue, *From Prairie to Corn Belt:
Farming on the Illinois and Iowa Prairies in the Nineteenth Century* (Chicago,
1963), 15; Paul W. Gates, *The Illinois Central Railroad and Its Colonization Work*
(Cambridge, Mass., 1934), 332; Evarts B. Greene, "Sectional Forces in the History
of Illinois," *Transactions of the Illinois Historical Society, 1903* (Springfield, Ill.,
1904), 75-83. On party regional strength see: Arthur C. Cole, *The Era of the Civil
War, 1848-1870*, Centennial History of Illinois, III (Springfield, Ill., 1919), 260-
271, and maps facing 60, 200, 270, and 414; Bogart and Thompson, *Industrial
State*, 5, 17; V. O. Key, *American State Politics: An Introduction* (New York,
1956), 218-226.

19. Late-nineteenth-century censuses give county-level data on the state of
birth of native-born Americans (all "races"), but not on the state of birth of native-
born parents of people born in Illinois. Hence, it is impossible to precisely disaggregate southerners from Yankees at the county level. Comments in this paragraph, therefore, are reasoned conjectures, based on my own analyses and the
works cited in notes 18 and 21, as well as the following analyses of popular voting
in late-nineteenth-century Illinois, which emphasize Chicago and do not focus on
legislative races: Jensen, *Winning of the Midwest*; Kleppner, *Cross of Culture*;
Tarr, *Boss Politics*, 21-47; Duncan McRae, Jr., and James A. Meldrum, "Critical
Elections in Illinois, 1888-1958," *APSR*, 54 (September 1960), 669-693. The bibliography in Robert P. Howard, *Illinois: A History of the Prairie State* (Grand
Rapids, Mich., 1972) lists the conventional sources in Illinois political history.

20. The Catholic and German variables explained 34 percent of the variance
in the Democratic vote and 15 percent in the Republican vote for house candidates
in 1892. The urban variable accounted for little additional variance, but the subsequent inclusion of North-South (a dichotomized dummy variable) in the regression
equation by the stepwise mode increased the total explanatory power of the model
to 54 percent in the Democatic vote and 40 percent in the Republican vote. Catholic and North-South registered beta weights of 0.55 and −0.52 with the Democratic vote and 0.55 and −0.58 with the Republican vote. The introduction of agricultural factors into multiple correlation models, which excluded Cook county (there
was no agricultural variation in Chicago) substantially reduced the ethnic betas
but left the betas for North-South virtually unchanged. Agricultural factors
(Wheat, Debt Ratio, Agincome) accounted for 29 percent and 22 percent of the

variances in the Democratic and Republican votes respectively after ethnic variables had first been introduced into the equation (Cook county excluded); but the relatively low betas for the agricultural variables indicated that their effect was largely the product of sectionalism. Zero-order correlations (Pearson r) between the 1892 vote for Democratic and Republican legislative candidates and selected constituency variables are given in the following tabulation, in which the first two columns refer to all districts and the last two columns to downstate districts only (see Chicago-Downstate in appendix).

	Republican	*Democratic*	*Republican*	*Democratic*
Urban	−0.25	0.49	0.17	−0.02
Catholic	−0.38	0.58	0.02	0.20
German	−0.30	0.49	0.02	0.14
Yankee	0.11	0.30	−0.31	0.15
Section	0.25	−0.09	0.54	−0.50
Farm Size			0.32	−0.23
Wheat			−0.50	0.54
Farm Owners			0.03	−0.18
Agincome			−0.07	−0.05

The special circumstances of Illinois sectional politics and the multi-member feature of the state's legislative districts resulted in universally low gamma associations between house party affiliation and constituency variables. See Campbell, "Political Parties," 46-47, 53.

21. Blaine F. Moore, *The History of Cumulative Voting and Minority Representation in Illinois, 1870-1919* (Urbana, Ill., 1919); Ernest L. Bogart and John M. Mathews, *The Modern Commonwealth, 1893-1918*, Centennial History of Illinois, V (Springfield, Ill., 1920), 288-295; George S. Blair, *Cumulative Voting: An Effective Electoral Device in Illinois Politics* (Urbana, Ill., 1960).

22. Party competition had been greater in 1884, when each major party ran two candidates in thirty-one districts. If the United Labor party is counted as a major challenger in the 1886 election, thirty-two districts each had a total of four candidates (not including other minor parties); elimination of Labor reduced the "competitive" districts to twenty-two, the same number as in 1892.

23. Substituting the number of party candidates for election turnovers as an index of competition provides similar results. The parties concentrated their two-candidate challenges in Chicago, the low Yankee districts in the north, and the high Yankee districts in the south, although in the south the pattern was relatively diffused. Statewide, the high Catholic and low Yankee districts locate ten of the twenty-two two-candidate challenges.

24. Only elections in districts whose boundaries remained fixed between pairs of elections are included in the Wisconsin index; see Campbell, "Political Parties," 73.

25. See Kleppner, *Cross of Culture*; Jensen, *Winning of the Midwest*; Tarr, *Boss Politics*; Wyman "Voting Behavior"; and Roger E. Wyman, "Wisconsin Ethnic Groups and the Election of 1890," *WMH*, 51 (Summer 1968), 269-293.

Compare these works with studies of other areas: J. Morgan Kousser, *The Shaping of Southern Politics: Suffrage Restriction and the Establishment of the One-Party South, 1880-1910* (New Haven, Conn., 1974); Melvyn Hammarberg, "Indiana Farmers and the Group Basis of Late Nineteenth-Century Political Parties," *JAH*, 61 (June 1974), 91-115; Samuel T. McSeveney, *The Politics of Depression: Political Behavior in the Northeast, 1893-1896* (New York, 1972); Stanley B. Parsons, *The Populist Context: Rural Versus Urban Power on a Great Plains Frontier* (Westport, Conn., 1973); James E. Wright, *The Politics of Populism: Dissent in Colorado* (New Haven, Conn., 1974). The impact of culture on American popular politics in a wider chronological context is synthesized by Robert Kelley, "Ideology and Political Culture from Jefferson to Nixon," *American Historical Review*, 82 (June 1977), 531-562. The motivational bases of ethnic group voting patterns are discussed by Richard L. McCormick, "Ethno-Cultural Interpretations of Nineteenth-Century American Voting Behavior," *PSQ*, 89 (June 1974), 351-377.

26. The possible political ramifications of the differential economic status of ethnic groups are discussed by James E. Wright, "The Ethnocultural Model of Voting: A Behavioral and Historical Critique," *American Behavioral Scientist*, 16 (May-June 1973), 653-674. For a contemporary suggestion that socioeconomic class affected voting behavior, see the *Chicago Times*, Nov. 7, 1888.

27. Key, *American State Politics*, 152.

28. Willet S. Main Diary, Sept. 25 and October 1888; "To the Catholic Voters of Iowa County," ca. 1887, and "A Correct Translation of a Circular Published in the Bohemian Language . . ." Nov. 5, 1895, broadsides, John Springer Papers, box 1, Special Collections Department, University of Iowa Library, Iowa City, Iowa.

29. T. A. Greiner to George D. Perkins, Oct. 9, 1891, Perkins Papers, IaDHA.

30. A. M. Jones to Shelby M. Cullom, May 16, 1892, and A. P. Dixon to Cullom, May 21, 1892, Cullom Papers, IllSHS.

31. See, for example, William C. ("Will") Brawley to Ellis B. Usher, Apr. 14, 1887, Edward C. Wall to Usher, Sept. 28, 1890, and Usher to Wall, Sept. 11, 1893, in Ellis B. Usher Papers, WSHS; also Edward C. Wall to William F. Vilas, May 1, 28, 1891, and Feb. 28, 1893, in Vilas Papers, WSHS. Also see: Wyman "Wisconsin Ethnic Groups"; Kleppner, *Cross of Culture*, 159-171.

32. Carter H. Harrison, *Stormy Years: The Autobiography of Carter H. Harrison, Five Times Mayor of Chicago* (Indianapolis, Ind., 1935), 118-119.

33. Tarr, *Boss Politics*, 10-47.

34. For Iowa: James S. Clarkson to John Fletcher Lacey, ca. fall 1891, Lacey Papers, box 248, IaDHA; "First Poll" books for 1897 and 1898, Albert B. Cummins Papers, container 1, IaDHA; For Wisconsin: Instructional broadside, ca. summer 1891, Wendell A. Anderson Papers, box 10, WSHS; "Democratic Campaign Documents: Wisconsin, 1894," WSHS. *The Chicago Daily News Almanac 1889*, 157-162, listed the nationality of voters by ward and precinct.

35. Ralph W. Scharnau, "Thomas J. Morgan and the United Labor Party of Chicago," *JISHS*, 66 (Spring 1973), 41-61; Henry David, *The History of the Haymarket Affair* (New York, 1958), 206-218, 538; Roy V. Scott, *The Agrarian Movement in Illinois, 1880-1896* (Urbana, Ill., 1962), 87-88; *Chicago Tribune*, Jan. 4, 27, 1887. Jerry M. Cooper, "The Wisconsin National Guard in the Milwaukee Riots of

1886," *WMH*, 55 (Autumn 1971), 31-48; Roger Wyman, "Agrarian or Working Class Radicalism? The Electoral Basis of Populism in Wisconsin," *PSQ*, 89 (Winter 1974-75), 827-829; Gerd Korman, *Industrialization, Immigrants, and Americanizers: The View from Milwaukee, 1866-1921* (Madison, Wis., 1967), 16-59, 82; *Milwaukee Sentinel*, Mar. 13, 16, 26, 1887.

36. Benton Wilcox, "An Historical Definition of Northwest Radicalism," *MVHR*, 26 (December 1939), 377-394; Chester M. Destler, *American Radicalism, 1865-1901* (Chicago, 1949; Quadrangle ed., 1966), 162-211; Jensen, *Winning of the Midwest*, 238-268; Bogart and Thompson, *Industrial State*, 179; Scott, *Agrarian Movement*; Herman C. Nixon, "The Populist Movement in Iowa," *IJHP*, 24 (January 1926), 3-107; J. Brooke Workman, "Governor William Larrabee and Railroad Reform," *IJHP*, 56 (July 1959), 231-266; Wyman, "Agrarian or Working Class Radicalism?"

37. Campbell, "Did Democracy Work?"

38. Ibid., 97, 108-109; Wyman, "Voting Behavior," 58-68; Kleppner, *Cross of Culture*, 15, 103-129, 138, 156; David P. Thelen, *The New Citizenship* (Columbia, Mo., 1972), 14-15. The zero-order correlation (r) between the Republican and Prohibition gubernatorial vote in the 1893 Iowa election was 0.38, and between the Republican and Prohibition vote for nominees for the lower house in the 1892 Illinois election it was 0.12. The structure of Illinois house districts and statewide patterns of popular voting behavior probably explain the low correlation in Illinois, which appears to underestimate the similarities between supporters of the two parties. Analysis of Republican and Prohibition candidates in the Illinois house elections of 1884 and 1892 suggests that the growing activity of prohibitionists tempered G.O.P. strategies. Republicans reduced their house candidates from two to one in eight districts between these two elections. Prohibitionists fielded only one house candidate in these districts in 1884 but ran nominees in all eight in 1892, where they averaged 4.4 percent of the vote, compared with their statewide showing of 3.1 percent. Five Democrats won election to the Wisconsin Assembly in 1886 in districts where the Prohibition and Republican parties together polled a majority of the Assembly vote. Also see chapter 6.

39. Wyman, "Wisconsin Ethnic Groups," and "Voting Behavior," 121-123; Kleppner, *Cross of Culture*, 159-171; Jensen, *Winning of the Midwest*, 122-148, 160, 219-221; Ballard C. Campbell, "Ethnicity and the 1893 Wisconsin Assembly," *JAH*, 62 (June 1975), 75-82.

40. See, for example, Wyman, "Wisconsin Ethnic Groups," 286-287.

41. Willet S. Main Diary, Nov. 5, 1890.

42. A. M. Jones to Shelby M. Cullom, May 16, 1892, Cullom Papers; Henry C. Payne to Jeremiah M. Rusk, Dec. 2, 1890, Rusk Papers, WSHS. Campbell, "Did Democracy Work?" 108-109. Kleppner, *Cross of Culture*, 252-260; Jensen, *Winning of the Midwest*, 154-237; Bayrd Still, *Milwaukee: A History of a City* (Madison, Wis., 1948), 297-304; *Chicago Tribune*, June 17, 1893, Jan. 19, March 3, 1895.

43. John Moses, *Illinois: Historical and Statistical* (Chicago, 1895), II, 1351-1352; Kleppner, *Cross of Culture*, 179-315; Wyman, "Voting Behavior," 162-169; Horace S. Merrill, *William Freeman Vilas: Doctrinaire Democrat* (Madison, Wis., 1954), 212-225.

44. *Burlington Hawkeye*, Mar. 12, 1892; *Chicago Tribune*, May 25, 1895;

Jensen, *Winning of the Midwest*, 158, 215-216, 292-295; Wyman, "Voting Behavior," 121. Also see Jean P. Kern, "The Political Career of Horace Boise," *IJHP*, 47 (July 1949), 237. Campbell, "Did Democracy Work?" 109-110 (quotation). Democrats regained control of the Illinois, Iowa, and Wisconsin lower houses in 1933; Illinois Democrats won a plurality of house seats in 1913.

3. The Lawmakers and Lawmaking

1. Forrest Crissey, *Tattlings of a Retired Politician* (Chicago: Thompson and Thomas, 1904), 307.

2. The appendix lists the sources of the data. If biographical information did not specify prior house membership, the rosters of representatives were compared between sessions. Rates of tenure and legislative experience in the lower houses between 1886 and 1895 averaged as follows. Reelection: Illinois, 25 percent; Iowa and Wisconsin, 30 percent. Proportion of members serving three consecutive terms: Illinois, 5 percent; Iowa and Wisconsin, 3 percent. Freshmen: Illinois, 68 percent; Iowa, 62 percent; Wisconsin, 75 percent. The numbers of freshmen (those without known prior legislative experience) in Illinois and Iowa are partial estimates because for some sessions information of possible service prior to 1884 was lacking.

3. In addition to the sources on the nineteenth century cited in Ballard Campbell, "The State Legislature in American History: A Review Essay," *Historical Methods Newsletter*, 9 (September 1976), 194, see: Ralph A. Wooster, *Politicians, Planters and Plain Folk: Courthouse and Statehouse in the Upper South, 1850-1860* (Knoxville, Tenn., 1975), 42-43; Gerald N. Grob, "The Political System and Social Policy in the Nineteenth Century: Legacy of the Revolution," *Mid-America*, 58 (January 1976), 14, n. 16; "The Blight on Legislatures," *The Nation*, 54 (1892), 460-461. For the twentieth century see: Samuel P. Orth, "Our State Legislatures," in Paul S. Reinsch, ed., *Readings on American State Government* (Boston, 1911), 42-47; Charles S. Hyneman, "Tenure and Turnover of Legislative Personnel," *Annals of the American Academy of Political and Social Science*, 195 (1938), 21-31; Charles W. Shull and Lewis J. McGuiness, "The Changing Pattern of Personnel in the Michigan Legislature: 1887-1947," *Michigan History*, 35 (December 1951), 467-478; William J. Keefe and Morris S. Ogul, *The American Legislative Process: Congress and the States*, 2d ed. (Englewood Cliffs, N.J., 1968), 136. For recent trends in Illinois, Iowa, and Wisconsin see: Gilbert Y. Steiner and Samuel K. Gove, *Legislative Politics in Illinois* (Urbana, 1960), 4; issues of *The Palimpsest* (The State Historical Society of Iowa), which appears biennially in October or November, devoted to sessions of the Iowa legislature in the 1950s and 1960s; *WB, 1964*, 266. See also Nelson W. Polsby, "The Institutionalization of the U.S. House of Representatives, *APSR*, 62 (March 1968), 144-168.

4. Ballard Campbell, "Ethnicity and the 1893 Wisconsin Assembly," *JAH*, 62 (June 1975), 79-81.

5. Sources of information on the legislators' ethnic backgrounds are given in the appendix.

6. Table II in Campbell, "Ethnicity," 79, gives the religious background of the 1893 Wisconsin Assemblymen. Paul Kleppner, *The Cross of Culture* (New

York, 1970), esp. 69-73; Richard Jensen, *The Winning of the Midwest* (Chicago, 1971), 58-85, 309-315; Frederick C. Luebke, *Immigrants and Politics: The Germans of Nebraska, 1880-1900* (Lincoln, Neb., 1969), esp. 65-67.

7. Core culture also included Unitarians, Universalists, Quakers, and Presbyterians. The intermediate classification also incorporated Dutch (when religion unknown), Episcopalians, Baptists, United Brethren, Christians, and religious liberals. Additional entries in the peripheral group were Lutherans and Reformed, unless national background dictated an alternate classification. The central and eastern Europeans who sat in these sessions were of Polish, Italian, Austrian, Belgian, French, and "Bohemian" origins. Slightly more than one-half of the sample served in five sessions: Illinois 1883 and 1893, Iowa 1894, and Wisconsin 1893 and 1895. Data refer to the occupants of seats in each session, and therefore individuals who sat in more than one session were eligible for multiple counting.

8. Three factors had a special bearing on the ethnic composition of the Illinois house: multi-member districts; the Democratic strength in southern Illinois, which was highly Yankee; and the classification of a large proportion of individuals in the "intermediate" category, partly because of lack of data on religious background.

9. Of the sixty-two Chicago seats held by Democrats in the five sessions of 1883 and 1887 through 1893, Irishmen occupied approximately forty-one. Twenty-seven of these men are known to have been Irish, and the national origins of the remaining seventeen were guessed at on the basis of names and supplemented in a few cases by known Catholic affiliation. Although such estimations must be done cautiously (the technique was not used in collecting the data profiled in table 3.2 or for subsequent voting analyses), the inclusion of men with such customary Irish names as Farley, Mahoney, O'Connor, Buckley, O'Toole, and Quinn with the set of known Irishmen is methodologically acceptable when the assumptions are specified and the generalizations are limited.

10. In the Illinois and Wisconsin houses prior to 1895, 31 percent (77 of 246) of the Democrats whose ethnic background was known were Irish; in the sessions of 1895 the proportion dropped to 21 percent (8 of 38). In Iowa, relatively few of the individuals whose national ancestry is known came from an Irish background.

11. Gamma coefficients for the association before 1894 and in 1894 or 1895 were as follows:

	Before 1894	1894 or 1895
Illinois	0.76 (257)	0.60 (59)
Iowa	0.69 (164)	0.68 (98)
Wisconsin	0.76 (207)	0.98 (62)

Figures in parentheses indicate the number of lawmakers on which each cross-tabulation is based. The calculation for the 1895 Wisconsin house includes only twelve Democrats, none of whom had a core background.

12. See for example: Michael F. Holt, *Forging a Majority: The Formation of the Republican Party in Pittsburgh, 1848-1860* (New Haven, Conn., 1969), 325-365; *Annals of Iowa*, 3d ser., 41 (Winter 1972), 886-888; "Rules of the Thirteenth

General Assembly . . . of Iowa," *Legislative Documents Submitted to the Thirteenth General Assembly of Iowa, 1870* (Des Moines, Ia., 1870), 24-26, and the legislative rosters in the same series for earlier sessions; John D. Buenker, "The New-Stock Politicians of 1912," *JISHS*, 62 (Spring 1969), 43, and *Urban Liberalism and Progressive Reform* (New York, 1973), esp. 24-25; Charles H. McCall, "The Indiana Legislature and Politics," in James B. Kessler, ed., *Empirical Studies of Indiana Politics: Studies of Legislative Behavior* (Bloomington, Ind., 1970), 14; legislative issues of *The Palimpsest*; Keefe and Ogul, *Legislative Process*, 127-131.

13. The sources of occupational information are discussed in the appendix. The single-entry occupational designations given in brief biographies and rosters of legislators do not report occupational histories. According to the *Iowa Official Register* for 1888, for example, Representative Abraham Owen was a farmer at the time of his service, but other sources reveal that he had also been a cotton-gin contractor in Mississippi, a saw mill operator, a carpenter, an "explorer," a "trapper and hunter," and a gold miner in California.

14. Horace B. Davis, "The Occupations of Massachusetts Legislators, 1790-1950," *New England Quarterly*, 24 (March 1951), 89-100; Anthony F. Upton, "The Road to Power in Virginia in the Early Nineteenth Century," *Virginia Magazine of History and Biography*, 62 (July 1954), 259-280; Ralph A. Wooster, *The People in Power: Courthouse and Statehouse in the Lower South, 1850-1860* (Knoxville, Tenn., 1969), 27-41, and *Politicians, Planters and Plain Folk*, 33-35; Orth, "Our State Legislatures," 42-47; Neil F. Garvey, *The Government and Administration of Illinois* (New York, 1958), 68; *WB, 1964*, 266; McCall, "The Indiana Legislature," 13; Keefe and Ogul, *Legislative Process*, 124. Allan G. Bogue and others, "Members of the House of Representatives and the Process of Modernization, 1789-1960," *JAH*, 63 (Sept., 1976), 284-285.

15. Orth, "Our State Legislatures," 43, 54.

16. The information on boardinghouses was found in "Rules and Standing Committees of the Twenty-first General Assembly . . . 1886," *Legislative Documents Submitted to the Twenty-first General Assembly of Iowa, 1886* (Des Moines, Ia., 1886), V, 28-30.

17. These comments on living and seating arrangements are based on an analysis of house seating charts, of legislators' biographical characteristics (sources given in appendix), and on newspapers.

18. Generalizations in this paragraph and the remainder of the chapter are based primarily on newspaper coverage of the session, house legislative journals, and the biographical sources listed in the appendix. Citations are confined mainly to quotations and to additional sources. On speakership races and other aspects of legislative procedure, see Ernest L. Bogart and John M. Mathews, *The Modern Commonwealth, 1893-1918* (Springfield, Ill., 1920), 297-304; Cyril C. Upham, "The Speaker of the House of Representatives in Iowa," *IJHP*, 17 (January 1919), 3-82 (esp. 10-29); John E. Briggs, "History and Organization of the Legislature in Iowa," in Benjamin F. Shambaugh, ed., *Statute Law-Making in Iowa* (Iowa City, Ia., 1916), 3-135; Ivan L. Pollock, "Some Abuses Connected with Statute Law-Making," ibid., 613-687. David T. Littler to Shelby M. Cullom, Dec. 4, 1886, and John R. Tanner to Cullom, Jan. 2, 1887, Cullom Papers, IllSHS; William O. Mitchell to John F. Lacey, Nov. 10, 1893, Lacey Papers, IaDHA.

19. Joshua E. Dodge to Ellis B. Usher, Nov. 10, 1890, Usher Papers, box 10, WSHS; see also Usher's outgoing correspondence for November and December 1890 in his Letterbooks, vol. 8.

20. Joshua E. Dodge to Ellis B. Usher, Dec. 25, 1890, D. W. Chency to Usher, Dec. 5, 1890, and John E. Wright to Usher, Dec. 10, 1890, Usher Papers; Usher correspondence for November and December 1890, Letterbooks, vol. 8, esp. Usher to George W. Peck (governor-elect) and John E. Wright, Dec. 9, 1890.

21. William F. Vilas to Ellis B. Usher, Dec. 4, 1890, Edward C. Wall to Usher, Dec. 28, 1890, W. Collins to Usher, Dec. 6, 1890, and Usher to Edward C. Wall, Dec. 29, 1890, Letterbooks, vol. 8, Usher Papers. Usher had had prior dealings with the railroads regarding legislative positions: Usher to Edward Keogh, Jan. 9, 1889, and Usher to B. G. Lennox, Jan. 8 and 9, 1889, Letterbooks, vol. 8; *Milwaukee Sentinel*, Jan. 14, 1891.

22. *IaHJ*, 1890, esp. 11, 30, 46, 79, 82, 83; *Davenport Democrat*, Feb. 20, 1890, and earlier coverage of the 1890 session. David Bradt, "Political Sketches," *IJHP*, 55 (1957), 351-353.

23. *Chicago Tribune*, Jan. 5, 7, 8, 9, 1891; *Chicago Times*, Nov. 23, 1890. John Moses, *Illinois: Historical and Statistical* (Chicago, 1895), II, 1317. *Illinois State Journal*, November and December 1892.

24. On the role of committees see: Upham, "Speaker of the House"; Briggs, "Legislature in Iowa"; Pollock, "Some Abuses"; and Bogart and Mathews, *Modern Commonwealth*, 309-310; Steiner and Gove, *Legislative Politics*, 58-83; Frank E. Horack, "The Committee System," in Shambaugh, *Statute Law-Making*. Moses, *Illinois*, II, 956-957, took a different and, I think, erroneous view of the influence of committees on the fate of legislation.

25. "Important" committees have been identified on the basis of newspaper coverage of the session, the timing of appointments, the size of committees, and the sources listed in notes 18 and 24.

26. The strict adherence to party in the election of speaker and the appointment of committee chairmen differs from the practice of some states in the early nineteenth century; see James H. Broussard, "Party and Partisanship in American Legislatures: The South Atlantic States, 1800-1812," *Journal of Southern History*, 53 (February 1977), 39-52.

27. Maureen A. Casilli, "The Composition of Standing Committees in the Wisconsin Assembly, 1864-1973" (unpublished seminar paper, Department of History, Northeastern University, Boston, Mass., 1975). Selection of chairmen in Iowa during the 1920s and 1930s bore little relation to seniority or to past committee service: on average, between 1925 and 1935 only 58 percent of incumbent (reelected) representatives who became chairmen headed committees on which they had served previously. See Charles S. Hyneman and Edmond F. Ricketts, "Tenure and Turnover of the Iowa Legislature," *Iowa Law Review*, 24 (1939), 683-684. Also see Douglas C. Chaffey, "The Institutionalization of State Legislatures: A Comparative Study," *Western Political Quarterly*, 23 (March 1970), 180-196. The relation between safe districts and chairmen did not hold true for Illinois, which is probably explained by the impact of multi-member districts on legislative career patterns.

28. Charles W. Moore to "Wife," Jan. 8, 1889, Moore Papers, WSHS;

Robert M. Bashford to William F. Vilas, Feb. 13, 1893, Vilas Papers, WSHS.

29. *WB, 1887*, 470-471; *WB, 1893*, 614-615; *IllHJ, 1893*, x-xi. Ethnicity played an important role in patronage decisions in Illinois and Wisconsin. See, for example, Shelby M. Cullom to George Schneider, July 11, 1892, Cullom Papers; William C. Brawley to Ellis B. Usher, Mar. 17, 1891, Usher Papers; Edward C. Wall to William F. Vilas, Mar. 25, Apr. 22 and 25, May 1, 1893, Vilas Papers.

30. *Milwaukee Sentinel*, Jan. 13, 1887.

31. *Catholic Sentinel*, Jan. 12, 1893; *Burlington Hawkeye*, Jan. 21, 1892; *Milwaukee Sentinel*, Feb. 18, 1887; *Davenport Democrat*, Apr. 16, 1890.

32. See Paul S. Reinsch, *American Legislatures and Legislative Methods* (New York, 1907), 126-128 and 228-274 for a summary of these views. James Bryce, in his *American Commonwealth* (New York, 1889), II, 398-661, and II, 37-44, leveled the classic indictment against state governments during the late nineteenth century. See also the following sample of other contemporary criticisms: *Burlington Hawkeye*, Jan. 19, 1892; *Catholic Sentinel*, Jan. 26, 1893; *Milwaukee Sentinel*, Mar. 30, 1895, quoting *The Philadelphia Press*; E. L. Godkin, "The Decline of Legislatures," *Atlantic Monthly*, 80 (July 1897), 35-53.

33. Moses, *Illinois*, II, 961 and 963 (quotations), 955-963.

34. *Milwaukee Sentinel*, March 1, 1895.

35. *Iowa State Register*, Feb. 9, 1886, quoting the *Chariton Patriot*; *Iowa State Register*, Mar. 2, 1888. See also *Iowa State Register*, Jan. 6, 13, 1888; *IaHJ, 1890*, 556, and *IaHJ, 1892*, 600-601; *Milwaukee Sentinel*, Jan. 9, 1895.

36. See *Burlington Hawkeye*, Feb. 2, 1892, and *Chicago Tribune*, April 12, 1893, and June 15, 1895, for the complaints.

37. Ernest L. Bogart and Charles M. Thompson, *The Industrial State, 1870-1893* (Springfield, Ill., 1920), 304-305, 495-500; Bogart and Mathews, *Modern Commonwealth*, 424-425, 511-515. U.S. Census Office, *Eleventh Census of the United States: 1890. Report on Wealth, Debt, and Taxation* (Washington, D.C., 1895), pt. II, 414, 416, 418, 464-474.

38. Bogart and Mathews, *Modern Commonwealth*, 319; Shambaugh, *Statute Law-Making*, vi-vii.

39. *Milwaukee Sentinel*, Apr. 19, 1895.

40. Journal of Archibald W. Hopkins, p. 221, microfilm, WSHS.

41. Diary of Willet S. Main, Jan. 7, 1889, box 2, WSHS. On this theme generally, see Samuel E. Patterson, "Party Opposition in the Legislature: The Ecology of Legislative Institutionalization," *Polity*, 4 (1972), 344-366.

42. See on Crafts: *Chicago Tribune*, June 4, 12, 13, 1893; *Illinois State Journal*, December issues, 1892; *The* (Chicago) *Daily InterOcean*, Jan. 5, 1893; *Kendall County Record*, Mar. 29, Apr. 19, 1893; *Chicago Tribune*, June 8, 17, 1893.

43. *Iowa State Register*, Apr. 13, 1886.

44. Ibid., Mar. 1, 1888.

45. *Chicago Times*, May 26, 1887; *Chicago Tribune*, May 26, 1887.

46. *IaHJ, 1890*, 159; *Chicago Tribune*, Mar. 8, 1895. The comments in this paragraph draw not only on newspapers but also on the explanation of votes inserted in Iowa house journals. On legislative role orientations generally, see Malcolm E. Jewell and Samuel C. Patterson, *The Legislative Process in the United States* (New York, 1966), 382-409; Heinz Eulau et al., "The Role of the Representa-

tive: Some Empirical Observations on the Theory of Edmund Burke," *APSR*, 53 (September 1959), 742-756; James D. Barber, *The Lawmakers: Recruitment and Adaptation to Legislative Life* (New Haven, Conn., 1965); Samuel C. Patterson, Ronald D. Hedlund, and G. R. Boynton, *Representatives and Represented: Bases of Public Support for American Legislatures* (New York, 1975).

47. Jewell and Patterson, *Legislative Process*, 339-357, 435-444; Warren Miller and Donald Stokes, "Constituency Influence in Congress," *APSR*, 57 (March 1963), 45-56; Patterson, *Representatives*; Wayne L. Francis, *Legislative Issues in the Fifty States: A Comparative Analysis* (Chicago, 1967), 8; James E. Wright, *The Politics of Populism: Dissent in Colorado* (New Haven, Conn., 1974), 92, 101. As Crissey's William Bradley put it (*Tattlings*, 123), "Any ordinary bunch of voters can forget to remember more things than a village money lender can remember to forget in making up a schedule of his personal property for the tax assessor." Charles Hipwell, member of the Iowa house from 1888 to 1892, acknowledged only two issues of major concern in his district: "My constituents are the easiest people in the world to please. Just so I vote right on prohibition and money questions I can do as I please on any other subject under the sun." Willis L. Hall, *Biographical Sketches of the Twenty-fifth General Assembly of Iowa* (Des Moines, Ia., 1894), 35.

4. The Contested Issues

1. A fuller discussion of the methodology appears in the appendix.

2. *IaHJ*, *1890*, 585-586.

3. I read one urban daily newspaper for the duration of each session and consulted other newspapers on specific matters. See appendix.

4. I use a stylistic shortcut in referring to the legislation and the roll calls classified according to the various subject categories. For example, the phrase "votes on Community Mores," in which the policy category is capitalized, is shorthand for "the roll calls on legislation classified in the category of Community Mores."

5. Numerous works have contributed to my ideas in this paragraph, but the following have been particularly helpful: Jacob M. Edelman, *The Symbolic Uses of Politics* (Urbana, Ill., 1964); Samuel P. Hays, "New Possibilities for American Political History: The Social Analysis of Political Life," in Seymour M. Lipset and Richard Hofstadter, eds., *Sociology and History: Methods* (New York, 1968), 181-227; Seymour M. Lipset and Earl Raab, *The Politics of Unreason: Right-Wing Extremism in America, 1790-1970* (New York, 1970), 428-483; and Joseph R. Gusfield, *Symbolic Crusade: Status Politics and the American Temperance Movement* (Urbana, Ill., 1963).

6. Unfortunately, there is no foolproof or universal technique for the categorization of public policy issues. See John C. Wahlke, "Policy Determinants and Legislative Decisions," in S. Sidney Ulmer, ed., *Political Decision-Making* (New York, 1970), 87-89. My classification decisions were based on the substance of controversy at stake in each bill and roll call, and not necessarily on the subject referenced in bill titles. When a roll call pertained to a topic different from that of its parent bill, the vote was classified separately under the appropriate subject. Many

bills embraced issues that could have been placed in several policy categories. Appropriations for state colleges, for example, touched both fiscal and education policy; legislation prohibiting habitual drunkards from practicing medicine was simultaneously a liquor and public health issue. The scheme used in this chapter is based on a primary system of classification, in which each issue was placed in a single discrete category. Difficult decisions encountered in implementing the procedure were resolved through experience in working with these materials, which gave me a sense of the policy category that best described the essence of each dispute. The drunk doctor bill, I decided, lay closer to the liquor issue than to any other.

These content categories and the classification decision for particular legislation, however, must be understood as a methodological operation designed to facilitate certain analyses in this study. The categorization scheme cannot be read as a finite statement about distinctions in policy content. Consequently, the discussion in later chapters is not locked into this topical framework, for it does not necessarily mirror the policy perceptions of lawmakers in the late nineteenth century. The technique of scaling roll call votes, which allows legislators to show linkages among legislative issues on the basis of lawmakers' voting behavior, helped to suggest when it was appropriate to make such adjustments.

These deviations are clarified by stating the objective of this chapter, which is to review the content and frequency of contested legislation. The larger question before the study, however, is analysis of policymaking, which examines the interaction between policy and the dynamics of legislative behavior in the late nineteenth century. My a priori content classifications are only one of several methodologies used to investigate these relationships. The appendix contains an explanation of scaling and its relationship to legislative content, as well as the sources used to identify the substance of particular bills.

7. Since the frequency distribution of bills and resolutions closely parallels the relative proportion of roll calls, I omit most references to bills when providing tabular and text indications of the frequency of contested issues.

8. For overviews of the liquor issue see: Norman H. Clark, *Deliver Us from Evil: An Interpretation of American Prohibition* (New York, 1976); and Gusfield, *Symbolic Crusade*. Also see chapter 6. I agree with Richard Jensen's observation: "It is possible to argue that from the 1830s to the 1930s no debate at the local level agitated this country more, year in and year out, than the question of controlling alcohol, unless it was the contests between Democrats and Republicans or Whigs." *The Winning of the Midwest: Social and Political Conflict, 1888-1896* (Chicago, 1971), xii.

9. Outlines of the temperance movement in late-nineteenth-century Illinois, Iowa, and Wisconsin appear in Ernest L. Bogart and Charles M. Thompson, *The Industrial State, 1870-1893* (Springfield, Ill., 1920), 42-51; John Moses, *Illinois: Historical and Statistical* (Chicago, 1895), II, 883-892; Dan E. Clark, "The History of Liquor Legislation in Iowa," *IJHP*, 6 (1908), 55-87, 339-374, 503-608; Alexander M. Thompson, *A Political History of Wisconsin* (Milwaukee, Wis., 1902), 219-228; David P. Thelen, *The New Citizenship: Origins of Progressivism in Wisconsin, 1885-1900* (Columbia, Mo., 1972), 12-16.

10. *Milwaukee Sentinel*, Apr. 12, 1895.

11. Ballard C. Campbell, "Did Democracy Work? Prohibition in Late Nine-

teenth-Century Iowa: A Test Case," *JIH*, 8 (1977), 108-110.

12. *Chicago Times*, Apr. 29, 1887.

13. *Milwaukee Sentinel*, Apr. 17, 1895; *Madison Democrat*, Apr. 17, 1895.

14. Leslie H. Fishel, Jr., "The Genesis of the First Wisconsin Civil Rights Act," *WMH*, 49 (1966), 324-333.

15. *Chicago Tribune*, May 8, 1895.

16. Supporters of a strong liability law during the sessions between 1887 and 1893 worked to reenact the 1875 law, repealed in 1880, which had eliminated the fellow servant doctrine. See Donald J. Berthrong, "Employer's Liability Legislation in Wisconsin, 1874-1893," *Southwestern Social Science Quarterly*, 34 (1953), 57-71; and Lawrence M. Friedman, *A History of American Law* (New York, 1973), 262-264, 409-427.

17. Thelen, *New Citizenship*, 176-201, 223-229, describes the municipal utility problem in Wisconsin. See also *Milwaukee Sentinel*, Apr. 17, 1895, Apr. 11, 1889.

18. *Milwaukee Sentinel*, Apr. 15, 1893, Apr. 11, 1889.

19. Ernest L. Bogart and John M. Mathews, *The Modern Commonwealth, 1893-1918* (Springfield, Ill., 1920), 433-450; Ivan L. Pollock, *History of Economic Legislation in Iowa* (Iowa City, Ia., 1918), 288-315; Thelen, *New Citizenship*, 39, 203-211; Robert S. Maxwell, *La Follette and the Rise of the Progressives in Wisconsin* (Madison, Wis., 1956), 98-99.

20. F. Garvin Davenport, "John Henry Rauch and Public Health in Illinois, 1877-1891," *JISHS*, 50 (1957), 277-293.

21. *Iowa State Register*, Apr. 1, 1886. *IaHJ*, *1888*, 973-975, *1890*, 495-496, *1892*, 687, *1894*, 977-978.

22. *Milwaukee Sentinel*, Apr. 14, 1887.

23. *Chicago Tribune*, May 27, 28, 31, 1887; Bessie Louise Pierce, *A History of Chicago*, vol. III, *The Rise of the Modern City, 1871-1893* (New York, 1957), 360-362.

24. *Chicago Tribune*, June 10, 1887, May 24, 1889.

25. Bogart and Mathews, *Modern Commonwealth*, 271; *Chicago Times*, Mar. 6, 1895.

26. *Milwaukee Sentinel*, Feb. 28, 1887.

27. Jerry M. Cooper, "The Wisconsin National Guard in the Milwaukee Riots of 1886," *WMH*, 55 (1971), 31-48.

28. *Chicago Tribune*, Jan. 16, 20, 1863; Pierce, *Modern City*, 310-313; Moses, *Illinois*, II, 1338-1341; *Chicago Tribune* for February through May 1889. The vials of dirty water were reported in the *Tribune* on May 25, 1889.

29. On urban streets, see Clay McShane, "American Cities and the Coming of the Automobile, 1870-1910" (Ph.D. diss., University of Wisconsin, 1975), 94-135, 301-308, and "Transforming the Use of Urban Space," *Journal of Urban History*, 5 (May 1979), 284-290.

30. On rural roads, see Bogart and Thompson, *Industrial State*, 354-362; Bogart and Mathews, *Modern Commonwealth*, 147-155. On Iowa and Wisconsin: John E. Brindley, *History of Road Legislation in Iowa* (Iowa City, Ia., 1912), 155-264; George S. May, "The Good Roads Movement in Iowa," *Palimpsest*, 46 (February 1965), 65-122; Ballard Campbell, "The Good Roads Movement in Wisconsin,

1890-1911," *WMH*, 49 (1966), 273-293.

31. *Iowa State Register*, Jan. 3, 25, March 8, 27, 28, 30, 31, Apr. 4, 1888; *Davenport Democrat*, Mar. 9, 12, 1890; *IaHJ, 1890*, 520-522.

32. *Chicago Tribune*, Mar. 5, 1895.

5. Party Voting

1. Ballard Campbell, "The State Legislature in American History: A Review Essay," *Historical Methods Newsletter*, 9 (1976), 193.

2. Frank J. Sorauf, *Party Politics in America* (Boston, 1972), 9-14.

3. A. Lawrence Lowell, "The Influence of Party upon Legislation in England and America," *Annual Report of the American Historical Association, 1901*, I (Washington, D.C., 1902), 323-324.

4. Malcolm E. Jewell and Samuel C. Patterson, *The Legislative Process in the United States* (New York, 1966), 419-422.

5. The index of disagreement is the percentage of Republican yea votes minus the percentage of Democratic yea votes, ignoring the sign. If, for example, both parties (or any other discrete pair of groups) cast the same proportion of yea and nay votes, 80 percent of the Republicans must respond yea and 80 percent of the Democrats must respond nay for disagreement to reach a difference of 60 percent. Again, if one party votes 100 percent yea, then the other party must vote no more than 40 percent yea for disagreement to meet a 60 percent difference threshold. The index of disagreement is the obversion of the index of likeness (i.e., 100-likeness), described in Lee F. Anderson, Meredith W. Watts, Jr., and Allen R. Wilcox, *Legislative Roll-Call Analysis* (Evanston, Ill., 1966), 44-45.

6. Lowell, "Influence of Party," 321-542.

7. Details of my recalculation of Lowell's data appear in Ballard C. Campbell, Jr., "Political Parties, Cultural Groups and Contested Issues: Voting in the Illinois, Iowa and Wisconsin Houses of Representatives 1886-1895," (Ph.D. diss., University of Wisconsin, Madison, 1970), 126-129. Lowell concluded that party divisions were infrequent in the states during the late 1890s ("Influence of Party," 337-339, 342). Similar assessments appear in Paul S. Reinsch, *American Legislatures and Legislative Methods* (New York, 1907), 276-277; and Ernest L. Bogart and John M. Mathews, *The Centennial History of Illinois*, vol. V, *The Modern Commonwealth, 1893-1918* (Springfield, Ill., 1920), 309. Apparently using Lowell's stringent definiton of a party vote and including every roll call taken in the sessions examined, Reinsch (*American Legislatures*, 276n) presented the following data, without further exposition, on party voting:

Iowa 1898	Senate	3 of 372 votes
	House	9 of 394 votes
Minnesota 1903	Senate	no party votes
	House	1 of 741 votes

8. James E. Wright, *The Politics of Populism: Dissent in Colorado* (New Haven, Conn., 1974), 94, 164, 178.

9. David W. Brady and Phillip Althoff, "Party Voting in the U.S. House of Representatives, 1890-1910: Elements of a Responsible Party System," *Journal of Politics*, 36 (1974), 755-756. The unweighted average for the seven sessions between 1881 and 1893 was 14 percent; for 1895-1913, the mean rate was 36 percent.

10. William G. Shade et al., "Partisanship in the United States Senate: 1869-1901," *JIH*, 4 (1973), 185-206. An important study by Jerome M. Clubb and Santa A. Traugott, "Partisan Cleavage and Cohesion in the House of Representatives, 1861-1974," *JIH*, 7 (1977), 375-401, which appeared after this chapter was written, confirms the level of congressional partisanship summarized in the paragraph.

11. William J. Keefe, "Party Government and Lawmaking in the Illinois General Assembly," *Northwestern University Law Review*, 49 (1952), 59; Malcolm E. Jewell, "Party Voting in American State Legislatures," *APSR*, 49 (1955), 780; Jewell and Patterson, *Legislative Process*, 420-421, citing David R. Derge, "Urban-Rural Relationships in the Illinois General Assembly" (Paper presented to the Midwest Conference of Political Scientists, 1958); Charles W. Wiggins, "Party Politics in the Iowa Legislature," *Midwest Journal of Political Science*, 11 (1967), 88; and John C. Wahlke, "Policy Determinants and Legislative Decisions," in S. Sidney Ulmer, ed., *Political Decision-Making* (New York, 1970), 100. A tabular presentation of most of these data may be found in Campbell, "Political Parties," 130.

12. Rates of party cohesion, calculated as the proportion of roll calls that manifested at least 90 percent party voting unity (80 percent by the Rice index of cohesion), for the five sessions of each state averaged as follows: Illinois, Republicans 29%, Democrats 24%; Iowa, Republicans 16%, Democrats 31%; Wisconsin, Republicans 21%, Democrats 26%. A more detailed presentation appears in Campbell, "Political Parties," 124.

13. The metropolitan data are presented in Campbell, "Political Parties," 205.

14. The observations about voting cohesion among farmers are based on five sessions, and the data for farmer-metropolitan (Iowa urban districts) disagreement rest on seven sessions. The computations for four of the sessions, Illinois 1891, Iowa 1888, and Wisconsin 1889 and 1891, appear tabularly in Campbell, "Political Parties," 204. Analogous calculations subsequently were done for the fifth session, Wisconsin 1893. Farmers achieved 80 percent voting unity (60 percent on the Rice index of cohesion) on 13 percent of the 322 roll calls in these five sessions. Republican farmers disagreed with Democratic farmers on 37 percent of the same set of votes. Farmers disagreed with metropolitan representatives (in Iowa, urban), at the 60 percent threshold level on 6 percent of the 471 roll calls taken in the five sessions listed above and in two others, Illinois 1893 and Iowa 1894. In these seven legislative meetings Democrats disagreed with Republicans on 34 percent of these votes. The observations about the voting of farmer-lawmakers may be marred by the fact that some of these men also had other occupations (see chapter 3).

15. A detailed discussion of the techniques of scale analysis used in this study appears in the appendix.

16. The twelve sessions subjected to comprehensive scale analysis were Illinois, 1887-1893; Iowa, 1888-1894; and Wisconsin, 1889-1895. Sixty-nine percent of the roll calls from the twelve sessions, including the supplementary votes, fitted

acceptably into a scale of four items or more. Additional scales were constructed for special subjects in several other sessions, but they are not discussed here.

17. A number of social, economic, political, and other (independent) variables, defined in the appendix, were used in these tests. Gamma coefficients were calculated for cross-tabulations between scale scores (grouped into ranked categories) and independent variables. See appendix.

18. In these tests, scale scores were transformed into interval indices, and the variance in voting responses attributable to party and urbanization was estimated by analysis of variance and regression. The technical details are given in the appendix. The technique was applied to all scales constructed for Illinois 1893, Iowa 1888 and 1894, and the 1891-1895 sessions of the Wisconsin Assembly. A scale in the 1894 Iowa house that concerned the liquor question (the mulct bill) is omitted from the discussion because Democrats abstained from voting on these roll calls.

19. Since party votes tended to scale more readily than nonparty votes, scale analysis may accentuate the true influence of party and devalue the real impact of urbanization as determinants of voting behavior on all the contested roll calls. On the other hand, urban correlations with scaled legislation sometimes were inflated by the effect of other variables. Analysis of the independent effects of party, urbanization, and other factors are discussed in chapter 7.

20. Leon D. Epstein, *Political Parties in Western Democracies* (New York, 1967), 130-166, 318-340. But party cohesion is generally higher among all parties in European parliamentary systems than in American legislatures.

21. Thomas R. Dye, *Understanding Public Policy*, 2d ed. (Englewood Cliffs, N.J., 1975), 196, 199.

22. Sidney Fine, *Laissez Faire and the General Welfare State: A Study of Conflict in American Thought, 1865-1901* (Ann Arbor, Mich., 1956), 353-354.

23. Sorauf, *Party Politics*, 356-360, 381-404; Theodore J. Lowi, "Party, Policy, and Constitution in America," in William Nisbet Chambers and Walter Dean Burnham, eds., *American Party Systems* (New York, 1967), 238-276; Joel H. Silbey, "Political Parties and Political History," in Lee Benson, et al., *American Political Behavior: Historical Essays and Readings* (New York, 1974), 206.

24. Lowi, "Party, Policy, and Constitution," 239, 274, 264.

25. Sorauf, *Party Politics*, 359.

6. Legislating Community Mores

1. *Chicago Tribune*, May 30, 28, 1891. Also see *Chicago Tribune* for June 19, 1887, May 21, 1889, and June 2, 1891.

2. *Iowa State Register*, Jan. 7, 1888, May 13, 1886, and Jan. 5, 1888 (sources of quotations); see also *Register* for March 5, 1886, Feb. 7, 1894. *Milwaukee Sentinel*, Feb. 17, March 12, 1887.

3. On Iowa, see Ballard C. Campbell, "Did Democracy Work?" *JIH*, 8 (Summer 1977), esp. 97-100, supplemented by *Burlington Hawkeye*, March 1, 1892, and *Dubuque Herald*, Oct. 21, 1893. On churches: *Chicago Tribune*, May 28, 1889; Ernest L. Bogart and Charles M. Thompson, *The Industrial State, 1870-1893* (Springfield, Ill., 1920), 42-50; Daniel F. Ring, "The Temperance Movement

in Milwaukee: 1872-1884," *Historical Messenger*, 31 (Winter 1975), 98; Alexander M. Thomson, *A Political History of Wisconsin* (Milwaukee, Wis., 1902), 223; George W. White, "The Churches of Milwaukee: Their Progress, Hindrances and Duty" (Address before the Milwaukee Ministerial Association, March 1893), WSHS; *Milwaukee Sentinel*, Apr. 1, 1895. On WCTU (sample only): *Milwaukee Sentinel*, Mar. 19, 1891, Mar. 20, 1895; David P. Thelen, *The New Citizenship* (Columbia, Mo., 1972), 18-19.

4. Illinois State Grange, *Journal of Proceedings* (1891), 52-53; Roy V. Scott, *The Agrarian Movement in Illinois, 1880-1896* (Urbana, Ill., 1962), 69. *Iowa State Register*, Apr. 9, 1886.

5. Personal liberty leagues: *Chicago Tribune*, Mar. 21, 1889; Dan E. Clark, "The History of Liquor Legislation in Iowa, 1878-1908," *IJHP*, 6 (October 1908), 568; *Milwaukee Sentinel*, Apr. 17, 1889. Wholesalers, saloonkeepers, and pharmacists: *Chicago Tribune*, June 2, 1887, Feb. 2, 1895; Edward C. Wall to William F. Vilas, May 1, 1891, Vilas Papers, WSHS; *Milwaukee Sentinel*, Apr. 5, 1895; *Iowa State Register*, Mar. 13, 1886; *IaHJ, 1890*, 552-553. Brewers and distillers: *Milwaukee Sentinel*, Apr. 12, 1895; Ernest L. Bogart and John M. Mathews, *The Modern Commonwealth, 1893-1918* (Springfield, Ill., 1920), 91, 102, 506; on their role in temperance movements elsewhere in the Midwest, see Lloyd Sponholtz, "The Politics of Temperance in Ohio, 1880-1912," *Ohio History*, 85 (Winter 1976), 13-18, and Larry Engelmann, "Dry Renaissance: The Local Option Years, 1889-1917," *Michigan History*, 59 (Spring-Summer 1975), 71-74.

CTAU: Rev. James M. Cleary to Bryan J. Castle, Feb. 25, 1884, Castle Papers, WSHS; *Chicago Tribune*, June 12, 1887; *Iowa State Register*, March 23, 1886; M. Justille McDonald, *History of the Irish in Wisconsin in the Nineteenth Century* (Washington, D.C., 1954), 229-235. Catholic press: *Catholic Citizen* (Milwaukee, Wis.), Nov. 14, 28, 1891, Dec. 31, 1892; *Catholic Sentinel* (Chippewa Falls, Wis.), various issues during August, September, and November 1892. Richard J. Orsi, "Humphrey Joseph Desmond: A Case Study in American Catholic Liberalism," M.A. thesis (University of Wisconsin, Madison, 1965).

6. Some representative selections: *Chicago Tribune*, Feb. 2, 1887, June 19, 1893, March 26, 1895; *Illinois State Journal*, Jan. 16, 1893; *Dubuque Herald*, Mar. 23, 1894; *Milwaukee Sentinel*, Jan. 8, 1889, Mar. 11, 1893, Apr. 8, 1895; *Catholic Sentinel*, Dec. 8, 1892; Harry H. Heming, *The Catholic Church in Wisconsin* (Milwaukee, Wis., 1895-1898), 289-290. Prohibition party platforms appear in the *Chicago Daily News Almanac, IOR*, and *WB*. Generally, see Paul Kleppner, *The Cross of Culture* (New York, 1970); and Richard Jensen, *The Winning of the Midwest* (Chicago, 1971).

7. The method of scale construction and analysis is discussed in the appendix. In addition to the items listed in table 6.1 and its adjoining text, the following legislation is included in these scales: Iowa—publication of the proceedings of county boards of supervisors and of the governor's inaugural address (both foreign language issues), alien ownership of real estate, orphans' homes, capital punishment; Wisconsin—use of foreign languages in official publications, jury trials in civil cases, veterans, marriage of second cousins. For these bills, as well as for other legislation, all roll calls on a particular bill do not necessarily fit acceptably into a scale.

8. Four scales on Community Mores are not reported in table 6.1. They are, with corresponding gamma values for party: Illinois 1887 Political Rights (1.00); Illinois 1891 Female Political Rights (0.49); Iowa 1888 Salary Discrimination against Female Teachers (0.03); Iowa 1894 Mulct (liquor; party not relevant). The mulct bill is discussed in chapter 7; the topics contained in the other three scales are addressed later in this chapter.

9. The debate over liquor at the statehouse described in these paragraphs is reconstructed from numerous sources, but it relies heavily on newspaper accounts of floor transactions, which I followed in the press for the duration of each session. Quotations are from the following sources: *Chicago Tribune*, May 22, 1889; *Milwaukee Sentinel*, Mar. 22, 1889; *Iowa State Register*, Mar. 20, 1886; Clark, "Liquor Legislation," 551, 552, 555; *Milwaukee Journal*, Mar. 8, 1893; *Milwaukee Sentinel*, Mar. 20, Apr. 12, 1895.

10. *Iowa State Register*, Mar. 17, 1888; *Chicago Tribune*, Mar. 17, 1887; *Chicago Times*, Mar. 12, 1887. Also see *Le Mars* (Iowa) *Semi-Weekly Sentinel*, Mar. 15, 1894.

11. *Davenport Democrat*, Feb. 27, 1890; *WisAJ, 1893*, 853-854. Also see *Burlington Hawkeye*, Jan. 21, 1892; *IaHJ, 1892*, 188-189, 507-508.

12. There is much literary testimony to this effect but no systematic inspection of legislative voting. Illinois: D. W. Lusk, *Eighty Years of Illinois, Politics and Politicians . . . 1809-1889* (Springfield, Ill., 1889), 411-412; John Moses, *Illinois: Historical and Statistical* (Chicago, 1892), II, 892; Bogart and Thompson, *Industrial State*, 42-44, 47. Iowa: Campbell, "Did Democracy Work?" 88-90. Wisconsin: Kleppner, *Cross of Culture*, 103-129; Thomson, *Political History*, 224; David P. Thelen, "LaFollette and the Temperance Crusade," *WMH*, 47 (Summer 1964), 291-300.

13. See the appendix for details.

14. Campbell, "Did Democracy Work?" 108-113.

15. For example, see Kleppner, *Cross of Culture*; Jensen, *Winning of the Midwest*; Joel Tarr, *A Study in Boss Politics: William Lorimer of Chicago* (Urbana, Ill., 1971); and Frederick C. Luebke, *Immigrants and Politics: The Germans of Nebraska, 1880-1900* (Lincoln, Neb., 1969).

16. One of the best accounts is Luebke, *Immigrants and Politics*, 50, 122-150.

17. See Campbell, "Did Democracy Work?" 103-108, for a detailed analysis of how these factors were related to legislative responses on prohibition.

18. Ibid., 93 (including n. 8).

19. *Laws of the State of Illinois, 1889* (Springfield, Ill., 1889), 237-238; *The Laws of Wisconsin, 1889* (Madison, Wis., 1889), chap. 519, 729-733. *Chicago Tribune*, Apr. 12, 24, May 25, 26, 1889; Roger E. Wyman, "Wisconsin Ethnic Groups and the Election of 1890," *WMH*, 51 (Summer 1968), 270-271. The Illinois bill did not evoke a contested roll call in the house; the Wisconsin Assembly passed the Bennett law by a voice vote.

20. Platform statements from *Chicago Daily News Almanac for 1891*, 164, 182, 183. Kleppner, *Cross of Culture*, 158-169; Jensen, *Winning of the Midwest*, 122-153; Wyman, "Wisconsin Ethnic Groups."

21. Based on *Chicago Tribune*, Apr. 27 through June 14, 1891, Jan. 13, Feb.

2, Mar. 24, Apr. 12, 13, 1893; analysis of house roll calls on the issue; and *Illinois Laws, 1893,* 178-179.

22. For Illinois, see *Chicago Tribune* issues cited in note 21 and the *Chicago Times,* May 17, 1891; *Illinois State Journal* (Springfield), Jan. 27, Feb. 2, 1893; *The Daily InterOcean* (Chicago), Jan. 6, 1893. For Wisconsin: *Milwaukee Sentinel,* Jan. 21, 23, 28, 1891; Heming, *Catholic Church,* 287.

23. *IaHJ, 1886,* 683.

24. *Iowa State Register,* Jan. 12, Feb. 10, 1886, Jan. 3, Mar. 8, 27-31, April 4, 1888. *Davenport Democrat,* Mar. 9, 12, Apr. 16, 1890. *IaHJ, 1888,* 892, 1016; *1890,* 235-237, 414, 419, 423, 424, 431, 433, 520-522.

Rural delegates showed greater preference for free and uniform books than did urban lawmakers in 1888, but only a small number of Iowa representatives served urban districts. When party and constituent ethnicity were controlled, urbanization explained only 13 percent of the remaining variance in the 1888 Iowa Textbook scale (seven votes) in regression analysis. The three factors jointly accounted for a third of the fluctuation in the voting scores. No clearly definable voting dimension on the 1890 Textbook scale came to light, however.

25. *IaHJ, 1888,* 900-901.

26. *Milwaukee Sentinel,* Mar. 4, 1893; *Milwaukee Journal,* Mar. 14, 1893.

7. Ethnicity and Dimensions of Legislative Voting

1. I have referenced pertinent literature on the subject in "Ethnicity and the 1893 Wisconsin Assembly," *JAH,* 62 (June 1975), and in note 9 of chapter 1. See also Andrew M. Greeley, *Ethnicity in the United States: A Preliminary Reconnaissance* (New York, 1974), and the literature cited therein.

2. The proportion (in percentages) of variance explained by legislators' ethnic background, controlling for party, on these scales was as follows:

	Mores	Pipeline	Commerce	RR/Silver	Government
Republicans	54*	11	19	11	15
Democrats	26*	31*	23	27*	5

Asterisks indicate relationships that were statistically significant (F test) at 0.05.

3. The Pearson correlation coefficients (r) between Party and the voting on the five scales were as follows: Mores, 0.83; Pipeline, 0.30; Commerce, 0.40; RR/Silver, 0.96; Government, 0.89.

The multiple correlation and regression analysis, which was performed on the voting of the full membership of the Assembly and separately on Republicans and Democrats, provides estimates of the variance explained by individual variables when the other variables in the equation are held constant. The four variables Urban, Ethnic District, Ethnicity (of lawmakers), and Party were entered, in that order, in stepwise clusters into the regression model, according to the procedures outlined in Norman H. Nie et al., *SPSS: Statistical Package for the Social Sciences* (New York, 1975), 343-345. With the exception of Party, which was not used in intraparty analysis, all variables were transformed into dichotomous "dummy" variables. Ethnicity (of lawmakers), for example, was divided into seven dichotomous pairings for analysis of the full Assembly, and into a lesser number of categories for intraparty calculations. Since beta weights, which are analogous to partial correlations, do not measure the combined effect of variables entered as a cluster in a regression step, beta underestimates the effect of lawmakers' ethnic background.

The variable Democratic Vote, an interval-level measure, was substituted for Party in intraparty analysis. The treatment of some variables used in this regression analysis of the 1893 Wisconsin Assembly was revised in the calculations used to compare voting patterns between states and sessions, discussed later in the chapter.

4. *Milwaukee Sentinel*, Mar. 30, Apr. 7, 13-15, 20, 1893; *Milwaukee Journal*, Mar. 23, 24, Apr. 6, 13, 1893.

5. Voting scores (in percentages) of Democrats, averaged by ethnic background, on the Pipeline scale were as follows:

Opponents
German Catholics and Lutherans	87 (12)
Others	82 (6)

Supporters
German Catholics and Lutherans	7 (6)
Continental Protestants	6 (7)
Irish Catholics	20 (9)
Yankees, British, and Scandinavians	11 (9)

Figures in parentheses indicate the number of legislators voting. Four Democrats whose ethnic background was not determined and three with absentee rates on the votes in the scale exceeding 50 percent have been excluded.

6. The data are presented more explicitly in Campbell, "Ethnicity," 86-88.

7. Edward C. Wall to William F. Vilas, May 1, 1891, Dec. 31, 1892; Rev. J. Schlerf, Nov. 29, Dec. 19, 1892, and H. Haber, Jan. 19, 1893, to Vilas, Vilas papers, WSHS. *The Catholic Sentinel* (Chippewa Falls, Wis.), Oct. 13, 1892. Horace S. Merrill, *William Freeman Vilas* (Madison, Wis., 1954), 116-117, 175, 188, 196; H. Wayne Morgan, *From Hayes to McKinley: National Party Politics, 1877-1896* (Syracuse, N.Y., 1969), 205. Roger E. Wyman, "Voting Behavior in the Progressive Era: Wisconsin as a Test Case," (Ph.D. diss., University of Wisconsin, Madison, 1970), 59-68, 121-127, and "Wisconsin Ethnic Groups and the Election of 1890," *WMH*, 51 (Summer 1968), 270, 274-276. The quotation is from: Edward Bragg to Ellis B. Usher, December (no day) 1892, Usher Papers, WSHS.

8. E. David Cronin, "Father Marquette Goes to Washington: The Marquette Statue Controversy," *WMH*, 56 (Summer 1973), 267-283. *The Catholic Citizen* (Milwaukee), Nov. 12, Dec. 3, 1892, Jan. 28, Feb. 11, 1893; *The Catholic Sentinel*, Aug. 25, Dec. 1, 1892, Jan. 12, 19, 1893.

The religious factor emerged in another incident. Assemblyman Michael Blenski, a Pole representing Polish wards in Milwaukee, changed his vote from

Mitchell to Bragg on the twelfth ballot and retained this position for the remainder of the canvas, even though two Polish Catholic priests from his home ward were admitted to the Democratic caucus to persuade him to reconsider. Mitchell's role in the erection of the Kosciusko monument in Milwaukee reputedly earned him the support of the city's Poles. *Milwaukee Sentinel*, Jan. 24, 25, 1893.

9. Aage R. Clausen, *How Congressmen Decide: A Policy Focus* (New York, 1973), 12-37. Recent applications include James H. Kuklinski, "Representatives and Elections: A Policy Analysis," *APSR*, 72 (March 1978), 165-177; and Barbara Deckard Sinclair, "The Policy Consequences of Party Realignment— Social Welfare Legislation in the House of Representatives, 1933-1954," *American Journal of Political Science*, 22 (February 1978), 83-105. For a useful synopsis of current models of congressional voting, with a suggested synthesis, see John W. Kingdon, "Models of Legislative Voting," *Journal of Politics*, 39 (August 1977), 563-595.

10. The agricultural variables used (for Illinois and Iowa only) were Agincome, Wheat, and Debt Ratio; see appendix. These indicators were chosen from a larger set of agricultural variables on the basis of lack of multicollinearity and their strength of association with roll call voting generally. Ethnicity was the personal cultural variable used for Wisconsin, Nationality for Illinois 1895, and Religion for Iowa 1894. Equivalent personal data were not available for Illinois 1887 and Iowa 1888. Yankee, German, and Catholic (Catholic + German Lutheran in Wisconsin) constituted the cluster of district ethnic indicators. Party, Occupation, and the personal cultural indices were transformed into dummy variables in the regression. Beta produced a "standarized" correlation for each individual variable, including the separate dummy variable categories of Occupation and Ethnicity, and did not measure the combined effect of clusters of variables (economic, cultural, etc.). On multiple correlation generally, see Nie, *SPSS*, chapters 20 and 21, and the literature cited therein.

11. It is difficult, for example, to disaggregate the effects of personal ethnicity from constituent ethnicity because of their high multicollinearity (for example, Yankee Republicans representing heavily Yankee districts) and because of small sample sizes. In the sessions for which data on personal ethnicity were available, it always increased the explained variance in voting after constituent culture had first been factored into the regression calculations. On the basis of various reorderings of the variables entered into the regression, I estimate that personal ethnicity statistically explained between 5 and 10 percent of the variance, on average, in intraparty voting on scaled legislation. In other words, legislator ethnicity had some, albeit a limited, impact on voting behavior.

12. Techniques of scale analysis are discussed in the appendix.

13. See for reference to this process: *Milwaukee Sentinel*, Jan. 8, Feb. 4, Apr. 28, 1887, Apr. 18, 1889, Mar. 4, 19, 1891, Jan. 8, 21, 1893, Mar. 28, 29, 1895; *Milwaukee Journal*, Mar. 27, Apr. 6, 1893. The paragraph also rests on my review of 314 roll calls in the Wisconsin Assembly.

14. Examinations of the urban-rural factor in twentieth-century midwestern legislatures include: Don S. Kirschner, *City and Country: Rural Responses to Urbanization in the 1920s* (Westport, Conn., 1970), esp. chaps. 4-6, which should be considered in light of Ballard Campbell, "The State Legislature in American His-

tory: A Review Essay," *Historical Methods Newsletter,* 9 (September 1976), 189-191; David R. Derge, "Metropolitan and Outstate Alignments in Illinois and Missouri Legislative Delegations," *APSR,* 52 (December 1958), 1051-1065; John C. Wahlke, "Policy Determinants and Legislative Decisions," in S. Sidney Ulmer, ed., *Political Decision-Making* (New York, 1970), 100-105. See generally Malcolm E. Jewell and Samuel C. Patterson, *The Legislative Process in the United States* (New York, 1966), 435.

15. Roy V. Scott, *The Agrarian Movement in Illinois, 1880-1896* (Urbana, Ill., 1962), 67-68.

16. *Chicago Tribune,* Jan. 6, 15, May 1, 1891; Ernest L. Bogart and Charles M. Thompson, *The Industrial State, 1870-1893* (Springfield, Ill., 1920), 179; Scott, *Agrarian Movement,* 103. In other sessions: *Chicago Tribune,* Feb. 3, 1887, Feb. 8, 1889, May 23, 1895; *Iowa State Register,* Feb. 29, 1888; *Milwaukee Sentinel,* Feb. 9, 1887.

17. Herman C. Nixon, "The Populist Movement in Iowa," *IJHP,* 24 (January 1926), 36; J. Brooke Workman, "Governor William Larrabee and Railroad Reform," *IJHP,* 57 (July 1959), 257; Leland L. Sage, *A History of Iowa* (Ames, Ia., 1974), 206.

18. Ballard C. Campbell, "Did Democracy Work? Prohibition in Late Nineteenth-Century Iowa: A Test Case," *JIH,* 8 (Summer 1977), 90, 108-113.

8. Economic Policy

1. The discussion of pressure activities is based largely on newspaper reports, which are cited selectively. *Chicago Tribune,* Mar. 18, 1887. *Iowa State Register,* Feb. 18, 1886, Feb. 8, 1888; *Burlington Hawkeye,* Mar. 13, 1892. *Milwaukee Sentinel,* Mar. 11, 1887, Apr. 22, 1891, Apr. 11, 1895; Will Rawley to Ellis B. Usher, Apr. 10, 1891, Usher Papers, WSHS; Albert R. Hall to Nils P. Haugen, Apr. 30, 1893, Haugen Papers, WSHS; Samuel Harper to James O. Davidson, Sept. 18, 1896, Davidson Papers, WSHS. Donald J. Berthrong, "Employer's Liability Legislation in Wisconsin, 1874-1893," *Southwestern Social Science Quarterly,* 34 (June 1953).

2. *Chicago Tribune,* May 25, 17, 1889; *Iowa State Register,* Feb. 3, 5, 7, 1888; *Milwaukee Sentinel,* Mar. 10, 27, 1893; Berthrong, "Liability Legislation." *Iowa State Register,* Feb. 4, 1886, Jan. 26, Feb. 29, 1888; J. Brooke Workman, "Governor William Larrabee and Railroad Reform," *IJHP,* 57 (July 1959), 251; Cyrenus Cole, *I Remember, I Remember* (Iowa City, Ia., 1936), 162. *Milwaukee Sentinel,* Feb. 24, 1887, Mar. 31, Apr. 6, 1893; David P. Thelen, *The New Citizenship* (Columbia, Mo., 1972), 35, 37; Stanley P. Caine, *The Myth of a Progressive Reform: Railroad Regulation in Wisconsin, 1903-1910* (Madison, Wis., 1970), 14-15.

3. *Chicago Tribune,* Apr. 21, 1887; *Iowa State Register,* June 12, 1888; *Milwaukee Sentinel,* Feb. 23, 1887, Feb. 26, Apr. 11, 1891. Also see Thomas C. Cochran, *Railroad Leaders, 1845-1890* (Cambridge, Mass., 1953), 193-196; Ivan L. Pollock, "Some Abuses Connected with Statute Law-Making," in Benjamin F. Shambaugh, ed., *Statute Law-Making in Iowa* (Iowa City, Ia., 1916), 624-630; and Robert Wiebe, *The Search For Order* (New York, 1967), 184. Earl S. Beard, in

"The Background of State Railroad Regulation in Iowa," *IJHP*, 51 (January 1953), 27-29, indicated that railroads hired full-time lobbyists by the late 1860s to oppose regulatory legislation.

4. *Milwaukee Sentinel*, Mar. 11, 1893; *Illinois State Journal*, Jan. 26, 1893; *Dubuque Herald*, Mar. 7, 1894; *Chicago Tribune*, Mar. 8, 14, 1893. On workers, see *Chicago Tribune*, May 10, 1889, May 9, 1891; *Iowa State Register*, Feb. 9, 1886, Mar. 16, 1888; *Milwaukee Sentinel*, Feb. 1, 1887, Feb. 20, 1891; Thelen, *New Citizenship*, 34.

5. *Burlington Hawkeye*, Feb. 18, 1892; *Iowa State Register*, Mar. 3, 1894. *Illinois State Journal*, Jan. 16, 1892; *Laws of the State of Illinois, 1891* (Springfield, Ill., 1891), 7. *IaHJ*, *1892*, 519; *Milwaukee Sentinel*, Mar. 12, 1891; *Chicago Tribune*, Feb. 3, 1887, May 22, 1891. Reuben G. Thwaites to William F. Vilas, Jan. 12, 1893, and Charles K. Adams to Vilas, Jan. 11, 1893, Vilas Papers, WSHS.

6. Taxes: *Chicago Tribune*, Jan. 25, May 22, 1887; *Milwaukee Journal*, Apr. 13, 1893. Regional claimants: *Chicago Tribune*, May 8, 1891, May 16, 1895; *Iowa State Register*, Mar. 4, 19, 1886, Feb. 15, 1894; *Milwaukee Sentinel*, Apr. 12, 1895. Urbanites: *Chicago Tribune*, May 3, 14, 1889, May 20, June 13, 1891; *Iowa State Register*, Jan. 28, 1888; *Milwaukee Sentinel*, Feb. 2, 10, 1887, Feb. 20, 1891, Jan. 17, Mar. 15, 1893.

7. *Chicago Tribune*, Apr. 24, 1891, Mar. 21, 1895; Bessie Louise Pierce, *A History of Chicago* (New York, 1957), III, 139. The flurry of contestants that entered the struggle over a proposed logging dam on the Wisconsin River is a classic illustration of entrepreneurial competition that resulted in an out-of-legislature compromise: *Milwaukee Sentinel*, January through Feb. 4, 1887. Also see V. O. Key, Jr., *Politics, Parties, and Pressure Groups* (New York, 1964), 145-147.

8. The point is illustrated in the following tabulation of mean gamma coefficients (signs omitted) for the association between all pairs of economic policy scales in each of six selected sessions. The mean gamma association between these scales and the Mores scale in the session is given for comparison:

	Scales (N)	Inter- association	With Mores
Illinois 1887	4	0.15	0.39
Illinois 1893	3	0.09	0.41
Iowa 1888	4	0.29	0.40
Iowa 1894	5	0.30	0.24
Wisconsin 1891	3	0.49	0.65
Wisconsin 1893	3	0.19	0.34

Further evidence of this diversity is given by other roll calls on economic issues that failed to fit acceptably into an economic policy scale.

9. The topical heterogeneity of the Mixed Economic policy scales resulted from the existence of small, interrelated clusters of roll calls on Commerce, Fiscal Policy, and Public Services, which did not correlate highly with the economic policy scales formed from votes in these policy spheres. To avoid several smaller

scales (of three votes or less), these small, partisan clusters were merged into larger Mixed Economic scales. The process is discussed further in the appendix.

10. These tests employed all the agricultural variables, as well as Party, Urban, Section, and various cultural indicators. See the appendix for definitions.

11. The intraregional correlations appear spurious, as they all occurred between Wheat and delegates from northern Illinois, a region where little wheat was grown. The three votes concerned appropriating money for the Illinois Dairymen's Association (Wheat −0.58, German 0.51), regulating rates for passengers boarding trains without tickets (Wheat −0.52, Catholic 0.50), and fixing the pay of election officials (Wheat 0.60, Party −0.71).

Correlations were also calculated separately for each party delegation, with similar results. Only a few votes registered coefficients of 0.5 or higher with agricultural variables. And since most of these roll calls concerned noneconomic issues, and cultural or other factors frequently correlated as highly with these economic votes as did agricultural variables, the influence of agricultural economics is questionable. Still, constituent differences in farm worth and agricultural specialties may have contributed to the intraparty divisions on the appropriations for dairymen, the regulation of fire insurance companies, the limitation of interest rates, and the redefinition of the "herd law," among other matters.

12. Generalizations in this chapter about voting on economic issues are based not only on the scale and correlation analysis reported in this section but also on disagreement and cohesion tests performed for all roll calls, using Party, Urban, cultural, and other indices as independent variables. Multivariate calculations, using analysis of variance and cross-tabulation techniques, were done for approximately fifty individual roll calls. See appendix for methodological details.

13. The following works were helpful in formulating the interpretation presented in this section and this chapter: Aage R. Clausen, *How Congressmen Decide: A Policy Focus* (New York, 1973); Thomas R. Dye, *Understanding Public Policy,* 2d ed. (Englewood Cliffs, N.J., 1975), 319; Jacob M. Edelman, *The Symbolic Uses of Politics* (Urbana, Ill., 1964), esp. 175-176, and *Politics as Symbolic Action* (New York, 1971), esp. 45, 63; Wayne L. Francis, *Legislative Issues in the Fifty States: A Comparative Analysis* (Chicago, 1976), 8; Morton Keller, *Affairs of State* (Cambridge, Mass., 1977), 422; Key, *Politics,* 134; Seymour M. Lipset and Earl Raab, *The Politics of Unreason: Right-Wing Extremism in America, 1790-1970* (New York, 1970), 462; Jerry B. Michel and Ronald C. Dillehay, "Reference Behavior Theory and the Elected Representative," *Western Political Quarterly,* 22 (December 1969), 759-773; Warren E. Miller and Donald E. Stokes, "Constituency Influence in Congress," *APSR,* 57 (March 1963), 45-56; John C. Wahlke, "Policy Determinants and Legislative Decisions," in S. Sidney Ulmer, ed., *Political Decision-Making* (New York, 1970), 108.

14. Legislators' grievances toward railroads can be followed in newspaper coverage of the legislative sessions and in the various bills filed there. For other commentary, see Roy V. Scott, *The Agrarian Movement in Illinois, 1880-1896* (Urbana, Ill., 1962), 16-20; Thelen, *New Citizenship,* 39, 203-211; Workman, "Larrabee and Railroad Reform." These works give a sampling of assertions about railroaders' control of state politics: Fleming Fraker, Jr., "The Beginnings of the Progressive Movement in Iowa," *Annals of Iowa,* 35 (Spring 1961), 578-593; Her-

man C. Nixon, "The Populist Movement in Iowa," *IJHP*, 24 (January 1926), 11-12; Herbert F. Margulies, *The Decline of the Progressive Movement in Wisconsin, 1890-1920* (Madison, Wis., 1968), 8; Caine, *Myth of Progressive Reform*, 5.

15. Ellis B. Usher to B. G. Lennox, Jan. 8, 1889, and W. Collins to Usher, Dec. 6, 1890, Usher Papers, WSHS. *Milwaukee Sentinel*, Mar. 22, 1893; Kenneth C. Acrea, "Wisconsin Progressivism: Legislative Response to Social Change, 1891 to 1909" (Ph.D. diss., University of Wisconsin, Madison, 1968), 120; Thelen, *New Citizenship*, 219; Cole, *I Remember*, 177-181. Also, David T. Littler to Shelby M. Cullom, Dec. 4, 1886, Cullom Papers, IllSHS.

16. Charles W. Moore to "Wife," Feb. 1, 1889, Moore Papers, WSHS. *Iowa State Register*, Mar. 17, 1886; *Milwaukee Journal*, Apr. 22, 1893. Diary of Willet S. Main, Mar. 13, 1889, WSHS; Edward C. Wall to Ellis B. Usher, Jan. 6, 1893, Usher Papers, WSHS. Legislator attitudes about passes are illustrated by the floor debate reported in the *Milwaukee Sentinel*, Mar. 21, 1895. Hall described the pace of his activity in quest of railroad reform: "have been so busy that I have not taken time to eat. Now I am very tired and still have oceans of work before me." Albert R. Hall to Nils P. Haugen, Apr. 12, 1895, Haugen Papers, WSHS. Also see Cochran, *Railroad Leaders*, 184-201.

17. Wisconsin outlawed passes in 1899, Iowa in 1906, and Illinois in 1913. Robert S. Hunt, *Law and Locomotives: The Impact of the Railroad on Wisconsin Law in the Nineteenth Century* (Madison, Wis., 1958), 258-259, and 160-162, 167-173 (generally on the relation of the Wisconsin legislature to railroads).

18. See for legislator commentary and description of the proceedings: *Iowa State Register*, Jan. 11, 1888, through March 1888; *IaHJ*, *1888*, 499-500, 501-502, 509-510, 678-679; Workman, "Larrabee and Railroad Reform"; Leland L. Sage, *William Boyd Allison: A Study in Practical Politics* (Iowa City, Ia., 1956), 212.

19. *Chicago Tribune*, Apr. 19, 1889. *Milwaukee Sentinel*, Mar. 29, 1889, Apr. 15, 22, 1891, Mar. 11, 1893. See for a sampling of newspaper editorial positions on "trusts": *Chicago Tribune*, June 4, 1887; *Chicago Times*, June 17, 1887; *Iowa State Register*, Mar. 2, 1888; *Catholic Sentinel* (Chippewa Falls, Wis.), Mar. 26, 1893.

20. The following tabulation shows the percentage of variance explained by selected variables in the voting on the Insurance scale in the 1888 Iowa house:

	All members	Republicans	Democrats
Party	0	—	—
German	20	18	26
Ethnic District	24	23	35
Urban	9	7	11
Section	25	17	42
Occupation	18	26	28
Farm Owners	2	6	0

See *IaHJ*, *1888*, 891; and, for legislator commentary on a related bill, *IaHJ*, *1894*, 754-755.

21. *Chicago Tribune*, Mar. 11, Apr. 19, May 2, 18, 1889. The North-South

association (gamma) with the three scaled issues were as follows: savings banks, 0.71; regulation of stockyards, 0.65; sanitary canal, 0.52.

22. *Chicago Tribune*, Mar. 11, May 8, 22, 1889; Apr. 15, 22, 1887. Demo-. crats voted 51 to 7 to strike the enacting clause from the building and loan association bill, a motion that Republicans resisted 24 to 46. The Pawn Shop scale generated a Party gamma of 1.00. The scale also included one vote on protecting trainmen from overwork and one vote on granting park commissioners authority to tax abutters for the improvement of streets leading to parks. Democrats supported both measures.

23. *Iowa State Register*, Mar. 3, 1886, Feb. 29, Mar. 2, 1888; *IaHJ, 1888*, 433-434, 463, *1892*, 179, 228-229.

24. *Chicago Tribune*, Feb. 24, Mar. 10, Apr. 8 (quotation), May 5, 1887. Pierce, *Chicago*, III, 289-290.

25. *Milwaukee Sentinel*, Apr. 15, 1893.

26. *Milwaukee Sentinel*, Apr. 8, 1887, Apr. 9, 1891, Apr. 1, 6, 8, 1893; *Milwaukee Journal*, Apr. 7, 1893. Hunt, *Law and Locomotives*, 155; Ezekiel H. Downey, *History of Labor Legislation in Iowa* (Iowa City, Ia., 1910), 62, 76-81.

27. *Chicago Tribune*, Mar. 23, 1887.

28. Ibid., Apr. 26, May 1, 1893. Clay McShane, "Transforming the Use of Urban Space: A Look at the Revolution in Street Pavements," *Journal of Urban History*, 5 (May 1979), 283, 287. A multiple regression equation constructed with the variables Ethnic District (three dummy variables), Nationality (five dummy variables), Urban, three agricultural indicators, and North-South explained 30 percent of the variance in the voting scores of all members, 55 percent in Republican voting, and 23 percent in Democratic voting.

29. Labor's preindustrial norms and ethnic balkanization during the era may have helped to blur such battle lines. See Herbert Gutman, "Work, Culture, and Society in Industrializing America, 1815-1919," *American Historical Review*, 78 (June 1973), 531-588; Gerd Korman, *Industrialization, Immigrants, and Americanizers* (Madison, Wis., 1967); Chester M. Destler, *American Radicalism, 1865-1901* (Chicago, 1949; Quadrangle ed., 1966), 162-211.

30. Twenty-three of the thirty-seven appropriation-bill roll calls qualified as party votes at the 60 percent disagreement level. Party produced the highest correlation with the voting on three scales constructed entirely or mainly of appropriation items. State party platforms were followed in the *Chicago Daily News Almanac*. See *Chicago Tribune*, Apr. 21, June 8, 1891.

31. For Crafts' activities on the Fair bill see *Chicago Tribune*, June 4, 1891, and succeeding issues. Scale analysis showed pronounced Chicago-downstate voting divergencies among Democrats on some or all of the items in the following scales: Pawnshops, and Tax Assessment Reform (1887); Stockyards (two separate scales), Fiscal policy, and the Chicago Sanitary Canal (1889); Mixed Economic issues (a potpourri of measures), and Government (1893). The Government scale included several proposals to call a constitutional convention, as well as legislation to increase the number of judges in Cook county and to prevent the conveyance of prisoners in uncovered wagons; all had special relevance to Chicago.

32. *Iowa State Register*, Apr. 1, 1886; *IaHJ, 1888*, 973-975; *IaHJ, 1890*, 495-497. Similar sentiments persisted into 1894, although the matter dropped out of the

contested-issue category: *IaHJ*, *1894*, 850.

33. *Iowa State Register*, Mar. 23, 1888; S. N. Fellows (Professor of Mental and Moral Philosophy, University of Iowa) to James S. Clarkson, Feb. 14, 1888, Clarkson Papers, IaDHA; *IaHJ*, *1892*, 687.

34. *Chicago Tribune*, May 20, June 11, 13, 1891. *Milwaukee Sentinel*, Apr. 1, 1887, Apr. 10, 1891. For a sampling of regional interests see: *Chicago Tribune*, Apr. 13, 1887, May 4, 1889, June 10, 1891; *Milwaukee Sentinel*, Apr. 5, 1889. On the propriety of financial aid to interest organizations: *Iowa State Register*, Apr. 1, 1894; *Milwaukee Sentinel*, Mar. 9, 1887, Mar. 21, 1889.

35. Ballard Campbell, "The Good Roads Movement in Wisconsin, 1890-1911," *WMH*, 49 (Summer 1966), 274-278, 282.

36. The following scores (mean percentages) illustrate how legislators' responses to the Apple bill varied by selected variable categories. High scores indicate support for the Apple bill. For Democratic Nationality, the category of Yankee includes British and Scandinavian.

	All members	Republicans	Democrats
Ethnic District			
Catholic and German	26	67	20
Yankee	72	67	83
Nationality			
Irish and German	37	70	19
Scandinavian and British	67	67	—
Yankee	75	75	75
Occupation			
Farmer	9	20	0
Lawyer	50	50	50
Merchant, banker	50	75	30
Professional	75	100	50
Urban			
City	26	67	12
Small town	60	80	40
Rural	46	58	33
Section			
Lake Shore	35	100	15
Central	52	87	33
Southwest	40	37	50
North	55	64	43

37. Samuel P. Hays's argument in "Political Parties and the Community-Society Continuum," in William N. Chambers and Walter D. Burnham, eds., *The American Party Systems* (New York, 1967), 152-181, fits comfortably with this interpretation.

38. Lee Benson, *The Concept of Jacksonian Democracy* (1961; Atheneum,

1967), 272-276; Chambers and Burnham, *American Party Systems*, 26-27 (Chambers), and 280-283 (Burnham); Cochran, *Railroad Leaders*, 199-201; Hunt, *Law and Locomotives*, 170; John A. Garraty, *The New Commonwealth, 1887-1890* (New York, 1968), 77, 121-122, 140-156; Edward C. Kirkland, *Dream and Thought in the Business Community, 1860-1900* (Ithaca, N.Y., 1956), 11-13, 216; John Tipple, "Big Businessmen and a New Economy," in H. Wayne Morgan, ed., *The Gilded Age* (Syracuse, N.Y., 1970), 13-30.

39. Thomas C. Cochran, "The History of a Business Society," *JAH*, 54 (June 1967), 11; Sidney Fine, *Laissez Faire and the General-Welfare State* (Ann Arbor, Mich., 1956), 354-362; Keller, *Affairs of State*, 371-438; Lewis R. Mills, "Governmental Fiscal Aid to Private Enterprise in Wisconsin: A Quantitative Approach, 1848-1954," *Wisconsin Law Review* (January 1956), 110-129.

9. The Issues of Government and the Roots of Partisanship

1. Fewer than 26,000 ballots were cast in the referendum, compared with 371,000 in the gubernatorial election in 1892 and 140,000 in 1889 over a constitutional amendment concerning the state supreme court. *WB, 1968*, 318-319. The Assembly voted on the issue of uniform laws for cities in each session between 1887 and 1895.

2. *Chicago Tribune*, Jan. 6, Feb. 7, 8, Mar. 6, 8, 1895; *Chicago Times-Herald*, Mar. 6, 1895. Ernest L. Bogart and John M. Mathews, *The Modern Commonwealth, 1893-1918* (Springfield, Ill., 1920), 271-274; Waldo R. Browne, *Altgeld of Illinois: A Record of His Life and Work* (New York, 1924), 206-207; Carter H. Harrison, *Stormy Years* (Indianapolis, Ind., 1935), 108-109, 129.

3. These remarks are based on newspaper reports, which I followed for all fifteen sessions studied, and, to a lesser extent, on secondary literature, unpublished manuscripts, and legislators' explanations inserted in the *IaHJ*.

4. *Chicago Tribune*, Apr. 13, May 12, 18, 25-27, 1893. Other illustrations: *Iowa State Register*, Mar. 17, 1886; *IaHJ, 1890*, 556; *Milwaukee Sentinel*, Feb. 23, 1887, Apr. 17, 1891, Mar. 8, 1893.

5. The tendency for roll calls on Government either to share very high intercorrelations or to show no interrelatedness removed much of the ambiguity in deciding whether various clusters of votes fitted acceptably into a scale, which was a greater problem when party did not dominate voting alignments. The low intercorrelations of the unscalable roll calls on Government, a fairly sizable collection, imply that a variety of idiosyncratic factors underlay responses to these issues.

6. Two recent investigations reference the literature on the subject: Sarah McCally Morehouse, "The State Political Party and the Policy-Making Process," *APSR*, 67 (March 1973), 55-72; and Helmut Norpoth, "Explaining Party Cohesion in Congress: The Case of Shared Policy Attitudes," *APSR*, 70 (December 1976), 1156-1171.

7. The two other sessions were the 1887 and 1889 Illinois houses. Legislators who were absent or abstained on more than one-half of the party votes were excluded from the analysis. As was explained in Chapter 5, there is no universally accepted criterion of a party vote. Nor do specific quantitative standards for identifying a party vote necessarily coincide with lawmakers' perceptions of their be-

havior on that vote. See Wilder Crane, Jr., "A Caveat on Roll-Call Studies of Party Voting," *Midwest Journal of Political Science*, 4 (August 1960), 237-249.

8. Variables are defined in the appendix.

9. The method of identifying important committees is explained in chapter 3, note 25.

10. The variables used in the multiple correlation models were as follows. The political model: (Illinois) Vote Margin, Party Competitiveness, Term, Steer, Chair; (Wisconsin) Democratic Vote, Term, Chair. The personal model: (Illinois) Occupation, Post Office, Nationality; (Wisconsin) Ethnicity, Occupation, Age. The district model: (Illinois) Catholic, German, Yankee, Urban, Wheat, Agincome, Farm Ownership, Section; (Wisconsin) Urban, Yankee (dummy variable derived from the Ethnic District indicator), Catholic and German Lutheran, Section. The comprehensive model drew selectively from these variables. Nominal indices were transformed into dummy variables. No more than eight variable categories were used in any model. The variables are defined in the appendix.

11. The percentages of variance explained by the two factors, averaged for the five sampled sessions, were as follows:

	Mores	*Non-Mores*
Republicans		
Ethnic District	16	8
Economic	5	4
Democrats		
Ethnic District	10	7
Economic	5	5

12. For this study party deviants were identified on the basis of their low party support scores and the number of actual votes they cast with the rival party. Since the distribution of support scores varied between parties and sessions, the criteria for deviancy were fixed in relation to each set of scores and not by a constant threshold. The sources of personal and constituent information used in this and the next paragraphs are referenced in the notes to chapters 2 and 3 and in the appendix.

13. Democratic party chairman Edward Wall's private observation that party disunity was partially due to "the sore resulting from the recent Senatorial squabble" supports this possibility. Wall to William F. Vilas, Feb. 28, 1893, Vilas Papers, WSHS.

14. Norpoth, "Explaining Party Cohesion."

15. Members of the steering committees are identified in John L. Pickering, *Souvenir of the Illinois Legislature of 1893* (Springfield, Ill., 1893), 41. The contrast in party voting between the steering committees and the full house membership may be partially due to the unrepresentative composition of these committees, the Democratic one especially. Of the thirteen members of the Democratic committee (including Speaker Crafts), six were lawyers and only one was a farmer. Also underrepresented were urban districts, electorally secure Democratic constituencies, and both southern Illinois districts and men of southern origin. Irishmen

and Yankees dominated the known ethnic affiliations. The Republican committee possessed a similarly skewed urban-rural profile and had an even greater predominance of lawyers. Ethnic backgrounds, however, included representative numbers of peripheral and core affiliations.

16. Publicly at least, commentators held the majority party responsible for shaping policy and the minority for "bothering" or embarrassing the majority when circumstances warranted; when a guideline to party action was needed, it should be the platform or "election pledges." See, for example, *Chicago Tribune*, Jan. 5, 1891, Jan. 4, May 11, 1893, Jan. 7, 1895; *Milwaukee Sentinel*, Mar. 18, 1887, Jan. 14, 1891; Thomas J. Cunningham to William F. Vilas, Feb. 16, 1887, Vilas Papers; Joshua E. Dodge to Ellis B. Usher, Nov. 10, 1890, Usher Papers, WSHS; Diary of Willet S. Main, Apr. 13-16, 25, 1891, WSHS; *WisAJ, 1895*, 930; *Iowa State Register*, Jan. 13, 26, 1886, Mar. 8, 1888; *Dubuque Herald*, Jan. 6, 1894.

17. Donald R. Matthews and James A. Stimson's hypothesis on the role of "cue giving" is pertinent here: "Decision-Making by U.S. Representatives: A Preliminary Model," in S. Sidney Ulmer, ed., *Political Decision-Making* (New York, 1970), 14-43, esp. 22-23.

18. Caucus activities were followed in newpapers, whose coverage of these meetings appears to have been spotty.

19. See the *Chicago Tribune*, April and May 1893, for detailed reports of these Democratic activities; letter from C. H. Robinson, printed in the *Pioneer Lawmakers' Association of Iowa: Fifteenth Biennial Session* (Des Moines, Ia., 1915), 59-63.

20. *Burlington Hawkeye*, Jan. 21, 1892; *Chicago Tribune*, Feb. 15, Mar. 7, 10, Apr. 28, May 11, 12, 27, June 14, 16, 1893; Harry Barnard, *Eagle Forgotten: The Life of John Peter Altgeld* (New York, 1938), 168, 176-177.

21. Wall's activities were reconstructed from press accounts and from correspondence contained in the Vilas and Usher papers. One reason for my focus on Wall is the existence of exceptionally detailed letters from him to William F. Vilas.

22. The *Sentinel* regularly prefaced references to Wall with "boss"; for example, Jan. 3, Apr. 11, 23, 1891, Apr. 8, 20, 1893.

23. *Milwaukee Sentinel*, March 29, 1893; Wall to Vilas, Mar. 19, 1893, Vilas Papers. And similarly, Wall to Vilas, Mar. 7, May 1, 1891, Vilas Papers.

24. Wall to Vilas, Feb. 28, 1893, Mar. 7, 1891, Vilas Papers.

25. *Milwaukee Sentinel*, Apr. 11, 16, 23, 1891, Apr. 9, 1893.

26. Wall to Vilas, Jan. 14, 18, 20, 1893, Vilas Papers; *Milwaukee Sentinel*, Mar. 13, 22, 1893; Clay McShane, *Technology and Reform: Street Railways and the Growth of Milwaukee, 1887-1900* (Madison, Wis., 1974), 47, 54, 60, 117; Horace S. Merrill, *Bourbon Democracy of the Middle West, 1865-1896* (Seattle, Wash., 1953), 226, 242; *Milwaukee Sentinel*, Apr. 16, 1895.

27. Wall to Ellis B. Usher, Sept. 21, 1891, Dec. 30, 1892, Usher Papers; Wall to Vilas, Feb. 28, Mar. 19, 1893, Vilas Papers.

10. Legislative Democracy in the Late Nineteenth Century

1. On alleged improprieties during senatorial nominations, see: *Chicago Tribune*, Feb. 3, 1887; and J. Gilbert Hardgrove, "General Edward S. Bragg Remi-

niscences," *WMH*, 33 (March 1950), 299. On the charges on the antitrust bills: *Chicago Tribune*, June 4, 1891, May 24, 28, 29, 1889, and May 8, 1895.

2. Specifically, two bills, proposed in 1895, authorized city councils to grant elevated and street railway franchises for ninty-nine years, instead of the prevailing twenty years. In an action sustained by the house, Altgeld vetoed both bills, announcing that they would create "a monopoly in Chicago of both the street railway and the elevated railway business for nearly a hundred years to come." *IllHJ, 1895*, 1139-1142. The story of the $1 million bribe, which more conservative estimates put at $500 thousand, probably was first printed in Forrest Crissey's fictionalized account in the *Chicago Tribune*, later incorporated into his *Tattlings of a Retired Politician* (Chicago, 1904), 307-325. Versions of the tale had been many times retold.

3. The legislatures of New York, Pennsylvania, and California are frequently cited in discussions of legislative corruption. James Bryce gave higher marks to the legislatures of New England and the Midwest than to those of other regions. *The American Commonwealth* (New York, 1890), I, 515-516.

Appendix on Sources and Methods

1. David L. Phillips, *Biographies of the State Officers and Thirty-third General Assembly of Illinois* (Springfield, Ill., 1883); J. B. Watson, comp., *Illinois State Legislators, Containing Biographical and Historical Sketches* (Chicago, 1893); John L. Pickering, *Souvenir of the Illinois Legislature of 1893* (Springfield, Ill., 1893), and *Directory of the Illinois Legislature of 1895* (Springfield, Ill., 1895); *Chicago Daily News Almanac* (Chicago, 1885-1895); *Blue Book of the State of Illinois, 1913-1914* (Danville, Ill., 1914), 388-398.

Frank D. Jackson, comp., "Rules and Standing Committees of the Twenty-first General Assembly . . . 1886," *Legislative Documents Submitted to the Twenty-first General Assembly of . . . Iowa, 1886* (Des Moines, Ia., 1886), V; D. M. Carr, *Biographical Sketches of the State Officers and the Members of the Twenty-second General Assembly of Iowa* (Des Moines, Ia., 1888); Willis L. Hall, *Biographical Sketches of the Twenty-fifth General Assembly of Iowa* (Des Moines, Ia., 1894).

2. Ballard C. Campbell, "Ethnicity and the 1893 Wisconsin Assembly," *JAH*, 62 (June 1975), 76-80.

3. Ballard C. Campbell, Jr., "Political Parties, Cultural Groups and Contested Issues: Voting in the Illinois, Iowa and Wisconsin Houses of Representatives, 1886-1895," (Ph.D. diss., University of Wisconsin, Madison, 1970), 310-317.

4. The following newspapers were read for the duration of each legislative session and frequently for pre-session political activities in the prior year, but only session years are cited: *Chicago Tribune*, 1887, 1889, 1891, 1893, 1895; *Iowa State Register*, 1886, 1888, 1894; *Davenport* (Iowa) *Democrat*, 1890; *Burlington* (Iowa) *Hawkeye*, 1892; *Dubuque* (Iowa) *Herald* 1894; *Milwaukee Sentinel*, 1887, 1889, 1891, 1893, 1895; *Milwaukee Journal*, 1893.

The following newspapers were consulted on a more selective basis. For Illinois: *Chicago Times*, 1887, 1891, 1892, 1893; *Chicago InterOcean*, 1892, 1893; *Illinois State Journal* (Springfield), 1892, 1893; *Illinois State Register* (Springfield), 1892, 1893; *Kendall County Record*, 1893. For Iowa: *The Carroll Herald*, 1894; *The Centerville Citizen*, 1894; *The LeMars Semi-Weekly Sentinel*, 1894; *Waukon*

Standard, 1894. For Wisconsin: *Milwaukee Journal*, 1889; *The Catholic Sentinel* (Chippewa Falls), 1892, 1893; *Catholic Citizen* (Milwaukee), 1892, 1893; *Madison State Journal*, 1895; *Madison Democrat*, 1895.

Not included in the list are innumerable local newspapers consulted mainly in conjunction with the search for biographical information about legislators.

5. Lee F. Anderson and others, *Legislative Roll-Call Analysis* (Evanston, Ill., 1966), 29-58, discusses these and other similar indices.

6. Duncan MacRae, Jr., "A Method for Identifying Issues and Factions from Legislative Votes," *APSR*, 51 (1965), 909-926. New students of the subject of legislative methodologies should see: MacRae, *Issues and Parties in Legislative Voting: Methods of Statistical Analysis* (New York, 1970); and Allan G. Bogue, "American Historians and Legislative Behavior," in Lee Benson et al., *American Political Behavior: Historical Essays and Readings* (New York, 1974), 99-119.

7. The issue is discussed at greater length in Campbell, "Political Parties," 338-341.

8. Leo A. Goodman and William H. Kruskal, "Measures of Association for Cross Classifications," *Journal of the American Statistical Association*, 49 (December 1954), 747-754.

9. *Census of Iowa for the Year 1895* (Des Moines, 1895), table 37.

10. Campbell, "Political Parties," 322-331.

11. U.S. Census Office, *Statistics of Agriculture at the Eleventh Census: 1890* (Washington, D.C., 1895).

12. The procedure documented in Ballard C. Campbell, "Did Democracy work? Prohibition in Late Nineteenth-Century Iowa: A Test Case," *JIH*, 7 (Summer 1977), 91, n. 7, was replicated for selected Illinois and Wisconsin sessions, but modified for thresholds and nominal categories as ethnic patterns of each state dictated.

The apportionment of nationality groups in Chicago districts followed the techniques described in Campbell, "Political Parties," 317-318, 322, 326, and used the nationality of registered voters, 1892, printed in Joel A. Tarr, *A Study in Boss Politics: William Lorimer of Chicago* (Urbana, Ill., 1971), 324-325.

13. Several techniques were followed in estimating the numeric approximation of German Lutherans. For Wisconsin Assembly districts of 1893 and 1895, the "communicants" of the Lutheran synods populated by Germans, as reported in U.S. Census Office, *Eleventh Census of the United States: 1890. Statistics of Churches* (Washington, D.C., 1894), were totaled and expressed as a proportion of the total district population. As is the case with Catholic "communicants," the index undercounts German Lutherans, but both indicators do provide a rough comparative apportionment of religious groups *among* districts. Unlike the other population indices created for Wisconsin, however, the German Lutheran population is not apportioned among districts formed within single counties; the variable is a county-wide indicator. For Milwaukee, the index was based on the operational assumption that German Lutherans were distributed in proportion to the whole German population in the city. Because of these crude provisions, the indicator was used principally as a component of Catholic + German Lutheran, and as one of numerous indices from which Ethnic District nominal classifications were created.

A similar accounting procedure of 1890 federal census data for churches was used to estimate the German Lutheran population in Iowa districts for 1888 and 1890. For the sessions of 1892 and 1894 the Scandinavian-born population was subtracted from the total Lutheran population (based on data in the 1895 Iowa state census) to provide a rough sense of the number of German Lutherans in each legislative district. Because these indices had low validity, they were used primarily as aids in the construction of Ethnic District, an index that was based on numerous demographic indicators. Data on church seating capacity in the 1885 Iowa census (table 7) served as an additional guide to religious populations in the creation of Ethnic District for Iowa 1886. German Lutheran was not used for Illinois.

INDEX

Age of legislators, 31

Agriculture, 5-6; issues concerning, 68-69. *See also* Economic factors; Farmers

Altgeld, John Peter, 14, 66, 191, 201

American Protective Association, 4, 29, 64, 100

Anti-Catholicism, *see* American Protective Association; Religion

Apportionment, 9-10, 53, 177, 196-197, 212

Appropriations, *see* Expenditures

Banks, 161-162

Bay View riot, 26, 75-76, 164

Bennett law, 28, 29, 62, 92, 114-116, 192

Bills, 54, 208. *See also* Contested issues

Boise, Horace, 28, 46, 106, 191

Brady, David W., 84

Bragg, Edward, 130-131

Bribery, 78, 200-201

Bryce, James, 1-2

Burrows, George, 50

Business (issues), 65-68, 151-153, 157-161

Capital punishment, 65, 121

Catholic Total Abstinence Union, 101-102

Catholics, *see* Ethnicity; Religion

Caucuses, 189-190

Chicago, 6, 10, 13, 21, 145, 166, 182-183, 212-213; issues concerning, 66, 70, 73, 75, 78, 141-143, 169-170, 176-177. *See also* Haymarket riot; Sanitary canal; World's Fair; Urban-rural conflict

Chicago Civic Federation, 75, 176

Cities, *see* Chicago; Milwaukee; Urban-rural conflict

Civil service, 75, 176-177

Clausen, Aage, 132

Commerce (issues), 57, 65-70, 93-94, 153-166

Committees, 44-45

Community Mores (issues), 57, 60-65, 92-93, 156-157; and legislative voting, 103-121, 136-141, 184-185

Congress (U.S.), 32, 84-85, 191

Constitutional convention, 22, 73, 178

Contested issues, 55-60, 158, 195-196, 200, 233n6. *See also* Commerce; Community Mores; Fiscal Policy; Government; Public Services

Cook County, Illinois, *see* Chicago

Crafts, Clayton E., 43-44, 48, 50-51, 165, 168, 190

Criminal Rights (issues), 64-65, 120-121